T0398646

WITHOUT THE STATE

Self-Organization and Political Activism in Ukraine

Without the State explores the 2013–14 Euromaidan protests – a wave of demonstrations and civil unrest in Ukraine – through in-depth ethnographic research with leftist, feminist, and student activists in Kyiv. The book discusses the concept of "self-organization" and the notion that if something needs to be done and a person has the competence to do it, then they should simply do it.

Emily Channell-Justice reveals how self-organization in Ukraine came out of leftist practices but actors from across the spectrum of political views also adopted self-organization over the course of Euromaidan, including far-right groups. The widespread adoption of self-organization encouraged Ukrainians to rethink their expectations of the relationship between citizens and their state. The book explains how self-organized practices have changed people's views on what they think they can contribute to their own communities, and in the wake of Russia's renewed invasion of Ukraine in 2022, it has also motivated new networks of mutual aid within Ukraine and beyond. Based on ethnographic fieldwork, including the author's first-hand experience of the entirety of the Euromaidan protests, *Without the State* provides a unique analytical account of this crucial moment in Ukraine's post-Soviet history.

(Anthropological Horizons)

EMILY CHANNELL-JUSTICE is the director of the Temerty Contemporary Ukraine Program at the Ukrainian Research Institute, Harvard University.

ANTHROPOLOGICAL HORIZONS

Editor: Michael Lambek, University of Toronto

This series, begun in 1991, focuses on theoretically informed ethnographic works addressing issues of mind and body, knowledge and power, equality and inequality, the individual and the collective. Interdisciplinary in its perspective, the series makes a unique contribution in several other academic disciplines: women's studies, history, philosophy, psychology, political science, and sociology.

For a list of the books published in this series see p. 277.

Without the State

Self-Organization and Political Activism in Ukraine

EMILY CHANNELL-JUSTICE

UNIVERSITY OF TORONTO PRESS
Toronto Buffalo London

© University of Toronto Press 2022
Toronto Buffalo London
utorontopress.com
Printed and bound by CPI Group (UK) Ltd, Croydon, CR0 4YY

ISBN 978-1-4875-0973-6 (cloth)   ISBN 978-1-4875-0976-7 (EPUB)
ISBN 978-1-4875-0974-3 (paper)   ISBN 978-1-4875-0975-0 (PDF)

Anthropological Horizons

Library and Archives Canada Cataloguing in Publication

Title: Without the state : self-organization and political activism in Ukraine /
    Emily Channell-Justice.
Names: Channell-Justice, Emily, 1986–, author.
Series: Anthropological horizons.
Description: Series statement: Anthropological horizons | Includes bibliographical
references and index.
Identifiers: Canadiana (print) 20220399379 | Canadiana (ebook) 20220399425 |
    ISBN 9781487509736 (cloth) | ISBN 9781487509743 (paper) |
    ISBN 9781487509767 (EPUB) | ISBN 9781487509750 (PDF)
Subjects: LCSH: Ukraine – History – Euromaidan Protests, 2013–2014.
Classification: LCC DK508.848 .C53 2022 | DDC 947.7086 – dc23

We wish to acknowledge the land on which the University of Toronto Press operates.
This land is the traditional territory of the Wendat, the Anishnaabeg, the Haudenosaunee,
the Métis, and the Mississaugas of the Credit First Nation.

Publication of this book was made possible, in part, by a grant from the First Book
Subvention Program of the Association for Slavic, East European, and Eurasian Studies.

Publication of this book was made possible, in part, by a grant from the Canadian
Foundation for Ukrainian Studies.

**Canadian Foundation
for Ukrainian Studies**

**Fondation canadienne
des etudes ukrainiennes**

University of Toronto Press acknowledges the financial support of the Government of
Canada, the Canada Council for the Arts, and the Ontario Arts Council, an agency of
the Government of Ontario, for its publishing activities.

 **Canada Council
for the Arts** **Conseil des Arts
du Canada**

ONTARIO ARTS COUNCIL
CONSEIL DES ARTS DE L'ONTARIO

an Ontario government agency
un organisme du gouvernement de l'Ontario

Funded by the   Financé par le
Government   gouvernement
of Canada   du Canada

 **Canadä**

To my mother, this book's first reader

Contents

Illustrations

Preface

The atmosphere in Kyiv is pretty tense. But I have the feeling that the threat of a military invasion will still be far away and is not a sure thing that will happen. But this very situation will exhaust the country economically, and the people morally. My feeling is that this is what is being done. I mean, it will be worse, but how soon it will be worse, I don't know. But we are going to hope for peace, and if you can't come in April, then in the summer or fall you will have the chance to come to Ukraine and you can come visit us. (20 February 2022)

After a visit to Kyiv in September 2021, I planned to return to Ukraine the following April to continue my new research project on state response to long-term internal displacement from the temporarily occupied territories of Donets'k, Luhans'k, and Crimea. I planned to travel to Mariupol for the first time to begin a secondary phase of research in a city that had seen its population expand with the arrival of many displaced people over eight years. And I planned to visit friends at their homes: most people did not really appear to believe that an invasion was coming, so I continued to make plans.

Four days after I received the message above, the Russian Federation, on the orders of Vladimir Putin, began bombing airfields near cities across Ukraine. Then, Russian bombs began falling on the cities themselves. Russian tank columns from the north threatened Kyiv. Bombs from the south – from Crimea, the Black Sea, and the occupied territories – fell on Kharkiv. Mariupol was besieged and thousands of its citizens were stuck in basements without supplies while the city was almost entirely destroyed. Millions of Ukrainians left their homes or became homeless in the wake of the invasion. Millions have been displaced within Ukraine, and millions more – women and children, as martial law prevents men ages eighteen to sixty from crossing the border – left the country for safety in Poland and other neighbouring countries. As of this writing in the beginning of April 2022, the world is just discovering the atrocities that took place during the Russian occupation and attack on villages and cities around Kyiv, including Bucha, Irpin, and Hostomel. Citizens are evacuating Mariupol in humanitarian convoys, but at least a hundred thousand people remain in the city, with dwindling supplies.

The events in this book focus largely on the events of 2013–14 in Ukraine: the Euromaidan protests. In the wake of the overthrow of the pro-Russian president Viktor Yanukovych at the end of those protests, Russian troops quietly invaded and occupied the Crimean Peninsula, which had been part of Ukraine since 1954 and remained part of independent Ukraine after the collapse of the Soviet Union in 1991. Russian troops supported the separatist movements in the Donets'k and Luhans'k regions, beginning a protracted but contained war that continued through February 2022. On 21 February, Putin recognized these occupied territories as separate republics. In his speech announcing this policy shift, he also clearly expressed his position that Ukraine should not exist as an independent country. His move to recognize the occupied territories and to fabricate a narrative of a Ukraine run by Nazis who need to be removed worked as Putin's justification for the full-scale invasion that began on 24 February.

Russian aggression towards Ukraine over the previous eight years of war did not make Ukrainians see themselves as part of Russia. Indeed, Ukrainian sentiments towards Russia declined progressively over these years, and there is little or no evidence of Putin's claims that Ukrainians wish to be part of Russia – even in the then-temporarily occupied territories, it was not necessarily a majority opinion.[1] In the wake of Euromaidan, Ukrainian public opinion became increasingly oriented towards Ukraine's future in the European Union. Internal politics focused on anticorruption efforts, curbing the role of oligarchs, and domestic reforms – including in the judicial and police sectors, as well as decentralization to give more powers to Ukraine's regions – were playing out with varying degrees of success and support. From 2014 to 2022, Ukraine saw two democratic transfers of power. President Volodymyr Zelensky, the TV comedian elected in 2019, brought a new perspective to reforms, earning the ire and disappointment of many when he was unable to fulfil campaign promises to end the war in Donbas.

Zelensky's approval rating was at an all-time low at the end of 2021.[2] After winning the presidency with nearly 75 per cent of the vote, and the majority in all but two of Ukraine's regions, people became disillusioned because of high rates of turnover in the government and failure to implement effective reforms in many sectors. Yet Zelensky was also Ukraine's most progressive president on, for example, LGBTQ+ rights (Channell-Justice 2020b), and he established the Crimea Platform, an effort to bring a global focus on the illegal annexation of the peninsula and the violation of sovereignty it represented. In other words, Zelensky was leading a democracy – he often faced disapproval, but he also often listened to his constituents when they pushed back against his initiatives.

Perhaps it was Zelensky's low approval ratings that led Vladimir Putin to think that Ukraine would easily give in to Russian threats and advances. Perhaps it was Putin's rage and Ukraine's clear movement towards democratic practices – however imperfect that movement was – that prompted him to act. There will surely be many books written on this question in the coming years. More relevant for the present volume is the question of the Ukrainian response. President Zelensky – despite many offers of safe passage – has remained in Ukraine, advocating for military and humanitarian aid to every possible audience. Petro Poroshenko, his predecessor, has picked up arms, as has Kyiv mayor Vitaliy Klitschko, along with his brother Wladimir, both well-known boxing champions.

More widely, the Ukrainian response to this war has elicited surprise from much of the world. The Ukrainian Army was not expected to succeed in defending Kyiv and other major cities from Russian forces, let alone retake any towns and villages from those Russian forces, as they have done in April 2022. Ukrainians have volunteered in droves to serve in the military, as well as in Territorial Defence Units, which are being mobilized across the country and doing everything from liberating previously occupied cities to evacuating civilians. Those who decided to remain in Ukraine are organizing humanitarian efforts, including delivery of necessary goods and medicine to places under siege, as well as organizing ride shares when information about cars to transport people to safe places is available. Ukrainians who are already abroad are helping organize resources available to refugees, such as housing information for people needing to resettle.

This response is not a surprise to many of us who watched the 2013–14 Euromaidan protests unfold. The key contribution of this book is about self-organization: when people have the ability or the resources to do something, and that thing needs to be done, they simply do it. They do not wait for the government or an international organization to come meet people's needs if they can do it themselves. The roots of the Euromaidan protests were in self-organization, and in this book I argue that the widespread use of self-organization in 2013 and 2014 has shaped people's engagement with political participation in Ukraine since the protests ended.

When I began new research in Ukraine in 2021, with a focus on the long-term implications of the internal displacement that began in 2014, many people I interviewed, especially Ukrainians who worked in international and non-governmental organizations that served internally displaced people (IDPs), referenced self-organization. One woman from Dnipro, a city in eastern Ukraine, told me about how the city allowed her to repurpose an unused dormitory to house IDPs from Donets'k and Luhans'k as they streamed into the city. Ordinary people mobilized to clean up the dorm, put up wallpaper, remove mould, and bring along basic supplies such as sheets and towels so that newly displaced people would be comfortable. This self-organized initiative existed before any Ukrainian government officials took over the distribution of services to IDPs. Indeed, the woman who recounted this story from Dnipro told me that representatives from various government ministries came to talk with her about the initiative, and that none of them wanted to take on the task of helping IDPs. Most government officials preferred to let self-organized groups handle such tasks.

In other words, self-organization is alive and well in Ukraine and is a robust part of the response to Russia's invasion. The proliferation of self-organized initiatives on Maidan prepared people to understand that there are many ways to be involved. Ivan Shmatko, a Ukrainian criminologist doing research there when the war broke out, described the importance of informal practices and local knowledge in making self-organized mobilizations effective. "While the armed forces were largely preoccupied with the war itself, millions of Ukrainians fled their homes. At the same time, more than one hundred thousand people rushed to sign up for the Territorial Defence Forces (TDF), a network of local volunteer units created to help the army protect cities and villages. These volunteers were often supplied with nothing more than automatic rifles. They also supplied the TDF with bulletproof vests, medical kits, and clothing. To do all this, volunteers relied almost exclusively on informal networks, not on state institutions" (Shmatko 2022).

As anthropologist Maryna Nading wrote, describing the hundreds of thousands of people who have mobilized to help one another, "I have been searching for a better word than *self-help* to describe this nonlinear, chaotic mobilization. 'Self' has expanded and subsumed individual families and neighbourhoods into a much larger entity that spans continents" (Nading 2022). Indeed, self-organization in this time of war subsumes individuality. It has gone beyond many selves acting outside of government entities, as characterized by the self-organization of

Euromaidan. Self-organization is part of the impulse to justify Ukraine's very existence.

It is impossible to predict what will have happened by the time this book is published, so I will not spend time speculating here. Instead, I want to return to 2014, when I was interviewing activists and included a question about how they saw the future of Ukraine. While many activists answered pessimistically – they were concerned about the rise of the far right, the diminished power of the left, and the long-term implications of war – one person, Svitlana, shared a more positive sentiment.

> It's 2024. Somehow Putin is not in power. None of his close descendants. Somehow the conflict is resolved. By 2024, I think we will have to connect with the European Union, [but] diplomatic relations with the Russian Federation are preserved. Someone else has power in Russia and they don't bother us as much. We are less dependent on Russian gas, resources. I think what would be important is if we have some kind of treaty with the EU that the borders are open, more people, especially young people, have the opportunity to study abroad. So, education for young people, opportunity to travel … I think a lot of people, there would be a big migration out of the country, but the believers would stay and try to change it in their lifetime, try to create opportunities and not look for opportunities in other places. Maidan helped promote these initiatives. So, peace, no Putin, opportunities to travel, to work, to study. (March 2014)

There is still time for Svitlana's vision to come true. Even nearly ten years after Euromaidan, her words are more poignant than ever.

Acknowledgments

Like most anthropologists, I am deeply indebted to many people who contributed to this book. And like many anthropologists, the most important contributors are my interlocutors whose words populate this text and who shaped my thinking about the problems addressed in it. While our research projects are of our own choosing and our own design, there is an element of luck in this one: it's the only explanation for how I got to work with people whom I have come to love so much and who have made an indelible mark on my person. A chance meeting nearly twenty years ago turned into lifelong friendships and the privilege of not just caring for, but with, the activists who are still trying to build a world in which they want to live.

Without Illia Vlasiuk, this book would simply not exist. He helped me navigate Ukraine from the beginning, and he facilitated my research project from its first days to its last. I am so grateful for our friendship. Of all the people in this book, I spent the most time during my yearlong fieldwork with Tonya Melnyk; their perspective was fundamental in how I experienced Maidan. I thank Tonya (and Masha) for patiently working through portions of this text to make sure it is representative and for reassuring me that its content presents an important point of view. Andriy Gladun similarly helped me think through many problems and perspectives, broadening my understanding of the left in Ukraine and connecting many of my thoughts to the bigger picture. I am thankful to have gotten to know Dafna Rachok and Ivan Shmatko during this fieldwork, and our discussions on the topics featured in this book have also contributed to how I think about my future research.

To protect their privacy, I refrain from naming the specific activists who participated in interviews, explained things to me, called me when something was happening, offered me help leaving the country, celebrated my birthday, and invited me to join them in their travels around Ukraine. I am thankful for each and every person who took interest in this project from its inception. I hope that the words in this book resonate with you all.

This book comes out of a dissertation that I completed at The Graduate Center, City University of New York (CUNY). My advising committee supported this research from its earliest days, and helped me orient myself as a researcher during the extremely difficult time when my fieldwork became focused on unexpected mass protests. Katherine Verdery encouraged my deep engagement with the concepts that make up this book, and challenged me to always write something that people want to read. Gerald Creed and Dána-Ain Davis gave me unique perspectives on research and writing. Julie Skurski's dissertation writing workshop helped me clarify so much about this project, and her careful reading was indispensable. Janet Johnson has been a positive force since I began this dissertation. During the writing process, Fabio Mattioli was the best partner I could have asked for. I am grateful for the support of Carwil Bjork-James, Andrew Hernández, Mohamad Junaid, Andrés León Araya, Estefania Ponti, Jose Vasquez, and Margarite Whitten during my dissertation research and writing.

At John Jay College and Bronx Community College, my colleagues were supportive of this project and helped me develop my pedagogy in important ways. I am grateful to have started my teaching career with the many motivated and invested students at CUNY. At John Jay College, Kirk Dombrowski provided me with an important fieldwork opportunity that improved my research and analytical skills. Avram Bornstein read early parts of this manuscript and offered many helpful comments, and Edward Snajdr supported my early career development. Thanks to Janet Johnson, Mara Lazda, Nanette Funk, and Sonia Robbins for inviting me to present material from Chapter 6 at the Gender and Transformation Workshop at New York University and for shaping the various versions of that chapter. In New York, Jessica Pisano offered creative solutions to some of the challenges I faced during my fieldwork. My friends and colleagues at Columbia University's Harriman Institute invited me to present parts of this book; I am particularly thankful to Ali Kinsella, Anastasia Tkach, and Kathryn Zehr.

My colleagues at Miami University were enthusiastic about this project at the moments I needed momentum the most. Stephen Norris, Venelin Ganev, Neringa Klumbyte, Benjamin Sutcliffe, Scott Kenworthy, and Zara Torlone read several chapters in this book and made me feel at home at the Havighurst Center. Carl Dahlman, Elana Resnick, and Jon Otto were an engaged audience and helped me reformulate some of my most challenging chapters. This book would never have been finished without the support of Amber Franklin. Charlie and Lynn Stevens helped me balance teaching and research in my first postgraduate job. Karen Dawisha gave me the motivation to persevere in the challenging job market, and I hope my work honours her contributions to the academic world.

At the Ukrainian Research Institute at Harvard University, I am grateful for the interest my colleagues have shown in my research, especially Serhii Plokhy, Tymish Holowinsky, Kristina Conroy, and Kostyantyn Bondarenko. Halyna Hryn helped me navigate the field of Ukrainian studies many years before we became colleagues at Harvard. Volodymyr Dibrova helped with a number of Ukrainian translation questions and gave me a love and appreciation for the process of translation. My discussions with Margarita Balmaceda encouraged me to take the time to finish this manuscript, and her support of my ongoing research has been invaluable. I deeply appreciate Benjamin Schmitt's enthusiasm for this project and for Ukraine.

Thank you to Hannah Chapman, Jacob Lassin, and Francesca Silano for your close reading of my work and for your encouragement. My friends and colleagues at the intersection of Ukrainian studies and anthropology helped create a strong network of which I am glad to be a part: Jennifer Carroll, J. Dickinson, Monica Eppinger, Deborah Jones, Sarah Phillips, Maria Sonevytsky, Cathy Wanner, and Jessica Zychowicz have all had an influence on this book and its research. Marian Rubchak brought the work of many young Ukrainian women scholars into the English-speaking academic world, and their contributions are an important framing, especially in Chapter 6. Nadia Diuk helped me understand the landscape of student activism outside of leftist groups.

I am indebted to many instructors who have helped me develop my Ukrainian language skills: Mar'ianna Burak, Nadia Khomanchuk, and Marta Panas (in L'viv, where I studied Ukrainian thanks to the Graduate Center's Doctoral Student Research Grant), and Yuri Shevchuk and Volodymyr Dibrova in the United States. I also appreciate Ali Kinsella's regular consultation on Ukrainian questions.

I was able to complete the majority of the research in this book thanks to a Fulbright-IIE grant. The support of the Fulbright program, especially Marta Kolomayets and Inna Barysh in Kyiv, was invaluable. Katie Hiatt Mattila and Jennifer Herrmann provided moral support during the many difficulties we faced together in Ukraine. I finished this manuscript at the University of Illinois thanks to a grant from the Open Research Laboratory on Russia, Eastern Europe, and Eurasia. Thanks especially to Jan Adamczyk, Donna Buchanan, and Jessica Greenberg for supporting my work during my time in Champaign. Thank you so much to my editor at the University of Toronto Press, Jodi Lewchuk, who has enthusiastically supported this manuscript and its publication, and to freelancer Barry Norris for his attentive reading and editing of the text. I also thank two anonymous reviewers for their comments, as well as Stephen Shapiro and Michael Lambek for their support for this book's publication.

I thank my dear friends who have stayed by my side throughout this project and beyond. Katherine McLean has been my companion through so many ups and downs, all around the world. Kara Newhouse is my buttress. Anne Pomathiod offered respite from my research at a crucial time that allowed me to reset and refocus. Richard Cochran inspires me to be true to myself.

This research and its publication would never have been completed without the support of my family. They trusted me to make decisions about being in Ukraine at a volatile period and continued to support my research despite their own uncertainties. They have supported the lengthy process of writing this book and of finding a home at Harvard over the course of many years. My mother, Kathi Regan, went to Ukraine with me at a crucial moment and helped me focus on all the various versions of this project. She was the first person to read this version of the manuscript and painstakingly commented on every chapter. It is a cohesive narrative thanks to her close reading. Her enthusiasm for this project has not abated over the seven long years of its gestation, and I will be forever grateful for her support. My father, Donald Channell, is a reassuring voice who has helped me stay grounded when I face challenges big and small. I am lucky to call Allison Racey both my sister and my friend. She inspires me to pursue my passions in both my professional and personal life. Rodney Racey has been a reassuring presence at some of the most challenging moments during this fieldwork and has remained so in the years since. Finally, Thomas Justice has never wavered in his commitment to me and to the life we have built together. He takes my research trips to Ukraine in stride, even being by my side in Kyiv during the most harrowing days of February 2014. He has supported every job application, every grant proposal, and every version of this manuscript. His patience and love through all these moments enabled me to pursue my goals even when I thought they might be unattainable.

Two grants support the publication of this book: the Association for Slavic, East European, and Eurasian Studies First Book Subvention and the Canadian Foundation for Ukrainian Studies (CFUS) publication grant. I especially thank the CFUS jury for their questions that helped clarify several points in the book. Substantial parts of Chapter 6 were previously published in the journal *Signs: Journal of Women in Culture and Society*. Some ethnographic illustrations from Chapter 3 were previously published in *History and Anthropology*; similarly, a small number of ethnographic illustrations from throughout the volume were previously published in *Revolutionary Russia*. All photographs used in the volume are my own.

Language Note

Transliterated terms and phrases are from Ukrainian except where otherwise noted. Ukrainian terms and phrases are transliterated using Library of Congress conventions, except in two cases. First, when an accepted spelling already exists (i.e., Kyiv, Zelensky), I use this spelling. Second, while the letters є (ie), ï (ï), ю (iu), or я (ia) begin a word or name, I use the following: ye, yi, yu, or ya. Following the first exception, many names that appear often in the text use this spelling (i.e., Yanukovych instead of Ianukovych; Yevropa instead of Ievropa [Europe]) to lend them more cleanly to an English transliteration.

All translations from the Ukrainian are my own, except where otherwise noted.

The names used in the text are pseudonyms, except in two cases, which are noted. Throughout the book, I typically use diminutive forms of names (i.e., Tonya instead of Antonina), as these are more common and more accurately reflect people's everyday communication styles.

WITHOUT THE STATE

"We provide the content of Maidan!"

On 29 November 2013, I stood on Kyiv's Maidan Nezalezhnosti, or Independence Square, with Hanna and Kostya.[1] It was one of those typical Kyiv winter days, with a deep, penetrating cold you could feel in your bones no matter how many layers of winter socks you had on. People were standing around the square below the independence monument, a large obelisk topped with a statue of a woman representing freedom, where people had placed signs and posters from the mass gatherings earlier in the week. Hanna, Kostya, and I stood outside the exit of one of Kyiv's many underground passageways to distribute a leaflet to passersby, some of whom would read it in front of us and some of whom would pocket them, perhaps to read later (figure 0.1). We hadn't known what to expect: just the night before, a group of feminist activists and their supporters who were attempting to participate in the mass gathering had been pepper sprayed, and Kostya had gotten the worst of it. The day before that, leftist, feminist, and anti-capitalist activists had been attacked when they attempted to hold a demonstration within the main gathering on Independence Square, and their signs had been damaged and destroyed. On the 29th, however, our flyer distribution was relatively uneventful. When it was so cold we couldn't stay outside another second, we went down the underground passageway and into the large, modern shopping mall to which it was connected to find something warm to drink. Amid the bustle of shoppers and other people who had been standing on the square and needed a steaming cup of tea, we discussed plans for future actions we might be able to organize that would bring a positive atmosphere to leftist protests and, we hoped, avoid further attacks. Little did we know that that very same night, riot police would enter the space of Maidan and viciously beat and arrest the protesters – mostly students – who had gathered there to stay the night.

Figure 0.1. Passersby examine a leftist flyer
Source: Author's photograph.

"The Substance of Our Protest"

Up until that point, the protest mobilizations that moved around Maidan were focused on then-president Viktor Yanukovych's refusal to sign an Association Agreement with the European Union. Protesters wanted to hold Yanukovych accountable for having promised to do so but instead turning towards Russia and Vladimir Putin's Customs Union. After the violence of the early hours of 30 November, however, most protesters turned their attention to Yanukovych's hold over police forces and his willingness to mobilize them to use violence against Ukrainian citizens. Later, people began to demand the resignation of Yanukovych and new elections. These themes melded together to shape the protests, known throughout this volume as Euromaidan, or simply Maidan.

This book is, in part, a testimony of the experience of Euromaidan, a completely unexpected event that became the centre of my research project. It includes a chronological description of the major events from November 2013 to February 2014. It asks, what were the Euromaidan protests, who participated in them, and what does this tell us about Ukrainian politics and society? What was the "Europe" that was envisioned on Maidan, and how did this vision change among groups of different political affiliations? Similarly, what other concepts – such as rights and freedoms – held significance for the protests, and why? These questions frame the volume, while, at the same time, I represent the experience of Euromaidan from the particular perspective of leftist activists, with whom I did the majority of my fieldwork. The flyer presented in figure 0.1 introduces their perspective on these major questions and the concept of "grassroots self-organization" (*nyzova samoorhanizatsiia*) that is central to this analysis.

At a fundamental level, self-organization is the idea that if something needs to be done and there is a person who has the capacity to do it, then it simply should be done, rather than waiting for someone else (particularly a state body or political figure) to do it. This notion ties together the various aspects of activism in this book, which range from critique of the police state to higher education reform to feminism to right-wing militarization practices. This book shows how self-organization is a mobile, fluid concept that can be applied to legitimize activism that criticizes particular kinds of regimes that have lost legitimacy; I also insist, however, on reconnecting self-organization in Ukraine to its leftist roots, which have largely been erased since the removal of Yanukovych from office and the end of Euromaidan.

This project began as a dissertation in which I intended to research student activism around Ukraine through social network analysis. I hoped to identify key sites of student activism and explore the scales of connection among the active groups in various cities. I began doing research with student activists in 2012, first with groups that consider themselves part of a broad spectrum of "left" that includes staunch Marxists and socialists as well as social democrats and anarchists, and those who simply see themselves as "left" or, to some extent, not sympathetic to the "right." The complexity of these definitions presented my dissertation project with its first challenges: how to define left and right in contemporary Ukraine, and how to study them both equally and fairly?

I never answered the second question, because when I returned to Ukraine in September 2013 to pursue ten months of fieldwork, the social network-based questions I had prepared for my interviews rapidly became irrelevant to understanding the organization of leftist student groups. While I had hoped to map out people's relationships through their coordinated organizing campaigns, discovering which activists were central to the student movement in different parts of the country, activists' commitment to their groups' non-hierarchical principles quickly made me realize that these were the wrong questions to ask.

Before I reorganized my interview questions, however, two months into my fieldwork Yanukovych refused to allow his political opponent,

Суть нашого протесту

Сьогодні усі ми вийшли підтримати "Європейський вибір України". Європейські цінності - це добре, вигідно, прогресивно і т.д. А конкретно? Давайте на мить затаємо подих і подумаємо, чого конкретно хочемо?

Ми не завжди усвідомлюємо переваги та недоліки договору Асоціації з ЄС. Це не дивно, адже ні ЗМІ, ні експрти, ні профільні департаменти досі не оприлюднили незалежного, ґрунтовного та критичного аналізу цього тексту. Ми чули, що в першу чергу йдеться про економічну співпрацю. Про налагодження торгівлі, тепліший інвестиційний клімат та кращі умови для великого бізнесу. Але хіба люди, які стоять разом на #ЄвроМайдані отримають безпосередній економічний зиск з угоди? Не варто забувати, що сумарний економічний ріст країни - це ще не гарантія рівного розподілу благ між громадянами: гроші накопичуватимуться там, де і були - у кишенях найбагатших.

Які конкретні спільні інтереси нас об'єднують? Ми вимагаємо рішучих політичних, соціальних та економічних змін! Прагнемо дійсного і постійного впливу на прийняття важливих політичних по рішень, які безпосередньо стосуються наших прав і свобод, умов та якості нашого життя. Прагнемо публічного врядування, що позбавить нас від мук бюрократії. Справедливого суду та припинення міліцейського свавілля. Ми прагнемо гідних умов та достойної оплати праці. Ми виступаємо за якісну та доступну освіту, розвиток культури і науки, та впровадження новітніх технологій. Вимагаємо екологічно свідомого використання природних ресурсів. Якісного, безкоштовного медичного забезпечення. Ми прагнемо зручної і доступної для всіх інфраструктури громадського транспорту. Ми мріємо жити у світі без кордонів. Та в решті решт, ми прагнемо коректного та толерантного ставлення одне до одного. Усе це і надає змісту нашій присутності на Майдані. *Ми надаємо зміст Майдану!*

Наші проблеми не вирішить ніхто, окрім нас. Наївно думати, що парламентські політики цього разу захищатимуть наші інтереси. Ми вже були на Майдані в 2004, ми вже побачили, що парламентська опозиція нічого принципово не змінює. Сьогодні політики знову пропонують обирати з двох зол, але перед нами стоїть якісно нова перспектива – низова самоорганізація та солідарність. Лише **безпосередня участь кожного здобуде справжню Європу. Асоціація з ЄС - перший крок.**

Долучитись до низової самоорганізації на #євромайдані: █████████

Figure 0.2. "The Substance of Our Protest"
Source: Author's photograph.

[Anonymous; translated from Ukrainian by the author; see figure 0.2.]

Today we all came to support "Ukraine's European Choice." European values are good, beneficial, progressive, and so on. But specifically? Let's catch our breath for a moment and think about what we want specifically.

We don't always recognize the advantages and disadvantages of the Association contract with the EU. This is not surprising, since neither the media, nor experts, nor relevant departments have published an independent, thorough, critical analysis of this text. We have heard that the first question is that of economic cooperation. Of establishing trade, a warmer investment climate and better conditions for big business. But will people who stand together on #EuroMaidan receive immediate economic benefits from the agreement? Do not forget that the total economic growth of the country does not guarantee equal distribution of wealth among citizens: money will accumulate where it already is – in the pockets of the richest.

What specific common interests unite us? We require decisive political, social, and economic change! We seek valid and permanent influence on the adoption of important political decisions that immediately concern our rights and freedoms, the conditions and quality of our life. We demand public governance that relieves us from the torment of bureaucracy. A fair trial and the termination of police arbitrariness. We demand dignified conditions and decent wages. We advocate for quality and accessible education, the development of culture and science, and the implementation of the latest technologies. We demand ecologically conscious use of natural resources. Quality, free medical care. We seek useful and accessible public transport infrastructure for all. We dream of living in a world without borders. Eventually, we seek civil and tolerant attitudes towards one another. All of this provides the content of our presence on Maidan. *We provide the content of Maidan!*

No one can solve our problems except for us. It is naive to think that parliamentary politics will protect our interests at this time. We were already on Maidan in 2004, we already saw that the parliamentary opposition fundamentally changes nothing. Today, politicians are again proposing that we choose between two evils, but before us stands a quality new perspective – grassroots self-organization and solidarity. **Only everyone's immediate participation will gain the real Europe. EU Association is the first step.**

Get involved in the grassroots self-organization of #euromaidan: [email redacted]

Yulia Tymoshenko – whom he had imprisoned on politically motivated charges – to travel to Germany to receive treatment for health issues she developed in prison. This refusal solidified that Yanukovych would not sign an Association Agreement with the European Union, a condition of which was that Tymoshenko would be released from prison. Instead, these actions expressed his intention to ally Ukraine with Russia and Vladimir Putin's Customs Union (*Mytnyi Soiuz*). The Association Agreement was expected to put an end to debates about whether Ukraine's future was with Europe or with Russia, and given Yanukovych's cooperation to that point with European leaders, most assumed that the Agreement would be signed. Surprise and disappointment at this decision prompted people to gather on Independence Square in Ukraine's biggest – and eventually most violent – mobilization since the country's independence in 1991. Some 1,500 people came to Maidan in the night following Yanukovych's decision, and hundreds of thousands would gather for protests throughout the next seven months. Ultimately, one hundred people were killed in the protests after standoffs with riot police and snipers, Yankovych fled to Russia, and a transitional government was put in place in February 2014. The protest camp on Maidan continued to exist throughout the rest of my fieldwork and was taken down the day after I left Ukraine on 30 June 2014.

Ukraine's physical location has placed it between two major geopolitical formations, Russia and the European Union (see Dunn and Bobick 2014). Its twenty-four regions or *oblasts* contain myriad ethnic and linguistic groups, all of whom were granted Ukrainian citizenship in 1991 (Arel 1995; Shulman 2002). However, their affiliations – to local, national, or supranational entities – were not unified upon Ukraine's independence. Many have studied this "regionalism" as challenging, if not detrimental, to establishing an effective Ukrainian national identity (Barrington and Herron 2004; Dickinson 2010; for a novel methodology to address this issue, see Schmid and Myshlovska 2019). It has led to a significant politicization of regional identities, in which stereotypes of "the East," represented most authentically by the industrial Donbas, portray the region as a bastion of Soviet nostalgia nurturing a desire to return to Russia. "The West" was brought into the Ukrainian Soviet Socialist Republic later than other regions and was also the area where nationalist, anti-Soviet resistance fighters had the greatest levels of support. This perceived schism has contributed to narratives of Ukraine as a borderland, pulled between Europe and Russia and powerless to decide its own fate.

In political terms, this division has strongly influenced Ukrainian governance. Many of Ukraine's most prominent political figures, including

Viktor Yanukovych and Yulia Tymoshenko, came from major cities in the East (Donets'k and Dnipropetrovs'k, respectively), where they contributed to oligarchic "clans" that made millions from the consolidation of industries after the fall of state socialism. Yanukovych's Party of Regions (PR) in particular was effective in further politicizing these regional differences. Specifically, the PR "position[ed] itself as representing Russophone voters generally, defending their identity and promoting their policy preferences" (Kudelia 2014, 20), which included promoting the status of Russian to an official language of Ukraine, as well as forging closer ties with Russia and delegating more authority to the regional level within Ukraine (Bustikova 2019; Kudelia 2014). It was on such promises that Yanukovych effectively mobilized this regional demographic in the 2010 presidential elections, appearing to represent those most disenfranchised in independent Ukraine and promising to stop the spread of fanatical nationalism, represented by Oleh Tyahnybok and the Svoboda Party.

When he ran for president in 2004, Yanukovych was widely perceived as incapable and undesirable as a representative of Ukraine. Famously poor at using the Ukrainian language, his criminal past discredited him as a positive political figure (Kudelia 2014, 20; Wilson 2005, 8), despite his support from Leonid Kuchma, Ukraine's second president. Viktor Yushchenko, his 2004 opponent who worked in the banking industry before taking up politics (Wilson 2005, 14–45), represented progress, as he promised to bring Ukraine into line with Europeanization policies that (theoretically) would allow Ukraine eventually to become a member of the European Union. Yulia Tymoshenko, who consolidated Ukraine's gas import business with oligarch Viktor Pinchuk in the 1990s (Wilson 2005, 19), supported Yushchenko and his European aspirations, lending a further "Ukrainian" air to their campaign with her peasant-inspired clothing and hairstyles (this despite her Dnipropetrovs'k origins, a city largely associated with Soviet industry).[2] Yushchenko and Tymoshenko attempted to represent a pro-Ukraine, pro-Europe perspective. Yanukovych and his support from Kuchma – whose own regime was responsible for the 2000 murder of the independent journalist Heorhiy Gongadze, which led, in part, to the "Ukraine Without Kuchma" movement to unseat the president in 2000–1 (Wilson 2005) – were a regression into oligarchy and Sovietesque relations with Russia.

On 21 November 2004, Viktor Yanukovych was declared the winner of the runoff presidential election against Yushchenko, who had been widely slated to win. With evidence of major fraud and the state-controlled media declaring Yanukovych the winner, some 300,000 people massed on Independence Square on 22 November (Quinn-Judge and Zarakhovich 2004; Wilson 2005, especially chap. 6). The tent camp they created there, filled with the orange colour of Yushchenko's campaign and giving the protests the name Orange Revolution, lasted for little more than two months. In late December, a new "third round" of voting was held, in which Yushchenko won over 50 per cent of the vote (Wilson 2005, 153). This moment was thought to herald a new era in Ukraine – the development of civil society organizations and a new enthusiasm for institutional politics, as well as putting the country on the path to Europe. However, infighting in the Yushchenko government led to the ousting of Prime Minister Tymoshenko and the creation of a coalition government in which Yanukovych gained power in conjunction with Yushchenko. The latter, unable to enact any substantive economic reforms, left office with some of the lowest approval ratings of any Ukrainian president. Thus, in 2010, Yanukovych's ascent to power came as a result of a more mobilized voting population in Yanukovych's home regions and because Yanukovych was seen as an antidote to the ills created by Yushchenko and Tymoshenko.

After consolidating power through reinstating the country's 1996 constitution, which gave more powers to the president (Kudelia 2014, 21), and by subordinating the judicial system to his government (23) – which allowed Yanukovych to prosecute Tymoshenko for abuse of authority during 2009 gas deals with Russia – the president appeared to have been instated successfully as a Putin-friendly head of the Ukrainian state. His approval ratings fell, however, and Yanukovych subsequently turned to Ukraine's European interests as a strategy to regain some of his former legitimacy. Importantly, the European Union's offer of an Association Agreement was contingent not only on economic reforms but also on the release of Tymoshenko from prison. But Yanukovych never fully gave up the possibility of integrating Ukraine into Putin's Customs Union (together with Belarus and Kazakhstan). Indeed, in November 2013, Yanukovych committed to the latter path: "Once again seeking Russia's financial assistance – including reduced gas prices – would offer a way to keep social payments up, utility rates down, and short-term debt safely rolled over" (Kudelia 2014, 28). Framing the deal as more immediately economically beneficial, Yanukovych attempted to gloss over the political implications of the agreement.

By 2013 Yanukovych and his regime had made it clear that it was time for Ukraine to be a borderland no longer but to take its inevitable place on the side of Russia. When it became apparent that Yanukovych did not intend to sign the Association Agreement, people again flooded the streets of Ukraine's major cities, particularly in the centre and west (Kyiv and L'viv in particular), but eventually in eastern cities including

Kharkiv, Dnipropetrovs'k, and Donets'k; in the southern centres Odesa and Kherson; and even in Crimea (see Onuch 2014a, 48). Not only did they declare their affiliation for Europe, which was supposed to be secured officially through the Association Agreement; they also declared that the state – meant to represent its citizens, who had elected its members democratically – was no longer representative of them.

Ukraine in Neoliberalism: State Criticism, Volunteerism, and Civil Society

The political context outlined above is deeply grounded in Ukraine's position in the post-socialist, neoliberal world. In this book, I argue that Ukraine's political trajectory since its independence exposes the nexus between the processes of post-socialist transformation and neoliberal development. The experience of socialism, as many have documented, continues to shape a variety of realities in now-independent countries that were part of the Soviet Union, as well as those satellite states that also implemented party communism. Indeed, social scientists of the region have developed an extensive body of literature attending to the state and economic systems since 1989, using these to explore the shift from a centrally controlled economic and political regime to, potentially, a market economy and representative democracy (Horváth and Szakolczai 1992; Humphrey 2002; Verdery 1996). And, while this market economy and representative democracy are often thought of as Western exports, imposed on fledgling post-socialist countries whose governments promised economic reforms and a crackdown on corruption, Johanna Bockman and Gil Eyal argue that reformist economists in eastern Europe were in dialogue with western European and North American counterparts, ultimately helping eastern European economists to implement neoliberal economic reforms and turning the socialist experience, as the authors argue, into a "laboratory" that "could be mobilized to support arguments about market regulations" (Bockman and Eyal 2002, 315; see also Johnson 2016). The dialogue between libertarian actors from the United States and market socialists from eastern Europe in the 1950s and 1960s led precisely to the development of *neoliberalism* in economic theory (Bockman and Eyal 2002, 333), which reformist economists conveniently imposed as economic reality in 1989 (337).

Here, I also draw from Jesook Song's research into the Asian debt crisis and neoliberal transformations in South Korea. She asks whether it is "correct to use the notion of neoliberalism in the context of late industrialized countries and former socialist states" (Song 2009, 11), and she argues that modern states do not necessarily have to go through the experience of a liberal economic system in order to become part of the global neoliberal economic order. As capital transactions are not constrained by national boundaries, and as workers are expected to be "flexible, adaptable, and 'self-governing'" (11) in a variety of political regimes, neoliberal economic systems are not necessarily grounded in a particular economic history. Thus, countries of the former USSR are not precluded from global neoliberal economics because they experienced socialism rather than liberalism in the twentieth century. Further, the presence of and reliance on international economic institutions are crucial in the cases of South Korea and of Ukraine and other formerly Soviet countries.

Bockman and Eyal argue that the "shock therapy" policies of total economic overhaul in the former Soviet Union enabled an erasure of the participation of eastern European reformist economists in the dialogues around economic reform in the 1950s and 1960s. In their place, Western institutions, such as the World Bank and the International Monetary Fund (IMF), became the ultimate authority in creating the standards for economic development in post-socialist countries. These institutions and actors believed that the socialist economies could not be reformed; rather, they had to be entirely transformed into market-driven economies with the state completely removed from policy decisions. Yet the presence of these institutions and their expectations of how neoliberal economies should develop led to new kinds of disenfranchisement that had not been present, for instance, under military dictatorship in South Korea or during the Communist Party's regime in the USSR. Song's book, for instance, focuses on homelessness and underemployment in South Korea following economic restrictions after the Asian Debt Crisis that began in 1997.

The advent and global spread of neoliberal economic policies, which propose that "human well-being can best be advanced by liberating individual entrepreneurial freedoms and skills within an institutional framework characterized by strong private property rights, free markets, and free trade" (Harvey 2005, 2), have led to an intertwining of economic and political systems (Greenhouse 2009). This intertwining is preserved by a state form that intervenes as little as possible in markets; at the same time, as Harvey argues, neoliberal economic policies are a "*political* project to re-establish the conditions for capital accumulation and to restore the power of economic elites" (Harvey 2005, 19). This has been true in eastern Europe and the former Soviet Union, as well: according to the Western representatives who came to the former USSR in the 1990s, "reformers should act to liberate the natural forces of the economy and civil society, the initiative and ingenuity of responsible citizens" (Bockman and Eyal 2002, 341). One of the major processes of this type of governance, documented in various global contexts, is the withdrawal or retreat of the "state" in society and its replacement by other actors (Harvey 2005, 3; this withdrawal goes along with major moments of deregulation and privatization). These actors have included non-governmental organizations (NGOs) and their representatives (Phillips 2008, 2011), other "civil society" actors linked with supportive government agencies (Song 2009), charities (Caldwell 2004), and civilian volunteers (Hemment 2009, 2012; Hyatt 2001).

Yet Song also argues that state actors are essential to the creation and reproduction of neoliberalism at both the economic and political levels. State agencies are responsible for implementing welfare systems, but their links remain with NGOs that take on other tasks no longer the responsibility of the state. Based on extensive research in Russia, Julie Hemment calls neoliberal projects in the post-Soviet world "uneven and contradictory" processes (Hemment 2009, 37). Exploring pro-Kremlin youth organizations, Hemment considers how "Soviet-style neoliberalism" develops through civil society organizations taking on the responsibilities of the state, while remaining deeply reliant on the state – what Hemment calls "not quite state yet not non-governmental" (37; Song makes a similar observation about civil society organizations in South Korea). These organizations help the state gain legitimacy, including regarding economic reforms, but they also help citizens see new ways of engaging with one another and change their expectations of what the state can and should do.

Similar developments in Ukraine led to an overvaluing of "civil society" as a mechanism to measure the success – based on the standards of Western economic institutions – of economic and political reforms after 1991. Katherine Verdery argues that civil society, like Europe, democracy, and nation, is a "key symbolic operator," rather than an "organizational reality" (Verdery 1996, 105). But the precise notion of civil society in post-Soviet Ukraine, in which "civil society" means non-government political actors that serve as a check on elected officials, cannot be said to have existed before 1991; it was an ideal established by those same Western reformers who arrived in the former socialist bloc intending to transform national economies. In Ukraine, civil society organizations are tasked with being the watchdogs that make sure the government implements the reforms required by the IMF in order to qualify for visa-free travel to Europe and monetary aid. Thus, international financial groups require certain actions on behalf of the "state," including both economic and political reforms in the case of Ukraine, but the expectation of accountability for implementing reforms is, to a large extent, placed properly on non-governmental actors.

Scholars of post-socialism have documented the various shifts that state forms have taken, particularly considering the state-citizen relationship and questioning what states' duties to citizens realistically can be (Haney 2002; Höjdestrand 2009). Some suggest that the post-socialist state is not in withdrawal but rather that people's expectations of state provisions are constantly being renegotiated as regimes attempt to stay in power (Cook 2007; Read and Thelen 2007). The creation of "civil society" and the establishment of expectations of what this non-governmental sector should do is an important component of this renegotiation. In Hemment's case, civil society groups use their positioning to help legitimize state actions, but in Ukraine such groups have tended to be critical of every presidential administration since independence. Here, we can see how civil society is a "key symbolic operator," rather than a concrete, measurable field of political activity: in both contexts, civil society must appear to be separate from the state, but in reality its existence is entirely intertwined with the state.

Privatization, Volunteerism, and State Processes

Social scientists are often cautious of language that reifies "the state" (see Abrams 2006), but here I use it extensively because it was central to elements of leftist activists' discourse that shape my analysis of Ukrainian politics. The "state" – in terms of what is expected of it as an institution, which bodies collectively become interpellated as the "state," and what those bodies do – shifts over time, growing and contracting depending on various social, political, and economic factors. In particular, throughout the Maidan protests, leftists used the language of a "police state" (*politseis'ka derzhava*) to criticize the use of force against protesters sanctioned by President Yanukovych. This language helped me see how people's view of the state – in this case, delegitimized because of the use of force against citizens – influenced their own actions. Because so many participants in Euromaidan saw the state as failing the citizens, they took up tasks of the state while also proposing a new vision of what could be expected of a state that was seen as legitimate. However, this post-Maidan reconstitution of the Ukrainian state intersected with other neoliberal political and economic reforms, which has meant that activists and citizens who participated in the Maidan protests did not create the state they might have hoped for, and instead have continued a complex negotiation with state bodies and the expectations of the state.

One of these complex negotiations includes the "privatization" of the state (Hibou 2004). Shifts in government from a centralized state body controlling welfare regimes or security services to privatized provisioning of such services, for instance, do not show a unidirectional state retreat. Instead, these processes are examples of a growing trend in which state bodies use privatizing mechanisms to redistribute and further reconsolidate power to new ends. They serve to diversify the state's influence and the actors that work in conjunction with the state, and the opacity created by these relationships is a crucial part of the power of the privatized state. This privatization of the state has developed over time; it is not simply a product of the neoliberalization of the global economy, but has long been entrenched in state forms and functions. Indeed, the globalization of economies – including foreign investment as a major contributor to state economies, as well as the intervention of international NGOs in state processes – further encourages the effective privatizing of the state. Those authors whose work describes a growing emphasis on individual autonomy and self-sufficiency are not necessarily suggesting simply that a state's retreat has displaced responsibility onto the individual. Rather, we can see this trend as part of the whole reconfiguration of the citizen-state relationship. Neoliberal governance includes a shifting relationship between governing and the governed in which the governed take an active role in creating the mechanisms through which such governance works (Ong 2006), a process I explore in detail in later chapters.

An important example of part of the ongoing process of "privatization" of the state, as well as a way to spread new discourses about how citizens should relate to their state, is civic participation – particularly the growth of volunteerism in Ukraine during and after Euromaidan. Volunteers who once criticized the state's inability to perform certain functions and completed them despite this inability are promoted through state discourses as those actors who were always meant to perform such duties. These processes absolve state bodies of their responsibilities, displacing those responsibilities onto citizens and civic groups, while drawing these actors more tightly into the state's power structure because they are now seen as necessary to the state's ability to govern (Eliasoph 2011; Hemment 2015; Hyatt 2001; Minakov 2018; Muehlebach 2012). Praise for the work of volunteers combined with the effectiveness of their organizational strategies helps naturalize citizens' responses rather than criticize the state's lack of responsibility.

At the same time, reliance on volunteerism reproduces further social stratification. In the context of Ukraine, volunteerism has a crucial gendered component. As I show elsewhere, militarized masculinity has been an important aspect of the image of Maidan (Channell-Justice 2017). The majority of the military volunteers in the Donbas have been men (Goujon 2016; Lebedev 2016), although several researchers have focused on the participation of female military volunteers (Marstenyuk and Grytsenko 2017; Rubchak 2014; UN Women 2015). Importantly, those who work behind the front lines, providing medical services, distributing food and clothes, and helping organize evacuations from the region, tend to be women (Shukan 2016a; Stepaniuk 2016). Ioulia Shukan's research among the "Sisters of Mercy" in Kharkiv shows an example of this tendency as well as the ease with which a women-run volunteer organization generates legitimacy (Shukan 2016a). These tendencies help encourage women to take on roles as caretakers, without remuneration, where state representatives have confirmed their own inability to provide these services even as people's lives and livelihoods are at stake. Natalia Stepaniuk (2018) suggests that the reification of traditional gender roles in volunteer groups through care work further prevents women from taking on decisionmaking roles, reinforcing the stereotypical assumption that women should not participate in politics or political decisions.

In sum, discourses about and practices of volunteerism benefit the new Ukrainian state in various ways. First, volunteer organizations take the burden of certain services away from the state and onto citizens. These range from simple collections of food for volunteer troops to the volunteer basis of much of the military action in the Donbas to the evacuation of Donbas inhabitants from the war zone. Second, the circulation of discourses that confirm volunteering as an essential part of good citizenship fits into the web of neoliberalization. Importantly, in Ukraine, the process of neoliberalization is linked with decommunization and Europeanization. The volunteer-as-citizen discourses that permeate neoliberal ideas about citizenship confirm that volunteerism in Ukraine, rather than being proof of the state's inability to provide properly for its citizens, shows instead that Ukraine is truly a European-style democracy.

Self-Organization in the Neoliberal World

This book is an ethnographic exploration of the Euromaidan protests that many refer to as a "revolution," notably naming it the "Revolution of Dignity" (but see Channell-Justice 2019b for a discussion of the suitability of this designation). Others have published work on these events, but many of these accounts tend to reinforce the widely disseminated image that the protesters were united in their goals, tactics, and expectations. In this book, however, I call that image into question by showing the pluralities within Maidan, rooted in very different visions of how to protest and what to demand. No other scholar from the United States was already working with activists when the protests began and continued to work with them during and after Euromaidan. Thus, my lens on the protests differs significantly from others' analyses of them. Some scholars who were already researching and publishing on Ukraine have also written about Maidan – see, for instance, Wilson's (2014) somewhat hastily published chronology of the events; Shukan (2016a), who presents a more measured analysis and continues into the post-Maidan period; Carroll (2019), who skilfully weaves Euromaidan into her larger discussion of addiction and public health; and Emeran (2017), who includes interviews with Euromaidan activists in her discussion of recurring protest movements in Ukraine. Others present a significantly more partial view, even romanticizing the "revolution" (Shore 2018). The Ukrainian novelist Andrei Kurkov (2014) has written what I consider to be the most resonant account of Maidan through his diary-like chronology.

My intervention in this discussion presents research that took place predominately from the perspective of activists who were long marginalized from Ukrainian political society and who thus had been ignored as significant participants in Euromaidan. Here, I argue that leftist activists infiltrated the protests expertly, by spreading the idea of self-organization in their initiatives in order to fight the state's violent crackdown. Sometimes they were successful; at other times their interventions were met with violence and harassment, ranging from destruction of their property to being pepper sprayed and physically assaulted. Yet many leftist activists continued to attend protest events throughout the winter. My ethnographic work uses various ups and downs among these activists on Maidan to explore the complexity of the protests and to reject a romanticized and simplified idea of the "revolution."

Yet, I also see that Euromaidan had great significance even after the removal of the tent camps in the summer of 2014. Participating in the protests led to a reorganization of Ukrainian political society, because people learned they have power and can wield it to achieve their goals. Of course, this power is tempered by economic instability, dissatisfaction with political figures, and fear of what might happen when masses make demands on the state again. But what has continued to resonate, I argue, is the idea that self-organization can be more fruitful than the existing political structures that make up what we know as the state.

Most simply, self-organization comes from the idea that, if something needs to be done and a person has the ability to do it, then the person should simply do it. Leftists have used the notion of self-organization as a way to take their experiences as activists and create new means of social and political engagement. One leftist activist told me that the success of leftist language around self-organization and anti-police violence was extremely important, even though right-wing figures themselves adopted this language later in the protests. She also felt that leftists had always recognized that political power is tied up with having money, that politicians have always gained their power with money, and that these themes also became prominent on Maidan. In an interview in June 2014, a leftist and feminist activist described to me the ways ordinary people had been affected by their experiences on Maidan: "When people get practical experience of protest and self-organization and actions with other people, they can't forget that and can't reject it. They treat it really seriously." In her view, people's engagement with self-organized protest changed their common sense about how they could interact with politics and government, whether they considered themselves activists or not.

For leftists in Ukraine, the notion of self-organization comes from socialist ideas of self-help at the same time that they draw from global anti-capitalist movements such as Occupy Wall Street to criticize the neoliberal or neoliberalizing state. Anti- or alter-globalization movements grew transnationally after what David Graeber (2009, viii) has referred to as the "watershed for global neoliberalism": the early 2000s. To a large extent, however, the countries emerging from state socialism were not included in the canon of new ethnographic research on social movements (see Casas-Cortés, Osterweil, and Powell 2008; Edelman 2001; Juris and Khasnabish 2013; Price, Nonini, and Fox Tree 2008). Research from the region focused on concepts such as "civil society" and building non-state actors' capacity to effect change (Minakov 2018; Way 2014). Because of the history of so-called leftist politics in the formerly socialist parts of the world, and because of the domination of narratives of nationalism and far-right resurgence that grew in the aftermath of socialism (Bustikova 2019), the existence of a post-socialist leftist politics that was part of the transnational alter-globalization movement was not evident. This trend began to be reversed with anthropologists' consideration of Occupy movements around the world (Juris 2012; Razsa and Kurnik 2012), a key moment in Ukrainian leftists' understanding of their own place in a global anti-capitalist movement.

Only more recently have anthropologists been interested in the growth of protest movements – including anti-national, radical leftist participation – around the post-socialist world that have developed after the humanist and modernist goals of the socialist world were not achieved (Kurtović and Sargsyan 2019). These authors have seen radical activists as fundamentally critical of the NGO-ization of political possibilities (Razsa 2015); they have shown that democracy is a project that is constantly under negotiation, rather than a measurable outcome of post-socialism (Greenberg 2014). Moving beyond earlier trends in studies of social movements to divide analysis between "new social movements" and resource mobilization (Edelman 2001), they adopt the notion of "prefigurative politics" (Graeber 2002) by taking seriously the worlds that activists are trying to build out of the socialist past (Kurtović and Hromadžić 2017; Razsa and Kurnik 2012). I follow this trend, and I also follow the suggestion that exploring a movement in formation – that is, thinking through how protest movements are shaped and how people begin to identify as part of a greater whole – elucidates what studying formal organizations cannot (Polletta 2006).

This book is part of a growing body of literature that focuses on the left, following Larisa Kurtović and Nelli Sargsyan, "not because we do not recognize that activisms fall on all sides of the political spectrum, but because we are specifically interested in how the loss of state socialism as a world-making project (and the subsequent failures of postsocialist 'civil society building') has impacted new generations of progressive, anti-nationalist, anarchist, and social-justice oriented activists" (Kurtović and Sargsyan 2019, 2). It takes seriously the worldbuilding that leftist activists envision, and it accepts that the future might look different from the so-called democratic institutions that are the focus of much development work in Ukraine today. It accepts that feelings of rage, disappointment, anger, fear – and of emancipation in the spirit of violence, as one activist described it after the peak violence of the Euromaidan protests in February 2014 – are part of radical activism against global political and economic inequality (Greenberg 2014; Kurtović 2015; see also Goodwin, Jasper, and Polletta 2001; Jasper 1998).

As the flyer shown in figure 0.1 expresses, leftists are critical of the accumulation of wealth in the hands of those who are already wealthy, a fundamental idea of the Occupy Everywhere mobilizations. At the same time that many Ukrainian leftists are actively engaged with other leftist and alter-globalization movements around Europe, they tend to be more focused on Ukraine's immediate concerns. The Euromaidan protests brought to the forefront Ukraine's relationship with the European Union, prompting leftists to consider whether the widely perceived good of becoming part of Europe would indeed help Ukrainians economically. Significantly, leftists targeted those already in power – those who made up the state *as well as* those who participated in political parties that made up the Opposition – as actors who were giving protesters on Maidan an either-or (Europe or Russia) choice. Leftists proposed alternatives, as they claimed with the expression, "We provide the content of Maidan!" Although even in the flyer leftists showed their preference for European association, they intended to enter into a relationship with Europe that would allow Ukrainians to make demands, rather than just acquiesce to the expectations of the EU and its leaders.

The Euromaidan mobilizations had various goals, strategies, and effects. One major goal of the protests and of the ensuing government was to prove Ukraine's place as part of Europe. But the idea of "Europe" is complex: what place does the nation-state have in an increasingly (at least for some people) borderless Europe? – see Asher (2005); Follis (2012); Shore (2004). Both the Europe presented during Euromaidan and the Europe of national referenda and Association Agreements are distinct from "actually existing" Europe or the lived realities of European citizenship. Euromaidan turned "Europe" into a contested political symbol or, as Verdery puts it, a "key symbolic operator," and leftist activists provided some of its most important critiques.

Leftists' criticism of Europe and "European values" is a crucial component of understanding how post-Maidan Europeanization processes have unfolded, including mass protests against post-Euromaidan president Petro Poroshenko's government in the winter of 2017–18 and the ensuing election of TV comedian Volodymyr Zelensky in 2019. How leftists made demands during Euromaidan and the ultimate outcomes of their campaigns tells the greater story of the reorganization of Ukrainian political activism after Maidan. Leftists' claim that "We provide the content of Maidan!" invokes a dual significance. First, it implores participants of all political ideologies not to let leaders claim to represent the diverse voices of protesters. Second, and more significantly for this book, the minority leftist community within the protests influenced the essence of the protests – and thus the future of Ukrainian political organizing – with their insistence on self-organization. Thus, this book is an analysis that uses one moment to answer bigger questions about political futures in a country in which stability still seems far away for many. It uses the lens of self-organization to explore the lasting effects of an event that continues to loom large in Ukraine's post-independence period.

Research Methodology during Maidan

November 21, 2013: Last night there were some gatherings on Maidan to protest the decision not to allow Tymoshenko to go abroad to seek treatment, thus ending the likelihood of signing the Association Agreement this month.

This was my first fieldnote entry mentioning "Maidan" – the shorthand often used to describe the mass mobilizations that took over my research for the next seven months. My lack of enthusiasm and detail reflect my scepticism; I can honestly say I did not anticipate that the small protests of 21 November would become anything more than a few disappointed young people who had hoped European accession was close at hand. I was wrong. Over the next few months, the protesters expanded into the tens of thousands, set up a tent camp, and, in the end, one hundred were killed at the hands of militarized riot police and the president fled the country.

Neither I nor my interlocutors anticipated the events that frame this research project. Rather, it began thanks to a serendipitous meeting when I first visited Ukraine as a teenager in 2004. I met Vitalii during a school exchange program in Kyiv just months before the Orange Revolution, and we became friends. I did not return to Ukraine until June 2011, when I visited Kyiv for a short week. When we met anew, Vitalii told me he had become an activist in his university and was interested in Marxism and other leftist ideologies. The problems he faced as an activist fascinated me, and I began to develop a research project to document the work of these leftist student activists. In 2012, following intensive language study in the western Ukrainian city of L'viv, I got the project under way. I spent a weekend travelling in the region with Vitalii and another comrade, who began to enlighten me about the state of leftist and feminist activism and scholarship at the time. After my language program, I spent several weeks in Kyiv with Vitalii, meeting other leftist activists in the student activist group Priama Diia (Direct Action). In August 2012, I attended Priama Diia's student organizing summer camp in Crimea, where I spent a week camping with over one hundred activists, the majority from across Ukraine and the rest from Russia. Here, I connected with activists from regional centres in Ukraine, including Simferopol (in Crimea), Kharkiv, and Odesa, as well as from the smaller but extremely active city of Khmel'nyts'kyi in western Ukraine.

I returned to Ukraine in September 2013, and began interviewing activists about their actions and networks, intending to map connections among activists in various parts of the country. I attended several demonstrations with leftist activists, and I began to participate in self-defence classes organized by and for leftists. On 21 November 2013, however, protests started on Independence Square in the centre of Kyiv. It rapidly became clear that the activists whom I knew from my research were going to participate. I began to follow leftists around Maidan during the protests and to their planning meetings; I visited Maidan nearly every day that I was in Kyiv until I left the country on

30 June 2014. I lived in an apartment a forty-minute walk, or two sub-way stops, from Maidan. Even on days when the subway and other transportation had shut down, I could still walk to Maidan, but the neighbourhood was also far enough from the protests that I could come and go safely.

Over time, I developed a symbiotic relationship with the activists who participated in my research. As activists who were so often ignored or misrepresented, they appreciated having someone write honestly about them and their organizations. They encouraged my close partici-pant observation by including me on listservs, Facebook groups, and sometimes even by calling me to make sure I would attend a particular event. I always brought my high-quality camera to protest actions and, as a person unknown to non-leftists, I was asked regularly to share with activists pictures of the protests, not only because activists simply ap-preciated seeing good photos of their actions, but also to photograph people who had attacked activists – and once even to track down a suspicious figure – to help protect organizers in the future. Because of these mutual investments, I felt confident that these leftist activists would do their best to ensure my safety during the mobilizations. I always checked in with particular activists I knew best before events to be sure I would endanger neither myself nor the other activists by my presence. When major violence broke out during Euromaidan, several activists contacted me immediately to make sure I was not in danger, and one even offered for his father to drive me to the airport if I needed to evacuate the country.

Thanks to this rapport I shared with these activists, I was able to com-plete effective research despite the unpredictable nature of the Ukrain-ian context. I did formal interviews with twenty leftist activists,[3] mostly in spring 2014, after the political situation appeared to have stabilized somewhat. I pursued a strategy of intermittent informal questioning throughout the course of Maidan. I asked similar questions of multi-ple activists at various times, which provided me a relatively holistic – while also fluid and flexible – view of Maidan, of individual activists' ideologies and positions, and what the left, most broadly, was doing and thinking on Maidan.

Aside from interviews and field notes, I generated several thousand photos from Kyiv's Maidan. These feature protest events (leftist, fem-inist, and otherwise) as well as posters and signs, the tent camp, and the constantly changing barricades. I visited occupied buildings (the Kyiv City Hall and the Ukrainian House), and I once spent the night on Maidan with some activist friends. I attempted to avoid contact with the police, but this was difficult, as they seemed to be on every corner

Figure 0.3. The occupied Maidan, December 2013
Source: Author's photograph.

in the city centre. I never spoke to a police officer because I did not want to show my temporary residency permit and reveal that I was American. I also used Facebook as a resource quite extensively. Many activists posted status updates about Maidan, protest events, or information about activism or life in general. As these were shared publicly, I used them to inform my analysis, but I have not relied on them without clarifying a person's stance through an interview, formal or otherwise. Facebook is an interesting tool to consider someone's public self-representation, but it cannot replace a deeper discussion of one's opinions and experiences, particularly during such a major moment as Maidan (figure 0.3).

The leftist activists whose work and ideas make up much of the ethnographic work of this book are indeed a small group. In Kyiv, I interacted with fifty or so on a regular basis; I met with activists in Odesa early on in my fieldwork, before Maidan began, and was planning to meet with an activist group in L'viv as well. Importantly, I had planned two additional field sites in Khmel'nyts'kyi and Simferopol, but nearly all the activists from these two cities had moved to Kyiv by the time I began my fieldwork or during its course. I did complete several interviews in L'viv, but most of those activists were regularly shuttling between Kyiv and L'viv during Maidan, so I talked to and interacted with them in both places. Outside of protest events and meetings, I spent time with activists at their communal apartments and at the homes of those who lived with their parents, at their jobs, and occasionally travelling with them. Since I left Ukraine in 2014, I have continued contact with many of the activists who participated in my research project, visiting them in Ukraine again in the summers of 2016 and 2017 and finally in the fall of 2021 to discuss this book project.

Outline of the Book

In the chapters that follow, I use the Maidan mobilizations and their aftermath to call into question the citizen-state relationship in contemporary Ukraine. The chapters provide a lens through which to look at Ukrainian politics, particularly as I follow leftists' attempts to create space for themselves in the protests. Self-organization provides a unifying concept that brings together the various threads of my analysis.

In chapter 1, I explore the concept of self-organization as it is grounded in historical and ethnographic experiences. I place self-organization in relation to other significant concepts for post-socialist Ukraine, including civil society and volunteerism. I link self-organization to the leftist activists with whom I completed the majority of my research, describing the presence of leftists on Maidan in ethnographic detail. Finally, I connect self-organization to the post-Maidan conflict, a theme to which I return in the conclusion.

In chapter 2, I delve into what it means to be part of the "left" in contemporary Ukraine. The chapter features two in-depth profiles of leftist activists, to show that there is no one path to becoming a leftist in Ukraine and no singular way the left is defined. Following these profiles, I use two ethnographic examples – a leftist-organized Free School and self-defence classes – to investigate leftist community-building practices. I use these profiles and examples to place the Ukrainian left in dialogue with other contemporary leftist movements in the post-socialist world and beyond.

Chapter 3 examines the essential place of decommunization in the development of Ukraine's national ideology since its independence in 1991. In theory, decommunization should have cleansed the Ukrainian political sphere of those affiliated with state socialism and the Communist Party and, by extension, those affiliated with Russia. The Yanukovych regime's refusal to implement such policies confirmed its own desire to remain attached in some way to Russia. Leftist politics, often associated with the communist regime in Ukraine, were caught up in the politics of decommunization before the Maidan protests began, marginalizing them from participating in mainstream politics.

In chapter 4, I delve into specific leftist initiatives that appeared on Maidan in response to two factors: the rise of right-wing groups and the receptivity of protesters to the notion of self-organization. I focus on the ways leftists shifted their own tactics during the protests to protect themselves from violence, which was widely present during the first weeks of the mobilizations. Contextualized in the growing use of force against protesters – and protesters' willingness to fight back against the police – I explore how leftists grappled with their own typically non-violent stance as the protests changed. Specifically, I examine three ethnographic incidents that enlighten leftists' complex relationship with the people and ideologies present on Maidan. First, I reconsider the failed attempt at leftist criticism of the protest camp and the pro-Europe stance that I described briefly at the beginning of this introduction. Then, I show how, in response to several such events, leftists begin to retract ideologically leftist statements and slogans from their protests and focus instead on promoting anti-state rhetoric and tactics for self-organization. Finally, I follow the leftist initiative called Varto u likarni (Hospital Guard), which was created in response to police using force against protesters. Varto grew into one of the most recognized self-organized initiatives on Maidan, distanced from its leftist roots but something that leftists most often identified as successful self-organization.

In chapter 5, I provide an extended example of the site where leftists have had the most success over the course of recent political regimes: activism for higher education reform. I use the example of higher education to explore further how activists have used self-organization to gain broader acceptance in the Ukrainian political sphere. This example shows that self-organization could also be used to work within the confines of the state, not simply against it and its representatives. By focusing on reform through legislation, a major compromise for leftists, higher education activists have used self-organization to garner more interest in their issues and to integrate higher education into the fabric of the larger Maidan mobilizations.

In chapter 6, I use a feminist lens to explore how gender-based activism was integrated into the protests. I focus particularly on feminists' ideas about Europe and the ways protesters' ideas about the nation clashed with their own views of gender equality. While feminist activists were often threatened with violence and harassment from other protesters, the mobilizations created the space for feminists to think about how to use self-organization to promote feminist ideas, even amid widespread support for the retraditionalization of gender roles and the glorification of militarized, masculine heroes.

In the conclusion, I examine some of the new self-organized initiatives that have developed since the end of Maidan in the context of an ongoing war in Ukraine's eastern regions, known as the Donbas. I consider the intersection of self-organization with civil society and volunteerism once again, focusing on several examples of leftist self-organizing that have served different levels (local, municipal, and national). I use these examples, bolstered by evidence of other forms of volunteerism in Ukraine, to show how such practices have contributed to the reorganization of the state and the reconceptualization of citizenship since Maidan. Leftists have turned their attention to more local concerns, rather than continuing their earlier anti-state activism. At the same time, many have begun to question whether or not a total avoidance of representative politics is useful or necessary.

Since the end of the Maidan protest camps in July 2014, self-organization has continued to define the political moment in Ukraine. This is largely thanks to the ongoing war in the Donbas, which is supported in part through donations and volunteer forces. To some, these efforts – and projects to help ordinary people displaced by the conflict – are an extension of the self-organization that enabled the Maidan mobilizations to be so successful. At the same time, many of these practices encourage the government to withdraw further from people's lives; people's self-organized practices continue to fill gaps left by a shrinking state with a declining economy and growing austerity practices, even as it is increasingly integrated into the European Union.

Chapter One

Without Any Help from the State: Self-Organization in Ukraine

I first met Maria in late November 2013, but I didn't speak with her until a protest march went badly. I went with a group of leftist activists to Independence Square, where mass protests against President Viktor Yanukovych's decision not to sign an Association Agreement with the European Union had begun just a week earlier. The protests had mostly focused on claiming that Ukraine was part of Europe (geographically and culturally) and on presenting the benefits of Europeanization for Ukrainians. Leftist activists wanted to try to orient the protests more towards social inequalities that might come to Ukraine with the adoption of the agreement. But most people protesting did not want to hear these negative counterpoints to their pro-European positions. The leftist activists were attacked that night, their protest signs smashed on the stone and their group surrounded by threatening, angry protesters who berated the leftists for bringing seemingly anti-Europe language to the demonstrations. Maria was completely frustrated, but she didn't seem scared. I, on the other hand, could feel adrenaline coursing through my entire body as I walked around the menacing protesters, taking photos to document the assault, while the leftist activists linked arms to protect one another. After the leftists' signs had been destroyed and their assaulters started to disperse (see figure 1.1), I found myself standing next to Maria, and I asked her if she had experienced something similar before. "It happens all the time," she said, referencing several previous examples of protests in which leftist activists were attacked with pepper spray or their signs destroyed.

Leftist activists typically have been marginalized in post-independence Ukrainian party politics. This marginalization materializes through the constant threat of physical violence, as in the interaction described above, and actual violence. The young, post-socialist leftist activists whom I worked with do not affiliate themselves or their organizations

Figure 1.1. Remnants of leftist signs after an attack on Maidan
Source: Author's photograph.

with the Communist and Socialist parties of Ukraine, and they have no representation in government at any level.[1] Yet, over the course of these mass mobilizations, leftist activists found ways to engage with the masses of protesters, eventually with more success than the violent episode in November. Their main contribution was political activism based on the concept of "self-organization" (*samoorhanizatsiia*). For leftists, this term originated from Marxist principles, but its most basic definition is that, if a person is capable of doing something, and that thing needs to be done, then that person should simply do it.

This book explores the idea of self-organization as a development of anti-regime political activism during the mass mobilizations of 2013–14 and the kinds of activism and organizing that have continued in the years since the protests ended. Leftist activists' idea of self-organization came out of a Marxist political ideology, but, as I show, the term became more fluid as the protests went on, and many groups used the idea of self-organizing to signify any anti-government political action. Eventually, self-organization was adopted by groups that were very far from leftist political orientations, including by far-right volunteer militia groups. In this book, I use self-organization to explore leftist political activism and the ways leftists negotiated for space during mass mobilizations that were generally unfriendly to their politics. Self-organization – and the ways leftists associate their actions with it – provides an analytical lens through which to look critically at the relationship between political organizing, volunteer work, and the increasingly popular idea of civil society in post-Yanukovych Ukraine.

This chapter elaborates on the concept of self-organization as I use it throughout this book. I focus on the definition established by a particular group of leftist activists in Ukraine, because their use of the term was grounded in a specific vision of a Marxist ideal. However, as we will see throughout the book, the concept of self-organization has been picked up by different groups, both in Ukraine and beyond; thus, the concept changes over time and space. Here, I start with one group's definition so that the term's later movement and applications can be better understood. This chapter explores the Marxist origins of the idea of self-organization, its usages in the Soviet period, and the new life it took on in Ukraine during Maidan.

I also introduce the leftist activists who participated in this research. As with any research project, this representation of leftists is inherently partial: I do not claim to represent the views of all leftists in Ukraine. I delve more into the diversity of leftist perspectives in chapter 2, and I have continued to clarify people's stances on specific issues and their self-identification as leftists in the years following the main component of this research. Occasionally, I use "leftists" as a shorthand in this and other chapters; in these cases, I mean to indicate the group of leftists that participated in this research. Despite widespread assumptions that there is limited leftist presence in Ukraine, the people who make up the left have wide-ranging views, opinions, and interests. This is precisely what makes leftist perspectives a worthwhile topic of investigation.

Maria was one of the activists who helped me better understand the leftist origins of self-organization. On a sunny day in June 2014, after the protests had largely ended, I sat down to talk to Maria alone about her activist background and her ideas about leftism. Resting on some rocks in a courtyard behind a Soviet-era apartment block in Kyiv, smoking, Maria elaborated on why self-organization was so crucial to leftists and how she found it becoming a major organizing principle for other forms of activism after the protests on Maidan ended. Maria had visited the Crimean Peninsula after Russian troops occupied the territory in February 2014 but before a referendum to support Russia's annexation of Crimea that took place the following month. She had gone there with a photographer friend to document women's experiences of occupation. As she told me, "I said to them, we want to talk to you, do interviews with you, photograph you. And they said, oh, girls, we can't now, we have these problems. There are five hundred people, and we need to get them out [of Crimea]." With the presence of Russian troops, a photography project no longer seemed so important, so Maria and her friend decided instead to help these people escape the occupation.

With several grassroots initiatives that had been established during the Maidan protests, including Euromaidan SOS and Krym SOS (discussed later in the book; the latter was founded to provide reliable information about the rapidly changing situation in Crimea), Maria and her photographer friend helped this group of women find transportation and funds to get out of Crimea and into the main territory of Ukraine. Maria pointed out, "and this was all only with the help of the internet, telephones, and communication with ordinary people who were just looking for opportunities. And it was done without any help from the state. And after that I understood that maybe the state needs to have less of a function." Maria was not alone in describing the ways ordinary people used their personal networks and the internet to solve problems that, theoretically, should come under the purview of government institutions. Even non-activists volunteered for self-organized initiatives, such as the Krym SOS hotline, which helped resettle those who left Crimea. One friend in the western city of L'viv, a philology student who supported Maidan but had not previously considered herself an activist, recounted how she volunteered for the hotline, finding a place in the city for a family with three children and their horse.

Whether the latter group of volunteers ever considered themselves activists is unlikely. They were drawn to this type of work by the idea of self-organization, in which one can work against the regime in many ways. Even the most everyday tasks, like staffing a hotline, were part of the self-organized anti-government mobilization: one didn't have to stand on the front lines facing riot police and snipers in order to participate. This accessibility made self-organization an idea that permeated the protests, even as it was detached from its leftist, activist roots. I argue, however, that these activist roots influenced the flow of self-organization in a way that requires us to consider this type of activity unique from – but in relation to – volunteer work or humanitarian organizing.

Activists such as Maria never detached self-organization from its political roots. She linked the effectiveness of the impromptu evacuation from Crimea that she helped organize and ordinary people's willingness to help others to the Maidan protests, the initiatives that grew there, and an overall change in mentality. As Maria put it, "even in this kind of event, mass protests like Maidan, when people get practical experience of protest and self-organization and actions with other people, they can't forget that and can't reject it. They treat it really seriously." To Maria, the major impact of Maidan – and of leftists' presence on Maidan – was that serious problems were being solved by ordinary people themselves because they knew they could find solutions. This was a new political attitude, borne out of necessity and sustained by the continued demand for creative solutions to everyday problems.

Defining Contemporary "Left"

This book presents a view of citizens' shifting relationship with the Ukrainian state that is anchored in the Maidan mobilizations of 2013–14. The ethnographic research that makes up this analysis is based largely on participant observation with leftist activists, with whom I have done research since 2012. I use the term "left" because my interlocutors use it to describe themselves, but it is a fluid concept. Young, twenty-first-century Ukrainian leftists encompass a broad spectrum of identifications, ranging from a generic "left" to socialist, communist, Marxist, anarchist, and democratic socialist. These leftists are not members of the Communist Party, and they do not support a return to the Soviet Union or even an economic association with Russia. They are all Ukrainian, they speak Ukrainian (as well as Russian and often English), have a Ukrainian education, and, for the most part, want to live in Ukraine. In other words, their leftism is not mutually exclusive with being Ukrainian.

Contrary to many assumptions about leftist activism in Ukraine, leftists as a group do not want Ukraine to become part of Russia. Indeed, most leftists have a distinctively anti-colonial perspective in their analysis of the Russia-Ukraine relationship, as well as of the relationship between Ukraine and the European Union. They would prefer to see Ukraine not be in a position of subordination to either of these two entities, and they encouraged me to use this framing in my analysis. At the same time, most leftists are vocally critical of political ideologies that place any version of "the nation" or of establishing a "legitimate" nation above the rights of ordinary people. For instance, whereas many of the slogans used during Euromaidan referenced "Ukraine above all" (*Ukraïna ponad use*), leftists were promoting slogans for LGBTQ+ rights, gender equality, and access to free and accessible education, health care, and transportation. In response to "Ukraine above all," many leftists began carrying signs with the slogan, "Human rights above all" (*Prava liudyny ponad use*; see figure 1.2).

Figure 1.2. Police barricade with protest signs; the centre sign is a leftist
poster with the slogan "European values are human rights above all"
Source: Author's photograph.

At the same time, what being a "leftist" means and what a "leftist"
should do are still topics of intense conversation among Ukrainians
who identify with a left spectrum. The stories activists told me about
how they became leftists reflect this fluidity – there is not one unique
path one must take to become a leftist. Rather, leftists come out of punk
music and anti-fascist groups, from reading Marx, Engels, and Trotsky, and from bad experiences with university administrations. Enacting the left can take many forms, too. Importantly, leftism also comes
directly from feminism: some leftist-feminist activists I interviewed
stated that they were feminists first and, when they went to university,
they found that leftist student groups were the most receptive to their
feminist perspectives. This led to an intertwining of leftist and feminist
views among young, educated activists in contemporary Ukraine (see
Channell-Justice 2017).

Of the activists with whom I worked closely, over half were originally
from Kyiv. Every person I interviewed formally and informally had
completed a university degree: approximately a quarter had completed
or were pursuing a master's degree or higher (and most of these degrees came from outside Ukraine, particularly from Central European

University in Budapest or from other English-language programs in central European countries). Their studies encompassed a large range of subjects: a majority studied in a social science or humanities field, such as sociology, economics, political science, history, or cultural studies, while other activists pursued biomedical engineering, fashion and design, film and cinematography, and computer science. At the time of my fieldwork, many of those with degrees in social sciences worked for one of two major left-oriented research organizations, the Centre for Social and Labour Research and the Centre for Society Research.[2] The youngest activist I interviewed was twenty, and the oldest thirty-one. The average age of activists who participated in an interview was twenty-five.

I did not delve into each activist's personal or familial background as part of my interviews; however, from informal conversations, I know that a disproportionate number of these activists' parents are members of university faculty, typically in their hometowns. In addition, these activists were set apart by the fact that many of them lived together in group apartments rather than with their parents. This was a response to both necessity and ideology: some of these apartments were referred to as "communal" living spaces, and the activists who inhabited them attempted to live a mutual, non-proprietary lifestyle. Some of these activists were from Kyiv and had moved out of their parents' homes in order to pursue this leftist way of living; others, however, were students who came from other cities to live in Kyiv to study and needed a place to live. Of the latter, several lived in dormitories but were displaced in the summer of 2012 for the European Football Championship, which led them to seek alternatives in shared apartments.

The group of leftists featured in this research, while a small community, attempted to live in a way that would allow them to practise their vision of the future (see Maharawal 2013). However, they were also tied to the expectations of ordinary life, and held jobs to pay their rent. Recently, anthropologists have turned their attention to such small communities, placing their political diversity within national and global political spheres while remaining cognizant of the everyday efforts of activists (Chushak 2013; Graeber 2009; Greenberg 2014; Razsa 2015). Such studies reflect the transnational flows of global anti-capitalist movements, particularly as fundamental ideas about solidarity and political change are adapted into local leftist practices. In this context, and having worked with leftists prior to the mass mobilizations, I entered the experience of Euromaidan with a distinctly leftist view of contemporary Ukrainian politics. These were the people with whom I stood on Maidan for seven months of protest, never knowing what might happen next but knowing we had to be there.

A Note "on Maidan"

Throughout this book, I refer to protests "on Maidan." Maidan means "square" in Ukrainian and is an alternative to the Russianized *ploshcha* (Rus. *ploshchad*). "Maidan" is a common word in various Turkic and south Asian languages that suggests an "open space."[3] The 2013–14 mobilizations were not the first time Kyiv's central square, Maidan Nezalezhnosti, had been the site of political upheaval. The locus of various so-called revolutions, this legacy began with the Revolution on Granite of 1990–1, a student movement in support of *Rukh*, Ukraine's Soviet-era independence movement that began in the late 1980s and culminated in a referendum declaring Ukrainian independence from the Soviet Union on 24 August 1991. Ten years later, the "Ukraine Without Kuchma" protests (2000–1) targeted Leonid Kuchma's presidential regime (1994–2005), following allegations that the president had played a role in the beheading of opposition journalist Heorhiy Gongadze in 2000. Finally, the Orange Revolution took place in 2004–5, when protesters called for new elections in response to allegations of fraud following Viktor Yanukovych's successful bid for the presidency (supported by Kuchma and Russian president Vladimir Putin) against Viktor Yushchenko, widely known to be the more popular candidate (see Wilson 2005). Each of these protest movements included tent camps in the space of the square, which was "occupied" largely by student protesters. None of these movements, however, is known as "Maidan." Only the most recent – and largest – protest movement, which was the only one to see the deaths of protesters at the hands of state forces, is referred to as "Maidan." The fact that the word refers to a physical space (rather than a group name or a presidential candidate or campaign) reflects the central role that space itself played in the protests.

I continue to use this terminology of being "on Maidan" for two main reasons. The protesters lacked a unified voice in terms of how they viewed the Ukrainian nation, as well as in their goals and demands for the protests themselves. There were people on Maidan from all backgrounds who had various goals for their presence and who took part in different kinds of actions and demonstrations (figure 1.3). I do not feel that the names used to describe the mobilizations, including (but not limited to) Euromaidan and the Revolution of Dignity, represent the multivocality of the protests; they even work to erase much of the diversity among protesters that continued throughout the winter. The other reason I insist on this terminology is because everyone I knew who participated in the demonstrations also referred to being "on Maidan" (Ukr. *na Maidani*) or going "to Maidan" (*na Maidan*); in other

Figure 1.3. Protesters occupy Maidan Nezalezhnosti, late November 2013
Source: Author's photograph.

words, the place of Maidan Nezalezhnosti worked as a synecdoche for the protests themselves. The place itself had the effect of unifying people far more than did slogans or demands.

I began to hear the word "revolution" (*revoliutsiia*) to describe the protests in late November (figure 1.4). The word was mobilized quickly in order to link previous mass demonstrations that took place on Maidan, particularly the Orange Revolution in 2004 that resulted in new presidential elections. Leftist activists, however, rarely used this word to describe Maidan, because most protesters were not demanding substantial change in the political system itself, only in representatives. To leftists, the result would be more of the same governance, which they did not see as revolutionary. I adopt leftists' hesitation to use the word "revolution" too swiftly, and I agree with their criticisms. My leftist colleagues also encouraged me to question the positive associations attached to the buzzwords of the protests, such as "democracy" and "Europe," while at the same time impressing upon me the significance of the moment with their constant insistence on participating even among unfriendly crowds. Following leftist activists' critical positions regarding the protests on Maidan, in this chapter I establish leftists' own conceptualization of self-organization, and I show some of the

Figure 1.4. "Revolution 2013" painted on a container on Maidan, 2 December 2013
Source: Author's photograph.

ways this framework expanded throughout the protests. The ongoing war with Russia, which began in April 2014, has continued to influence self-organization and the possible mechanisms of political engagement with the Ukrainian state.

The Socialist Origins of Self-Organization

From the earliest days of Maidan, leftists used self-organization to suggest that other protesters stop looking to party leadership to help them get Yanukovych out of power. Instead, protesters should decide what they want and work together to demand it. Leftists' view of self-organization was the basic notion that, if a person has an ability or skill that is needed in a given context to help others, that person should contribute according to his or her ability. Ideally, if all people in a community contribute according to their abilities, the community could sustain itself without the intervention from, for example, state entities. This conceptualization was inspired by leftists' reading of Marxist texts, with one activist explicitly citing the framework, "From each according to his ability, to each according to his needs" (*Vid kozh-noho za ioho zdibnostiam, kozhnomu za ioho potrebamy*).[4]

The leftist activists I worked with in Ukraine made explicit connections to self-organization's Marxist ideological origins. In their view, their current activism was driven by a vision of the world in which wealth was distributed more equally, social services helped people access what they needed, and no one took more than he or she contributed. Thus, the leftist idea of self-organization was distinctly political and intentionally critical of existing power relations. These origins show how self-organization differs from volunteerism or civil society activism, both of which can – and often do – exist in harmony with exploitative labour practices in capitalism.

How, then, did self-organization become such a widespread designation over the course of Maidan, even being used by right-wing organizations? Self-organization began to be used to indicate a refusal to interact with any state institutions or political parties, rather than expressing an affiliation for leftist politics or criticism of capitalism. This avoidance of the state created a new space for political organization that could be built around non-party, anti-regime activism, only in exceptional cases influencing the government itself.

The notion of self-organization reflects a different relationship that Ukrainian activists have with the state, which, I argue, is a response to Ukraine's specific trajectory towards neoliberalism after socialism. Whereas the Soviet state's project was (theoretically) premised on providing for people's needs, that people should and would take only what was needed, and that they should contribute according to their abilities, the states that have developed in post-socialism have never adhered to any similar promises. Thus, the original basis of self-organization adheres to a desired ideal political structure that challenges the formation of neoliberal states around economic questions of austerity and new definitions of deservedness and need.

Self-organization as a criticism of the state has come largely in the form of activists assuming the role of the state when state bodies are incapable of fulfilling promises to citizens, as in the case of Maria's helping people leave Crimea. Self-organization also presents a new, unexpected form of agency that might enlighten some limitations of neoliberalism. Greenhouse (2009, 3) identifies "social fragmentation and democracy deficit" as well as the "valorization of the individual" as concurrent processes that result from privatization and the growing economic gaps in neoliberal societies. But she also argues that neoliberalism provokes new kinds of political power that can be harnessed against the actors promoting the social forms that result from neoliberal economic processes: "Self-identity, community, and capital are contingently precarious in relation to each other, giving rise to new forms of agency with political import yet not necessarily in political arenas as conventionally understood" (7). I suggest that self-organization, particularly following the complex generative path I pursue here, presents one of these kinds of agency that might be geographically and temporally contingent, but also must be understood as a challenge to global economic transitions.

Leftist activists had been part of self-organized, non-partisan (*bezpartiini*) groups since before Maidan began. The concept became more intriguing during Maidan because Opposition party leaders – those whose parties had been in opposition to Yanukovych's Party of Regions since his election in 2010 – increasingly lost credibility in the first few months of Maidan due to continued compromises with the Yanukovych regime. Leftists made connections between Opposition leaders who touted "European values" and pro-Yanukovych representatives, suggesting that *both* benefited from the current economic system, in which wealth is unevenly distributed among citizens, as was pointed out in the flyer described in the Introduction. Leftist activists used the concept of self-organization to place the mass of protesters at the centre of the demonstrations, setting this mass protest apart from previous mobilizations such as the 2004 Orange Revolution, which was driven by a political figure (Viktor Yushchenko).

Leftist language about self-organization reflects the influence of Soviet-era practices and discourses that promoted active engagement with communities and the state as "good citizenship" and the way towards becoming New Soviet Men and Women (Sinyavsky 1990). Soviet regimes, from the early Leninist period (Gorsuch 2000) and throughout the Stalinist period (Fürst 2010; Hellbeck 2009; Yekelchyk 2014), targeted each new generation with novel rhetoric about how its social and political participation would bring about the revolution. The most influential institutional mechanism through which such rhetoric was promoted was the *Komsomol*, or Communist Youth League (Rus. *Kommunisticheskii soyuz molodyozhi*). Youth political participation became a central element in discourses promoting the socialist revolution, but young people's actions and practices reflected a complex relationship with such discourses – shown in detail in Yurchak's (2002, 2006) work on late socialism.[5]

Indeed, while these discourses were hegemonic throughout state socialism, people living under communist regimes negotiated within and beyond them in order to challenge state-determined notions of citizenship and to create self-organized forms of social and political participation. Youth practices combined an engagement with state ideology and everyday practices that allowed young people to find meaning in socialist values outside state discourses. Young people were continually negotiating the ideals placed upon them throughout the socialist period, even as they embraced socialist principles to become productive participants in an actually existing version of increasingly global socialism. Although state control over resources and opportunities mattered, people were still able to create their own forms of meaning, and their own meaningful ways of being, in socialist states.

Diana Georgescu, studying children's socialization in post-Stalinist Romania, shows how youth practices created "a middle path between approaches that emphasize formal engagement with ideology and those that uncover meaningful lives and appealing socialist values" (2015, 29). Georgescu's historical examples – including diaries from student ethnographic programs and children's camps – show that both students and teachers contextualized their lives in a "general climate of political apathy," at the same time that some of the ideas promoted by the Ceausescu regime resonated with them, such as "professional fulfillment and self-realization, the ideal of cultured life, the role of education as an engine of upward social mobility, the centrality of children and youth to family and social life, as well as patriotism, national allegiance, and pride" (30). But young people were able to dissociate these elements of life from the delegitimized communist regime of the 1980s, leading them to see these characteristics as part of "universal human and cultural values," rather than ones associated specifically with state socialism.

In a related process, Alexei Yurchak traces the ways Soviet citizens in the late 1980s "were not supposed to be good at inventing and running private businesses because their generation was raised in a society in which private business was practically nonexistent" (Yurchak 2002, 278), yet these young people were indeed able to create functional and successful private businesses in the 1990s. As Yurchak argues, people had acquired an "entrepreneurial language" during the Soviet era thanks to their interactions with that system. He documents a hybridity in the ways Komsomol secretaries, for instance, adhered to state laws that they felt were productive and useful, whereas they subverted or skirted laws that were a drain on the ways resources could (or should) be used. In Yurchak's framing, young people in late socialism "were less critical of the system because they no longer experienced its ideological claims as ideas to be taken at face value" (285). While Soviet ideology and its ensuing structures still constrained or enabled their access to resources, once certain people gained access, they were able to "create their own alternative universe of meaning" (285) in practice.

Thus, those in positions as Komsomol secretaries used the flexibility that had guided their engagement with the state to find ways to create and run successful businesses once the economy opened in the late 1980s during *glasnost*. For instance, economic reforms allowed Komsomol committees to control their own finances; many Komsomol secretaries, already in a position of power in relation to other Komsomol members, "managed to transfer the financial resources of the Komsomol into starting capital for their future businesses, making these operations invisible to the higher Komsomol bodies and to the rank-and-file Komsomol members, depriving them of an opportunity to lay claim to these resources" (Yurchak 2002, 292). This allowed certain strata of Komsomol representatives to gain an advantage not only during *glasnost* but also after the fall of the Soviet Union and the greater opening of regional markets.

Such accounts suggest a rethinking of the ways people living under state socialism were able and willing to think beyond seemingly all-encompassing ideology in order to create new forms of sociality that both incorporated and subverted the state forms that represented this ideology. Butterfield and Sedaitis (1991) describe the concurrent rise of social movements during *perestroika*, when the social policies of democratization enabled those invested in government representation to use the newly adopted election cycles to change institutional structures from within. In their view, Communist Party–based organizations such as the Komsomol, while historically contributing to a totalitarian state, now worked as "transmission belts" to greater social participation in criticism of the state (7). Importantly, however, Bova (1991) suggests that such "opening" and "restructuring" were more a reflection of Gorbachev's interest in creating "an alliance between the reform-minded leadership at the top and a newly assertive public at the bottom" (29), generating "just enough 'democracy' to stir up managerial interest in reform but not so much as to totally undercut the key institutions of the Soviet party-state" (32).

This last point is crucial in understanding the apparent lack of mass participation in effective social movements in the Soviet Union and other formerly communist countries after 1989, including feminist social and political activism (see chapter 6). As the economies of these newly independent countries shifted throughout the 1990s, many scholars documented a weakening of civil society and demobilization of civic activism coinciding with major distrust in state institutions (Petrova and Tarrow 2007). Petrova and Tarrow, however, follow more closely the views of Georgescu and Yurchak, suggesting instead that the development of civil society is more effective in the region when based on "lateral ties" – that is, "among civil society groups" – and on "vertical ties between these groups and public officials" (2007, 78–8). This enables an interpretation of effective social movements and activism that is *not* based on the numbers of people who have mobilized, but instead on the strength of ties among groups and in the relationships that are most beneficial to both state and civic groups. Particularly, the authors document "a richer picture of transactions consisting of coalition formation around single issues, network formation, and negotiation with elites on the part of civic groups in Central and Eastern Europe than would be predicted from the levels of individual participation that have been observed" (80).

Such a formulation provides a better vantage point for understanding how self-organization works in Ukraine today. Moving away from its leftist roots and adapting to meet the demands of varied groups of activists, self-organization has allowed people to mobilize larger groups laterally to help one another, rather than to support a politician or political party. While most activists promoting self-organization had not experienced state socialism themselves, their parents lived in Soviet Ukraine, and contemporary Ukrainians still see the lasting effects of state socialism. The rapid integration of post-socialist Ukraine into a global economy created greater stratification between rich and poor, exacerbated by the governance of regimes such as those of Yanukovych and his predecessor, Leonid Kuchma. Thus, contemporary leftist notions of self-organization combined these socialist origins with more recent global, anti-capitalist protest movements such as Occupy Wall Street. For instance, leftists linked *all* political parties to the global capitalist political economy, making them all equally culpable for Ukraine's current political and economic problems. Leftists also combined self-organized activism and issues of higher education, presenting the marketization of higher education as a problem for activists that must be solved without the influence of parties. As we will see later, this latter example presented a challenge for leftists, as legislative change came to be seen as a necessary part of sustainable higher education reform.

For some of these reasons, self-organization drew in non-leftist political groups as well. Particularly over the course of Maidan, right-wing and nationalist groups also lost their trust in the political opposition and were drawn to the idea of self-organization, although only when it was detached from its Marxist origins. For instance, the Right Sector, an umbrella nationalist organization that unified several right-wing groups, was also self-organized inasmuch as it did not, during the protests, represent a political party or have a singular figurehead. Its organizing, however, was styled after military practices and resulted in the division of many right-wing groups into *sotnia*, or hundreds – the typical way to organize military brigades. Thus, the notion of self-organization to these groups prioritized working around or outside state forces, but it was still based on the idea that each person should contribute according to his ability. Without the leftist origins of their organizing practices, though, these groups did not have such goals as redistribution of wealth, social democracy, or anti-capitalist action. Further, their vision of revolution was to create a Ukrainian state based on nationalist principles and focusing on the territorial integrity of Ukraine.[6]

Leftist Self-Organization on Maidan

The protests on Maidan were touched off by the question of an Association Agreement with the European Union. While years of negotiation had led many to believe that then-president Viktor Yanukovych would sign the agreement, pressure from Russian president Vladimir Putin led to Yanukovych's last-minute about-face. Instead, Yanukovych decided to sign on to Putin's Customs Union, along with Belarus and Kazakhstan, in exchange for a cash influx of US$15 billion. Although the protests began in response to the lost accession to the European Union, they were motivated by a more general anger at the continual pressure from Russia and the inability of politicians to extract themselves from Putin's influence (see Ganev 2014). Leftists saw an opening for a broader social protest that promoted complete government overhaul and economic reforms that would encourage the redistribution of wealth in Ukraine, particularly out of the hands of oligarchs.

Leftists used the framing of "self-organization" from the earliest days of the protests. In the Introduction, I described the flyer entitled "The Substance of Our Protest," which I helped leftist activists distribute on Maidan in late November. In this flyer, leftists describe "grassroots self-organization" (*nyzova samoorhanizatsiia*), which denotes a position in which activists do activism because they feel they can create better political structures than can the state. Similar to Georgescu's and Yurchak's examples, leftists have worked within the structures available to them to analyse and criticize how those structures work. From these criticisms, leftists have used the notion of self-organization as a way to take their experiences as activists and create new means of social and political engagement.

The idea of grassroots self-organization presented both leftist and non-leftist protesters with effective language to criticize the state – in this case embodied in the Yanukovych regime, which no longer served their interests. One activist, Danylo, described self-organization in a way that reflected the notion of personal responsibility:

> It would be really good if they developed so that pressure on the government, the mechanisms of pressure on those who make decisions, on legislative initiatives, that the pressure continues, and the government doesn't relax. And only in this way when each citizen[7] feels his or her own responsibility and takes a personal part in the decisions of questions and takes part in political life. And then some changes are possible.

Danylo's understanding of "responsibility" presents an interesting reflection of the social fragmentation and valorization of the individual that Greenhouse (2009) describes as a social effect of economic neoliberalism. To some extent, Danylo's perspective reinforces the significance of the individual and an idea of "personal responsibility" in which each citizen is responsible for his or her own well-being. But we can also interpret Danylo's idea of "responsibility" (*vidpovidal'nist'*) in a collective way, especially in the context of self-organization. When citizens begin to care about governmental politics – which Danylo saw as unrepresentative of citizens' concerns – only then can ordinary people change how politics works in Ukraine. This can only be done, as Danylo and many other leftists saw it at the time, through self-organization, rather than by joining political parties and attempting to change the system from within. Ultimately, the tent camps and ongoing protests themselves became "self-organized" because they did not rely on the presence of leaders or parties to unify people. Danylo continued,

> I think that three months of protests, from the beginning almost two months of peaceful protests, and then another month, even more now, some tents stand on Maidan, the [occupied city hall] lives, in all of this there was really a lot of self-organization. A lot of initiatives to hold this Maidan, these barricades, these tents, this existence, car tires…in other words, a lot of this was without order from politicians, or from someone. I think that this is a very useful experience and it will help in the future, the next protests.

For Danylo, not only that people practised self-organization, but that it *worked*, was the most important aspect of Maidan as a whole. Another activist even suggested that Maidan made people change their entire view of government:

> I see a lot of positive things which this Maidan experience gave people. Self-organization. People left in a situation where they have no one to take

responsibility for them, they are forced to self-organize. People don't see government as something sacred. I think it's a very good turn.

These explanations help clarify why self-organization was so widely adopted on Maidan, even among non-leftists. Right-wing participants were also critical of political parties and felt empowered by the success of their own organization, and even many people elsewhere on the right-left spectrum no longer felt that political figures had their best interests in mind.

While many leftists saw these anti-government turns as positive, they also recognized that self-organization had been adopted by groups with whom they had significant ideological differences. They did not always reflect positively on the broad use of self-organization. As one activist put it, "not all self-organization is good," specifically referencing the way groups such as Right Sector used self-organizing discourses to legitimize their actions because self-organization distanced them from political parties. Because so many politically diverse groups used the language of "self-organization," the term has become associated with the Maidan protests at large (see Diuk 2014), but the concept has been detached from the leftist roots described above.

New *Subbotniki*: Local Self-Organization

Following the end of Maidan – after police-protester violence in which one hundred people were killed and Yanukovych fled Ukraine for Russia – self-organization continued, albeit in shifting forms. Some self-organized practices grew around the military mobilization in eastern Ukraine, others focused on smaller-scale practices, targeted at local, district-based initiatives around Kyiv. Sasha, a student and feminist activist, commented that she felt "decentralization" was taking place in every district in the city. She recounted that several self-defence brigades had reorganized after Maidan, particularly around city districts, in a sort of community policing initiative.[8] Sasha also wanted to get more involved in these district-based initiatives, focusing on a dilapidated stadium area where leftists occasionally had held concerts and other events. Organizers were attempting to make the stadium area into a commons for the neighbourhood, which had no other parks, in order to prevent high-rise apartments from being built there.[9] Activists began to hold gatherings every Saturday to encourage the community to support the initiative and to reclaim the space through improving its appearance.

Some activists made the connection between these processes of reclamation and earlier Soviet practices of *subbotniki* – weekend volunteer work that was expected to help instil revolutionary values into Soviet citizens and promote the idea that each person was an essential part of communism. These campaigns began in Moscow in 1919 as localized, grassroots movements to work on railway lines, and were expanded to Ukrainian railways in 1920 (Chase 1989). Over time, the *subbotniki* were organized by Communist Party institutions, and participation became mandatory, distancing these campaigns from their voluntary origins (Kaplan 1965). The language of self-organization appeared in descriptions of *subbotniki* (cited in Chase 1989, 121), and Soviet-era writers in Ukraine referred to their contributions as "necessary for victory over the enemies and the formation of the high moral qualities of the builders of a socialist society," in addition to contributing to increased labour production (Freilikher 1968, 93). Although the *subbotnik* campaign officially ended in 1921, mandatory labour requirements were still referred to as *subbotniki* throughout the Soviet period, including in language condemning the extra work as forced labour (Siry 1978).

Some contemporary leftists clearly had a romanticized vision of the *subbotniki*, although they were not alone in connecting the notion of self-organization with voluntary labour. Lobanov (2002) quotes a regional representative referring to self-organization and self-governance as "doing the good tradition of carrying out *subbotniki*" in urban areas. This framing helped leftists reconnect self-organization to its Marxist roots in the context of an expanded definition of the term following Maidan. Maria framed several post-Maidan volunteer events in the language of a *subbotnik*. Even in her own apartment complex, where many people owned their apartments, Maria said that a lot of residents had been involved in Maidan and it changed their consciousness (*svidomist'*). She described their spring *subbotnik*, in which residents painted benches in the courtyard and then had a picnic – usually, she said, "it was maybe about ten people who came. And this year, there were so many people!" Maria praised the social effects of the event; as she put it, "very often people say it's some kind of Soviet tradition, but it's very pleasant when you go out with people you know, with your neighbours. Why not paint something, a bench, or a fence?"

Maria's explanation of the *subbotnik* is itself detached from the activist orientation of self-organization, even as it is connected to the idea's Marxist origins. Many leftists participated in this new kind of *subbotnik* after Maidan, and they linked practices of making change for themselves with the socialist motivation of contributing to the greater good. The significant distinction in this usage is that new *subbotniki* are not organized for the state but for the benefit of one's community, however defined. Here, leftists use the idea of each person's contributing based on ability not to motivate activism, but to fill in the gaps left by the state. Their description of this work as "self-organization," however, expresses their rejection of the neoliberal connotations of volunteer work and their criticisms of the state.

For many activists, even something as banal as painting a bench became symbolic of a shift in consciousness, especially for those who had been committed to activism since before Maidan began. Maria's neighbours had never been able to make any sense of what she did as an activist until they also participated in similar kinds of actions and felt that their presence had been effective. As Maria put it, people "can't forget it and can't reject it." Even as participants were filling the gap of the state by their self-organized efforts, they were also forming new socialities based on being active contributors to their communities – a change in consciousness that came from having seen the effects of mass mobilization. All these kinds of local, self-organized initiatives were undertaken without the help of the state or any political party, which led leftists to conclude that self-organization had been broadly successful in infiltrating the protests and their participants.

The new socialities that were formed outside of a relationship with the state, however, are not necessarily novel in the greater post-socialist sphere. As others have documented, throughout post-socialism, informal networks regularly have functioned outside of the state (Humphrey 2002; Ledeneva 2006; Wanner 2005). That such networks are now being understood as more effective than official practices reflects a fundamental questioning whether the Ukrainian state is needed to ensure social well-being. This attitude towards the state benefits Russian aggression in Ukraine, as it encourages further fragmentation and localization of social solidarities; additionally, it confirms the decreased significance of European aspirations among Ukrainians who participated on Maidan, as they are no longer confident that any government, including the European Union's, can adequately meet their needs. This is not to suggest that Ukrainians should look to the state to discourage fragmentation, but simply that local self-organization is actively changing the nature of the relationship between citizens, states, and international forces.

War and the Contraction of the State

The protests on Maidan resulted in the ousting of Viktor Yanukovych, the establishment of an interim government, and, in May 2014, the presidential election of Petro Poroshenko. At the same time, conflict began in southern and eastern Ukraine, starting with Vladimir Putin's annexation of the territory of Crimea in March 2014. In April 2014, separatists and militants established the Donets'k and Luhans'k People's Republics in the Donbas. The Ukrainian government's efforts to regain control over these regions – known as the Anti-Terrorist Operation, or ATO – has continued to the present. The ongoing conflict has troubled the nature of the post-Maidan state, as the government's resources cannot meet the demands for equipment and troops in the Donbas and, at the same time, provide for its citizens and their theoretical path to Europe. Elizabeth Dunn and Michael Bobick suggest that these effects were precisely the kinds of goals Putin had in mind in annexing Crimea and encouraging separatism in the Donbas, creating "a prolonged sense of liminality that provokes anxiety and fear on a national scale" (Dunn and Bobick 2014, 410). Such fear, further, "may well force the post-Maidan Ukrainian government to capitulate to Russian demands, and, in doing so, will damage its autonomy as much as if Russia had in fact invaded" (ibid.; see also Fournier 2018; Shukan 2018).[10]

Putin's interest in Ukraine, as these authors document, has strongly influenced the role of state institutions in serving their expected purposes. The post-Maidan government focused on implementing IMF-required austerity measures, on passing the Decommunization Laws (discussed in chapter 3; see also Channell-Justice 2015), and on its attempts to win the war against, or at least quell, the advancing separatist and Russian troops. These issues took priority over long-term economic restructuring and people's demands for state support as the economic situation took a turn for the worse after February 2014.

The shifting post-Maidan state has opened Ukraine to multiple new forms of political organization and action. A host of new political parties developed in various forms for the 2014 elections (both presidential and parliamentary), with varied levels of success. The integration of volunteer groups – ranging from military brigades to simple crowd-funding sources – into governance, or even into oligarchic circles whose inhabitants wish to influence governance as effectively as possible, is an uncertain process whose development will certainly affect the future stability of any version of a Ukrainian state. Finally, the shifting state has changed the ways activists of all kinds, including leftists, engage with the Ukrainian government. This last development is the major interest of this volume. The transformations brought on from these new kinds of political activism and its influence on the Ukrainian government will extend beyond Ukraine and its borderlands with Russia, to Europe and the EU's own stability.

Chapter Two

Twenty-First Century Leftists

In 2012 and 2013, before the protests on Maidan began, about a half-dozen leftist activists had been attacked by violent right-wing gangs. Some of these attacks happened at protests; others took activists by surprise when they were walking home or otherwise alone. One of these activists was Ivan, a philosophy student who had just finished his degree in Kyiv. During his years at the university, Ivan had been involved in the leftist student union Priama Diia. But like many other Ukrainians who were born or grew up following independence in 1991, Ivan was a nationalist when he was in grade school in a small town. As he described it, nationalist activism was the only political position available to him. His father was a nationalist who voted for the Svoboda Party in parliamentary elections, and they both had negative views towards the left when Ivan was growing up. "The whole left-wing [vocabulary] was written by the Soviet Union, … like capitalists are West and they are awesome, they are wealthy, and communists killed our grandfathers and there was no freedom and it was horrible. At this time, I believed this." When he was young, Ivan had no other way of understanding leftist politics other than mainstream anti-Soviet political rhetoric.

As a pre-teen during the Orange Revolution – the 2004 mass protest for new elections – Ivan said he experienced a feeling of solidarity with the protests. He did not participate, but ten years later he still remembered the effect of the protests on his young mind. It led him to seek out further political engagement when he left his family home and moved to Kyiv, where he discovered a whole spectrum of ways to be politically active. Ivan's story was typical of young leftists, particularly those who grew up outside Kyiv. The Orange Revolution played a central role in their realization of a political consciousness, and many were drawn into politics through nationalist organizations and parties. These nationalist groups often appeared as the only option for engaging in politics. Many young people did not know a left even existed outside the Communist Party, in part because the Party marginalized a critical discussion of leftism in contemporary Ukraine by presenting its version of communism as an authentic extension of the Ukrainian Communist Party from the Soviet era.

Many leftists explained to me that, even when they were teenagers, long before Maidan, they felt limited in their political options because they were already learning a kind of national ideology that privileged a dichotomy between a pro-Ukrainian, anti-Soviet stance and any position that could be interpreted as sympathetic to the Soviet Union. Maidan created a space for some of the most active right-wing sympathizers in Ukraine to promote this kind of national ideology, which relied on a narrative of repression, venerated the figures who challenged that repression, and demonized Ukraine's Soviet past because of the USSR's role in repression. Contemporary leftists recognized the increasing dominance of this type of narrative. As one leftist described, on Maidan leftists were unable to promote their own ideas because of the popularity of groups such as Right Sector, which was able to achieve this hegemonic force because of the ways it mobilized popular, albeit divisive, images and discourses from Ukrainian history. (In the next chapter, I explore the construction and amplification of this national ideology in the years leading up to and during Maidan.)

What constitutes the left in contemporary Ukraine or, more accurately, what did the left look like in 2013–14? As many activists describe, what "the left" is, has been, and could be are extremely varied, and this research can capture only a partial picture of even this small group of dedicated people. In this chapter, I describe what several activists told me about how they became leftists, and I present two profiles of leftists, who describe their activism and their affiliation with the left in their own terms. I then discuss two leftist initiatives that were organized outside the Euromaidan protests and created significant space for leftists to live in a world they had made for themselves. I look at the *Vil'na shkola* (Free School) that leftists had been organizing since 2012, and I discuss leftist-organized *krav maga* self-defence classes in which I participated during my fieldwork in 2013–14. These initiatives show how activists attempted to create spaces for a leftist community to grow despite the adversity they faced in Ukraine's political arena.

"But definitely left": Contextualizing the Ukrainian Left

Danylo became an activist later than many other leftists. At twenty-five, he had finished university and worked for a number of years before confronting leftist politics and joining activist circles. Like many others, he began to realize his leftist affiliations by participating in solidarity actions where many student and leftist activists were in attendance. "Basically, I am of leftist views. But the spectrum of 'left' is really big, and I only became politicized so strongly in the last year and a half, and especially during the time of the events on Maidan ... But to what level and which direction exactly, I haven't finished deciding. But definitely left." I interviewed Danylo after spending the previous six months getting to know him at leftist events related to Maidan. While many leftist activists had very clear identifications when I asked them to describe their political ideology, Danylo presented a general idea of the "left" that recognized how fluid the idea could be.

Ukrainians who used "leftist" to describe themselves had a remarkable depth in their discussions about what it means to be on the left in contemporary Ukrainian politics. Within anthropology and social sciences more broadly, there has been a focus on the rise of the far right, especially through the lens of populism and the success of right-wing parties across Europe (Pasieka 2017). At the same time, however, attention has been turned to new leftist movements, especially among scholars of eastern Europe (Graeber 2009; Kurtović and Hromadžić 2017; Razsa 2015; Razsa and Kurnik 2012; see also Coronil 2011; Juris 2012). Social movement studies have often framed political movements as fighting dominant groups, although such anti-authority movements can fall into either "right" or "left" designations. Many of the movements featured in social movement studies would be characterized as "left" by the Ukrainian activists with whom I spoke because of their focus on socio-economic issues and rejection of dominant powers and hierarchies.

I insist on a deep discussion of the idea of the left in this context because of the dynamic way it is being reborn in post-Soviet activism in Ukraine. Following Fernando Coronil's expansion of Norberto Bobbio's (1996) conceptualization of right and left, I also consider this "left" as "a fluid sign to identify actions directed toward universal equality and well-being and thus toward forms of political life without which these goals cannot be achieved, including democracy, diversity, justice, and freedom" (Coronil 2011, 233). As Coronil notes, these terms are no more fixed than the meaning of the "left," and it is these exact concepts that are the core of the debates among leftists in Ukraine. Further, "there are now multiple 'leftist' ways of imagining an ideal society" (233), and activists in Ukraine and beyond the post-socialist realm are contributing to those imaginings in novel forms.

As the following stories of how young Ukrainians became leftists show, leftists are committed to the ideas Coronil describes even if they are not united in their idea of the "left." Later in our interview, Danylo told a story that reflects the terms Coronil associates with the left.

> But in the last year and a half, when I met activists from Priama Diia, the student union … Maybe especially it was the action for International Human Rights Day that made an impression on me, at the end of 2012. There was an action against the Law 8711, that's the so-called homosexual propaganda, and human rights activists as well as Priama Diia activists came. And there was a Nazi attack. And it became clear to me that leftists support human rights and anti-discrimination, while the ultra-right does not … And then it became more interesting to read different [leftist] articles, sites, materials, so I started to go to actions … and I realized I sympathized with these themes, these people. It's close to me.

For Danylo, it was not only that the ultra-right did not support ideas such as human rights and anti-discrimination, but also that they supported the use of violence against peaceful protesters: "Just violence, it was not clear to me why they jumped us, used tear gas. There wasn't any kind of provocation, just an attack." The ultra-right attack on a human rights demonstration showed Danylo that right-wing groups were not supporting tolerance and non-discrimination. It solidified to him that leftists, on the other hand, did support these things. Although leftists do not necessarily talk about a unified vision of "human rights," from Danylo's perspective this meant stances such as countering anti-Semitism and racism. His work with high schoolers on the concepts of tolerance and anti-discrimination allowed Danylo to enact his political positions in his daily life and to help encourage a younger generation of Ukrainians to be more understanding of difference.[1]

Danylo's story also presents the problem of a violent radical right that responds to peaceful protest with attacks. Other peaceful demonstrations, including Kyiv's LGBTQ+ Pride Parades before 2016, also faced attacks by well-organized, violent right-wing groups (see Channell-Justice 2020b; Leksikov 2020). The context of becoming affiliated with the left is a violent one, and this violence shapes the nature of leftist activism. Leftists must be aware of the threats towards them, making any type of active recruitment extremely difficult. Despite that, many activists discovered leftism because of an event or in trying to organize for a cause; as the profiles below show, there is no single path towards becoming a leftist, and leftist politics is an ongoing process that relies on both theory and action to continue to exist.

The two leftist activists I profile here have different stories about how they saw the left and how they saw themselves as leftists.[2] In these profiles, I foreground the activists' own words, for two reasons: first, it shows how leftists think critically about their own position within leftist activism, and, second, it shows the extent of their influence on the trajectory of this book. Both activists bring up themes that are essential, grounding components of this study, and I return to them multiple times throughout the volume.

Andriy: Social Democracy and Anti-dogmatic Leftism

When I first met Andriy in November 2013, he struck me as a smart and thoughtful person who was critically engaged with leftist politics in Ukraine.[3] Over the years I have known him, our conversations have been essential in my understanding of leftist movements and goals, as well as how to conceptualize the place of the left in a larger conversation about Ukrainian politics. We first talked at length after a conference that month called "New Trade Unions and Democratic Lefts: Historical Roots and Ideological Questions," held in Kyiv and organized with the participation of several trade union confederations from Ukraine, Russia, Belarus, and Georgia. I wrote a blog post about the conference in which I asked questions about democracy and universality, as well as the potential movement to European reforms that Ukraine was facing at the time (the conference was held twenty days before the Euromaidan protests began). In the blog, I wrote at length about social democracy as a so-called European ideal that would not be easily transported to Ukraine. This prompted a longer discussion with Andriy about social democracies and, more important, the variety of self-identifications among leftists. He said he found that there were too many factions, including social democrats, but also Leninists, Trotskyists, anarcho-leftists, etc., and each group has its own point of view (*svii pohliad*); most don't want to come together or understand one another. This issue of factionalization is a theme in our discussions to this day. As he later said in our interview in 2014,

> There is too much dogma about the leftist movement, people have read something that worked somewhere else, but the conditions are completely different, and nobody tries to analyse what's going on in Ukraine and try to fit some perspective of any kind of ideology, from a Bolshevik one to an anarchist one. Anything could work depending on the conditions. I guess it's a huge problem of the movement that everyone's too embedded in those theoretical traditions rather than trying to analyze what's happening.

A defining feature of many of our conversations was this analytical angle; Andriy was always ready to consider critical perspectives of the events and groups that surrounded us. I continued these conversations with Andriy at our self-defence classes, when we were often the first to arrive. We participated in several leftist-organized events of the Euromaidan protests, especially in November and December, when leftists were attempting to share anti-capitalist, Eurosceptic slogans during the protests. We agreed to do a formal interview in May 2014, months after we first met, and after many of the major events of Euromaidan. In the interview he reflected on the experience of Euromaidan and the successes and failures of the left. Importantly, a major event that had happened days before our interview was the fire in the Trade Unions building in Odesa, in which several people were killed, and the "pro/anti-Maidan" lines had become very blurred (I discuss the events surrounding the fire and leftist factionalization at greater length in Channell-Justice 2019a). This event made us both conscious of how far things had gone in the protests and whether or not Ukraine was going in a good direction.

In this first interview, Andriy elaborated on how he became affiliated with the left. Given the post-independence marginalization of leftist movements in Ukraine, this was an important question that showed that leftists could come from anywhere. Andriy entered into leftist politics through Priama Diia, the independent student union. I asked Andriy how he came into contact with PD:

You must have heard of the laws for higher education which were, like the one that was passed recently, and there were three other versions of it. And one was by deputies of Party of Regions and was an awful law, and there were protests about it somewhere, I think in 2010 and 2011 … There were three organizations that were doing that – FRI, Foundation of Regional Initiatives, *Vidsich*, and PD. And PD were the ones who were mainly organizing those marches and pickets and demonstrations, and this is how I first found out about them. There was a huge gap between the time that I first found out about them before I joined. I was going to some events they organized, more or less reading the site, I kind of supported them, but I wasn't a member. It wasn't directly linked to PD, but I had a conflict with the dean of my department in the university … Problems with bachelor's theses. The teachers we were dealing with were not the ones who were sitting when we were defending – it worked really badly. Some other fellow students and I got [fed up] with the bureaucracy. More troubles with my work. It wasn't directly linked with PD but troubles with education. I thought maybe I should work in a more systematic way. So I decided to join in 2013, but there was nothing they could do about that situation, and I don't think there is something that the student trade union should do in that particular situation because it was more of a personal conflict.

Like many other student activists, Andriy became an activist through personal concerns about higher education, as well as self-education about left-oriented theory and practice. Specifically, he became interested in working for certain causes in a "more systematic way," among other concerned actors, rather than just analysing or theorizing those situations. What is important in this story is that Andriy knew about and participated in the mass student mobilizations that fought against the unsupported higher education reform law, and it was after having seen PD's success and knowing what it stood for that he joined officially.

The topic of Andriy's (and my own) political philosophy or affiliation is something we have rehashed multiple times. In 2014, he said the following:

> AG: I can say that I have a mixture of various leftist beliefs. I would call myself socialist, but I kind of cannot link myself to one particular ideology, like Trotskyism, or something else, because I don't think that one fits into our particular situation. But I would call myself a democratic socialist.
>
> ECJ: How did you get to the point of identifying yourself as a democratic socialist?
>
> AG: I guess it was some time during my university education I got more interested in various writings, besides some sociological theories, I guess it was some analysis of our current situation, mostly through the [leftist academic] *Spil'ne* journal,[4] and stuff like that. So I started reading those leftist sites and I got into contact with some people, from *Spil'ne*, [from the] Centre for Social Research where I currently work, I got persuaded by those arguments.

In 2020 I asked if he still considered that answer true, and he said he had an even less consistent political philosophy now, although he would most closely affiliate with the idea of social democracy. More specifically,

> I'm not sure that I have any plan in mind of how you can actually abolish capitalism, and I'm not even sure that that would be a desirable thing anymore, I guess ... So I wouldn't even call myself socialist now I guess, even. Social democrat, and that's it. Just being completely honest.

Our conversation in 2020 focused on many of the policy priorities that concern and interest Andriy now, rather than on a specific political ideology. They included social issues such as "the undoing of the welfare state ... making it more targeted and ... certain things becoming less of a right and more of a safety net, as people in the World Bank tend to say." We discussed political violence, especially at the hands of the far right, economic inequality, working conditions, the cost of and access to utilities (especially energy), and certain reforms – notably, of the police and judiciary – that are taking place in Ukraine today. While these issues are far from the problem of higher education reform, they are a clear extension of Andriy's concern for the growing social inequality present in Ukraine in 2013–14.

We discussed his views of the left in Ukraine in both 2014 and 2020. In 2014 he hoped that the leftist movement in Ukraine could be

> a party that linked to mass organization, and the party should be as weak as possible so it would simply represent on a legal level some people from below. I think that grassroots organizations should spread more and more, talking to people in their usual language, not using all that stuff that is not understood by anybody.

He elaborated:

> I think we should even limit our demands a little bit. I do support the idea of a classless society, but I don't see how it could be implemented in the short run. I think that something like moving to a welfare state, that kind of demand could be supported by many people, but it needs many years to be built. I think that some kind of organization could be built in ten years … I can see how we can work our way and propose new institutions that could work in this particular country, which would later turn out to be something different … There are people who don't have a clear vision but are very willing to do something to achieve something that they don't know how it looks.

Andriy's major concern was that the left would not be able to promote any unified platform because there was never a clear vision of what a leftist future would look like. I was not especially surprised when I asked him in 2020 to describe the left today and he said, "In a word? Irrelevant." He elaborated on why there had never been real interest in leftist ideas in post-independence Ukraine:

> It's a combination of the fact that for some people who tend to be more politically mobilized, everything left wing is associated with the Soviet Union, as it has always been, it never really went away. If anything, Maidan just generated a wave of anti-communism. And … just the fact that Ukraine is a society where people don't trust other people, you don't trust government, you don't trust political organizations, you don't trust them to represent you, that's why hardly any movement has any popular support because people don't do that stuff. They're not members of anything, you trust your narrow circle of friends and family, and … I think it's

hard for any movement, it's not just the left that doesn't have any sort of popular base, broad support.

Andriy is an example of a leftist whose views have shifted with time and distance from Euromaidan. Although he never affiliated with the most radical or the strictest factions of leftists, he has always thought very critically about the left and his position within the broader leftist movement. Like many other leftists with whom I have worked closely, he has focused much more on specific issues in recent years, rather than on building up a wider leftist political presence in Ukrainian politics, which, as he points out, is not likely to succeed.

Tonya: From Anarchism in General to Intersectional Anarcho-Queer Feminism

I met Tonya when I started my fieldwork with leftist activists in 2012, when I was staying in Kyiv with a student activist and attended student organizing camp in Crimea. Tonya always struck me as kind, but as I got to know her more over 2013 and 2014, especially during English Discussion Club and working with the Free School discussed later in this chapter, I learned that she was a dedicated activist who never shied away from thinking through challenging subjects and from discussing critiques of the leftist movement. As we have stayed in touch over the ensuing years, we discussed her interview from fall 2013 in January and September 2021. Tonya talked about how her views had changed, and her shifting perspective is an important component of the dynamism of social activism in Ukraine.[5] In 2013, I asked her how she became an activist.

> Well, the problems of people's lives, and especially students, have always bothered me. When I was younger, when I went to university. I met one experienced activist who had previously taken part in many protests, in many actions, with other organizations. At that time there was no Priama Diia. And [that activist] told me that he and his brother were going to start an independent student union that would fight for student rights. And at the same time, they were going to campaign against a bill, a bill for the new Labour Code. And he told me about this bill, and I was interested in it. I was thinking, "Yes, something needs to be done about this." And I went to the first action for myself … When I went to the actions about the new Labour Code, I was also one of the organizers. That is, I gave them money, painted banners, we organized a concert … Well, somehow I got into all of this, and I was one of the first active activists of Priama Diia, from the origins of this independent student union. And since then, I just can't imagine my life without activism.

In 2021 Tonya still considered themselves an activist, but they pointed out that they had a different understanding now of the concept of activism. It was necessary to develop this new conceptualization, they said, because of a major feeling of *vyhoran*, burnout, after a decade of activism. As they framed it in September 2021, "not all activism is public, and not everything public is activism." Together with their partner, Tonya had established a sewing cooperative that worked on activist projects and commissions alike. Thus, Tonya described,

> all my life, every day is activism [because] the whole concept [of a sewing cooperative] is an alternative economic system with alter-capitalist perspectives at the centre of the concept. It wasn't like I stopped student activism and entered into "real life" or normal life.

Now, however, Tonya's activism is "slow," and their daily activism (*shchodennyi aktyvizm*) incorporates self-care (*samozberezhennia*) to help prevent burnout. This way, Tonya said, the sewing cooperative creates alternatives and supports their community in a way that is different from student activism. There is a widely held perception, Tonya pointed out, that to be an activist

> you have to be this energetic cheerful person to be cool. But it's a capitalist paradigm. It's normal to be passive, angry, or sad. To not want to talk. You learn about all the discrimination against female-socialized people and others in the world and you can't be happy all the time.

But Tonya continued to hold on to strong political views. In 2013, she described her political views in this way:

> First of all, I see myself as an anarchist. That is, it seems to me that a society is possible and would be ideal if there is no government, and all problems, all issues can be resolved within that society. Society can be divided into certain initiative groups, which could be called, for instance, syndicates, like anarcho-syndicalism. And these groups, they will work for themselves, and they will work together. This is very general.

Priama Diia is structured as a non-hierarchical organization. That is, while one person is registered as the leader of the group on official documents, in reality the group works largely without hierarchical structures. I asked for Tonya's thoughts on whether or not this type of organization worked in the real world, given her interest in building an anarchist society.

I think it's the best option, because in this case, it generally works well because people come together who already know the ideas and principles of anarcho-syndicalism. So they expect that everything will be horizontal. For example, there is a meeting, and a certain number of people come. It's understood that not everyone will come to the meeting … it is not obligatory. Certain issues are resolved, and then the issues are posted to the Google group discussion board, and in the discussion board, any union member can discuss [the issues], whoever wants to take part. Everyone can speak, and as a result, according to the rules of consensus, everything is decided. There have always been certain problems, there always will be, but … when are there not problems? They can always be solved.

Of course, she admitted, certain people are more or less active and proactive within this horizontal structure, and this can sometimes lead to a closed structure in which the most active people communicate only with the most active people, because they know things will get done this way.

It just so happened that I belong to a group of mostly active, proactive people. On the one hand, I understand that this is our mistake, that such active, proactive people as we are, by taking our own initiative, we take away the possibility to show it to other people. But on the other hand, we are always faced with the question, "If not us, then who? Who will do it but us?" So it is like a vicious cycle.

Later in the interview, we discussed the major issues facing the student movement. One recurring theme was the passivity of other students, who were inclined to participate in political action only if it affected them directly. Tonya already understood that her own actions in Priama Diia reinforced this – just as she said in the previous quote, they created a closed structure of activists because the most active people only worked with one another. When speaking about a successful campaign against a higher education reform bill – which included a provision to pay for services such as laboratories and library access – that was not supported by most students and that ultimately was not passed in the Verkhovna Rada (or just Rada, parliament), I asked why she thought it was so successful.

Because, I think, these bills were very brazen. That is, they were painful points for students. I mean … a student is poor. Does he have extra money to pay, for example, for the library, or for a computer class? Can a student pay more for tuition every year? So [these bills] were seriously painful from the point of view of students. And that's why it mobilized students, because they definitely didn't want it. In general, people are so passive, but when they are really pressed, they begin to move. For better or for worse, unfortunately.

When we spoke in 2021, they pointed out how problematic this perspective was. They said, "I was really like this then ... but I am not very happy that these words came out of my mouth." We discussed the many reasons that people might seem "passive," from disability to a lack of funds or free time, or different priorities. Indeed, this opened a larger discussion about Tonya's shifting political perspective, particularly after a long bout with COVID-19 in 2020 made daily activities extremely difficult. Tonya's views became very influenced by intersectionality as an organizing concept, and they termed their political views in 2021 as "intersectional anarcho-queer feminism." This intersectionality incorporated queer – which Tonya pointed out was not really part of the leftist lexicon in 2013 as it is now – as well as non-binary and disabled perspectives. Of course, said Tonya, "I see that, ideally, there would not be a government, that everything is organized around horizontal, cooperative work," so anarchism still rang true for Tonya, "just with a lot of 'buts.'" Enacting anarchism can also mean a daily practice of running a sewing cooperative – it does not need to mean that everyone must be in the streets every day.

Feminism and gender (in)equality has always been a recurring topic of conversation over the course of our friendship, and these conversations challenged me to express my perspectives on feminism better in Ukrainian. In 2013 and 2014, she helped me think more about what it was like to be a woman in a male-dominated activist sphere in which many men thought, because of their leftist positions, they were feminists themselves, without doing any work for gender equality. In 2013, Tonya put it this way:

When I first came to activism, the majority of the most proactive activists were men or boys. And, well, it was really hard for me ... in the first place because, even though they were leftists and they should be feminists, they are not and never were. Honestly, they can laugh at something that you proposed, and that was the situation, many times. So I understood what it's like to be a girl, especially if there aren't more girls in activism. But, with time, the main thing is not to lose heart, to keep your head up, not to allow yourself to be humiliated ... and to make people pay attention to this, say it's discrimination ... And then in due course, they will see who you are, how you carry yourself, what you do, and they will evaluate you based not on your appearance but on your merit, on your activity. And now people evaluate me on what I did and what I do, and not on whether I'm a woman or a man.

In 2021 Tonya was hesitant to speak too directly against the male-bodied activists from Priama Diia or any other activist movement, as they recognized the negative impacts of gendered socialization on everyone. Instead, they said simply, "Sometimes people really want to prove that they are worth listening to. It's a very privileged position." Here again, the sewing cooperative is designed to be a space of daily feminist activism where such hierarchies are directly challenged and where queer, non-binary perspectives are primary.

Discovering the Left in Theory and Action

Some leftists were explicit about ideological labels with which they identified themselves. Petro, from a city in western Ukraine, told me outright that he identified as a socialist, communist, and Marxist. He stated: "I stand in favour of a system which will be based on fundamental differences from capitalism." Whereas Danylo found leftist affiliation through action and only after that began to explore leftist texts, Petro discovered leftist theories in his youth. He told me: "In middle school, I already identified as a socialist, as left. … In school I was kind of a nerd and I read a couple of books which were politically left. The first Marxist one was *The Origins of the Family, Private Property, and the State*, and then Fromm, Kropotkin." This reading coincided with major political events in Ukraine, particularly unfolding activism against Ukraine's second president, Leonid Kuchma, in the early and mid-2000s.

> I was already sympathetic to the movement against President Kuchma after the murder of the journalist Heorhiy Gongadze, Ukraine Without Kuchma. A couple of times I went out there, but already in my hometown there were oppositional actions in which an absolutely eclectic coalition of people participated, from leftists to nationalists, and which eventually grew to support the so-called Orange Revolution.

The "Orange Revolution" took place in Kyiv in 2004, when fraudulent elections led to Viktor Yanukovych – Kuchma's hand-picked successor – winning the presidential vote. People in Kyiv took to the streets to demand new elections, building a tent camp and standing in the cold for two months until new elections were granted. In January 2005, Viktor Yushchenko, opposition and pro-Western candidate, won the new elections. But for Petro, this was not necessarily a victory:

During the Orange Revolution, I was sceptical about Yushchenko, but I was also strongly against Kuchma/Yanukovych. But I had already come to Kyiv, I had access to the internet, I met more of these kinds of [oppositional] groups in Russia and Ukraine. The first action I got involved in was a picket against a conference that brought together different Ukrainian oligarchs and Francis Fukuyama. We wanted to tell Fukuyama what we thought about the "end of history."

Petro's idea of the left is based much more strongly in broadly leftist critiques of capitalism as a system of inequality and political marginalization of socialist alternatives. But his observations and later participation in political movements – first Ukraine Without Kuchma in 2000 (when he was twelve) and the Orange Revolution of 2004 (when he was sixteen) were essential in his progress linking the theories he was reading to an activist mentality.

Many activists, particularly those who grew up outside Kyiv, pointed to the Orange Revolution as having an important influence on their politicization. They described a feeling of solidarity with others in the street, having positive interactions with people who supported Yushchenko, and that the desire to reproduce such feelings impelled them towards other activists. While all of these activists were critical of Yushchenko's term in office and were generally quite sceptical of the effectiveness of political representatives, the Orange Revolution remains a common point in many of their stories of becoming politicized. Their association with leftist politics, however, came alternatively from interacting with leftist texts, as Petro did at an early age, or participating in an action that allowed for their political sympathies to become clear.

Most of the leftists I worked with tell a story that features theory and action coming together to politicize them as leftist activists. Together, leftists have developed a praxis that has created the space for diverse political identities to come together as the "left," especially around specific issues such as the Pride Parade or higher education. Where Petro was influenced by theory to seek out oppositional activism as a teenager, Danylo experienced a leftist protest he felt very sympathetic to and sought out texts to clarify his political identity following that action. Widespread access to the internet in Ukraine enabled leftists who were seeking to clarify their views, like Danylo, or who were entering into a new world of politics, like Petro, to find forums for discussions about leftist issues as well as reproductions of classic texts that they otherwise would not have been able to access. The internet has also served an important organizational purpose in connecting people organizing events while also protecting them from right-wing organizations seeking to disrupt leftist protests.

Importantly, education has long been a prominent site that encouraged the politicization of young activists, as Andriy mentioned earlier. This is not to say that activists read radical leftist texts in their university courses, but rather that the space of the university and the problems people confront there have led to interactions with other activists and the possibility of self-organized resolution of students' problems. Groups such as Priama Diia drew left-leaning students into their actions across campuses in Kyiv. How did universities encourage students to become more involved with activism, and why did they give them a place to develop their leftist sensitivities?

Universities Open Doors: Politicization through Education Activism

When I first asked Ania, then a twenty-one-year-old student in Kyiv, for an interview in the summer of 2012, nothing I said could convince her to do it. She did not consider herself enough of an activist to be useful to my research. She was, as she said later, "just present." I interacted with her at several meetings and actions in early 2013, and she was later a nearly constant presence with leftist groups throughout Maidan. She became a leftist simply by associating with other leftists in an informal sense, but these actions fighting against problematic university administrations and in solidarity with students had a real impact on her moving from passive participant to active activist. She had been a peripheral activist in Kyiv for several years when the following event took place and she began to prioritize activism as she had not before. When she finally agreed to an interview in spring 2014, she described her path towards activism in this way:

> A few years ago, I just met people and I got involved but I didn't do activism, we were just hanging out ... I just attended actions, meetings, so on. I didn't really do something, I was just present ... But I still thought activism was the thing you should do. There was this action organized by the university administration of Taras Shevchenko University at the campus near the Exhibition Centre against these temporary kiosks.[6] At the action, students came to shout, but Priama Diia joined in on the action because they had a history with the [university] administration, who hates them. Two or three [PD] girls climbed on the roof of the metro and had a banner against the commercialization of education. The other students [not from PD] didn't know what was going on, so they were shouting the same slogan – and the administration didn't like it, but the students didn't understand that those girls weren't part of the university action. It didn't achieve much but it was the first time I was in an action

for a long time … It was important for me and I felt I had a future as a leftist activist.

Events such as these made peripheral people like Ania see that they could participate actively in university-related activism and feel effective. She began to think about big-picture problems such as the commercialization of education and what she as an individual activist could do about them.

Other activists told stories of negative interactions with authorities at their universities that impelled them to seek out help from the student union Priama Diia, whose members were known for supporting students in various complaints against universities. Ivan, along with a half-dozen other students, ran a campaign in his university to change students' excessively heavy class schedules. This was Ivan's first step into the activist community, as it was for the other unorganized activists, who eventually became Priama Diia members at Kyiv-Mohyla Academy (KMA), one of the most prestigious universities in Ukraine. After they won the issue of changing the schedules, Ivan told me, they turned to other problems in the university, such as paying extra fees.

Ania's description of herself as "just present" for quite some time, even though she believed in leftist ideas, could be applied to many other activists. Andriy also discussed his regular participation in student-organized protests about education, but he was hesitant to join Priama Diia until the fall of 2013. He also talked with me a few times, before the protests on Maidan began, about not appearing at events where right-wing groups would be present because, until then, those groups did not know his face. Despite their sympathies with the left, both Ania and Andriy feared the results of their overt participation with Priama Diia, as so many of the group's members had been targets of right-wing attacks. Both of them, however, became official or more active members in Priama Diia before the mobilizations on Maidan began, suggesting that the impetus for stronger politicization was based on a possibility of action with a mutually supportive group of like-minded activists. Both used Priama Diia as the starting point to get more involved with other forms of activism, and they parlayed this momentum when student organizing on Maidan needed core participants to help move some more radical ideas into the forefront of the protests.

These stories are examples of the diverse iterations leftism can take in contemporary Ukraine. They reflect some of the debates going on within leftist groups as well as some of the ways leftists view their place in the contemporary Ukrainian political scene. I turn now to two sites built for and by the leftist community that show some of the dynamics among leftists as they self-organized before Maidan.

«Вільна школа» - це абсолютно новий, альтернативний освітній проект, який пропонує різноманітні дисципліни, курси, лекції, воркшопи. «Вільна школа» - це також осередок нових знань та знайомств. Місце, де немає поняття «вчитель», який знає усе, й «учень», який у всьому має слухати «вчителя».

Тут немає парт, поставлених в ряди і один за одним, немає контролю «знань». Але й немає хаосу, недисциплінованості та нудних занять. Кожен, хто приходить, може висловлювати свою думку по темі або якісь побажання щодо проекту.

Разом ми створюємо освітній простір, який є цікавим та комфортним для нас.

Проект має на меті забезпечити людям доступ до **БЕЗКОШТОВНИХ курсів** як з найбільш затребуваних загальноосвітніх предметів, так і з спеціалізованих дисциплін університетського рівня. Передбачено різні види курсів, які можуть зацікавити різні аудиторії, а також одиничні зустрічі, презентації, кінопокази на різноманітну тематику, актуальну сьогодні.

Наразі «Вільна школа» проводить курси англійської, німецької, французької мов, англійський дискусійний клуб, заняття з історії, релігієзнавства, психології, курс сучасного мистецтва та театральні тренажі. Детальний розклад занять дізнавайтесь на сайті та в групах ВК і ФБ.

Figure 2.1. "The Free School"
Source: Author's photograph.

Building a Community Together: The Kyiv Free School

"The Free School" is an absolutely new, alternative education project that offers diverse disciplines, courses, lectures, and workshops (figure 2.1). It is also a centre for new knowledge and acquaintance, a place where there is no notion of a "teacher" who knows everything and a "pupil" who must listen to everything the teacher has to say; here, there are no desks placed in rows one by one, no test of "knowledge." But neither are there chaos, indiscipline, and boring lessons. All who come can express their opinions on the topic or their wishes for the project.

Together, we are creating an educational space that is interesting and comfortable for ourselves.

The goal of the project is to guarantee people access to FREE courses both in the most popular general subjects and in specialized disciplines at the university level. Different types of courses are provided of interest to different audiences, as well as meetings, presentations, and film screenings on diverse themes relevant to today.

Currently, The Free School offers courses on English, German, and French languages, English discussion club, lessons on history, religion, psychology, a course on contemporary art, and theatrical training. A detailed schedule of classes can be found on the website and in the VKontakte and Facebook groups. [translation by the author]

According to Tonya, the original idea for the Free School came from a Priama Diia activist who was interested in education in general and was inspired by liberation pedagogy. In particular, the group of activists who founded the project drew from A.S. Neill's *Summerhill*, which Tonya described as "building living conditions together, becoming more responsible even in childhood to choose [one's] profession [oneself]." The founders saw education as a process based on the exchange of knowledge and as free and accessible to all. Further, Priama Diia was an activist union and, as Tonya put it, "we were suffering from authoritarian principles in the university. There was lots of unnecessary work, just wasting time." She and other activists wanted to take pleasure from gaining knowledge, so in 2012 they started the Free School. Activists in other cities, including Khmel'nyts'kyi, Simferopol, and Chernivtsi created free universities, as well.

The Free School is based strongly on principles of liberation pedagogy and the work of Paulo Freire, who, Tonya pointed out, worked with proletarian society to teach language and science in a free and accessible way. Tonya and other activists had discussed Freire and liberation pedagogy in detail in 2012 at a student organizing camp I attended in Crimea.[7] In their words, these principles included the following:

- rejection of enforced discipline, influence on moral or religious grounds;
- no obligation to attend class;
- no exams, no tests of knowledge;
- questions and answers come from both sides; teachers and students both offer questions so that it is a conversation;
- open meetings to solve issues connected to personal problems, not just related to education;
- no authority, no imposing enforcement of dogma;
- horizontal principle of work based on education to overcome the difference between teacher and taught;
- search for a new outlook, a new model of society, new possible solutions for controversial situations;
- overcoming a culture of silence, which Freire connected with ignorance: the culture of silence is a consequence of social-economic dependence, poverty;
- overcoming stereotypes;
- personal work and personal creativity.

The three presenters talked about the experience of trying to create the Free School in Kyiv based on these principles. As they described, many activists were still not familiar with them, and even though organizers held meetings to define which classes and workshops should be offered, many people still did not have a clear vision of what was needed and waited for others to tell them what to do. This response, the Free School organizers pointed out, comes from an educational system based on memorization in which there must be a clear hierarchy in the teacher-student relationship. It can be challenging to convince people to find answers themselves; people often prefer to wait for an answer to be given. Only with a permanent process of rejecting this hierarchy, as one activist put it, can it be overcome. As Tonya argued,

> the idea of overcoming the relationship between the teacher and student can't just be literal, it can't work without a coordinator, who gives information about the field. But overcoming the division means that no one feels privileged to be in that position, imposing their views and thoughts as the only way. The person who already has the knowledge has an obligation not just to give it but to show the ways he or she got it.

The presentation was followed by a lively discussion about the nature of education: how can we evaluate what students have learned without testing? How can we learn from examples in Latin America or Finland, for instance? A tall activist named Misha argued that liberation pedagogy can increase students' efficiency, but it has to be measured by some kind of evaluation. Nastia from Moscow responded that giving marks is not the same as an evaluation of knowledge, and evaluations are also important so that students' backgrounds are taken into account by the lecturer or facilitator.

Importantly, leftists recognized the role of authoritarian and totalitarian regimes in developing seemingly benevolent literacy programs that, in reality, were ways to minimize individuality and expand state power (see Clark 2000). One activist described liberation pedagogy as "giving human personality a way to grow," which is the crucial point that divides it from a totalitarian system, which prepares people for a narrow, specialized place in society that they must follow. Liberation pedagogy has the possibility to help people break out of the existing social system from below, thus making it potentially transformative of capitalism itself.

This discussion shows that leftists took seriously the theoretical foundations of their educational projects, and they wanted to build something that challenged capitalist structures of hierarchy and authority. Although the Free School clearly offers classes that are desirable to activists and others, especially foreign language classes, the ideas behind the structure of the school are equally important as its content. When my research began, the Free School did not have a permanent location, so its regular course offerings were limited. I participated in the English Discussion Club that was held most Monday evenings at 5 p.m. at a small library off Prospekt Peremohy. The club was a place to speak with non-activists who were interested in practising English, and our topics of discussion ranged from basic conversation to politics to a film screening of *Paris Is Burning*, followed by a discussion.

Earlier in my research, many people had big ideas about how the Free School should function. In mid-December, around the time that the Maidan protests had begun to be entrenched for the winter, I met up with one organizer, Misha, and Larisa, who was going to join the community as a teacher. Larisa was interested in doing excursions to historical sites in Kyiv, such as the House of the Chimaeras, a unique building across from the presidential administration building on Bankova – a street that had already seen violence against protesters at the hands of the police and would remain closed to civilians for most of the winter. Even then, I noted that it didn't seem to be safe to be wandering around the city centre; in another part of the centre, we tried to access the city hall (*Kyïvs'ka mis'ka derzhavna administratsiia*, KMDA), but it was already occupied by protesters. Although Larisa made it clear that she would be a good instructor, nothing ever came of this meeting as far as I know from further discussion with Free School organizers.

One space that Free School organizers used was known as the Solidarity Centre, a shared space used by other leftist and political organizations in downtown Kyiv. After meeting Larisa, Misha and I went there to have a meeting with Free School organizers, including Tonya and two other women. As I learned, they had many courses lined up for the next year: French, Spanish, German, English, plus chemistry, economics, Left Liberatory Theory, and possibly gender studies. They wanted to make some rules or requirements or conditions for participating in certain courses, because often people would tend to come and sit without talking or participating. Especially in courses such as Left Liberatory Theory, participants were at various levels: some people came in with a base in leftist theory, others were completely new to the material. One of the organizers proposed having lectures about the more basic concepts to Left Liberatory Theory, including consumerism, Marxism, and globalization, to help participants have a shared understanding of foundational ideas. The organizers never resolved this problem, however, because they were not sure who would volunteer to organize and run these base-level courses.

At this meeting, other courses were proposed, including a programming class suggested by Misha, who was already taking such a class but wanted to adapt that work to the Free School. Tonya advocated for bringing back the gender studies course, which had been very popular in its first iteration, but she was not willing to take on the work herself because of other commitments. Another attendee, Nastia, volunteered to run the class. In addition to these new classes, they discussed continuing their very popular Esperanto classes, which were held at the Solidarity Centre, as well as their French lessons, for which they had to approve a new teacher. I noted that the sheer number of volunteers who were invested in the project reflected well on the organizing, although I am not sure how many courses continued through the year because of Maidan.

Nastia, Misha, and Tonya were all enthusiastic about the prospect of taking the Free School to Maidan, especially as an Open University had been set up there behind the main stage. Tonya planned to propose a dual talk about Left Liberatory Theory with another student activist, who would present the more theoretical component while Tonya would talk about the practice of the Free School. Nastia was hesitant to support the idea, as she feared it would be considered a provocation because it referenced a leftist perspective. She anticipated that right-wing people on Maidan would come to the lecture and make it unsafe for the presenters and attendees. Tonya clarified that she wanted to focus on liberation pedagogy, using the Free School as an example of practice of the theory, which, while still leftist, was far enough from "the left" that Nastia ultimately approved. However, when Tonya proposed this to the Open University organizers later, she told us at an English Discussion Club meeting that they had asked her for a biography and summary of the presentation. She concluded that the Open University wasn't so open after all, and the lecture never took place.

This meeting shows some of the challenges of the Free School – namely, that a small group of people was responsible for a rather large organization that served many people in Kyiv. The challenges of bringing the principles of liberation pedagogy into practice led to some stagnation in course planning, although how much influence Maidan had on the lack of follow-through is hard to say. I know of at least one researcher whose lecture was cancelled at the last minute because attendees wanted to plan for the next day's protests. English Discussion Club continued to meet through the winter and spring of 2014, and I continued to attend, if only to get a break from thinking about the protests.

Tonya and Misha remained committed to the project, and in June 2014, I met with them and a few other activists after English Discussion Club to talk about the Free School. That day, at the English Club, we were joined by a young man from France who wanted to propose a new method for teaching math and physics as a Free School course or lecture. But his condescending attitude and clear lack of understanding of the Ukrainian context derailed what could have been an interesting pedagogical conversation. While Tonya was describing her participation in feminist activism, he kept pushing her on the kinds of actions that feminists in Ukraine do, so she mentioned recurring demonstrations on 8 March, the Free School course on gender studies, and publications about feminism. The French guest refused to see any of this as action, rejecting Tonya's long commitment to feminism and the hard work of feminist activists in Ukraine (see chapter 6 for a longer discussion of feminism in Ukraine; see also Channell-Justice 2017, 2020a).

Despite the negative part of this conversation, what happened next was perhaps more crucial in terms of understanding the role of the Free School. A young Ukrainian named Lyosha had been attending the English Discussion Club for several months. He was not an activist or a leftist, and he attended a pedagogical university in Kyiv. But his participation in the club had opened his eyes to many issues that leftists often take for granted, and this discussion of feminism was an important one for him. He had told me before that he was taking an interest in LGBTQ+ issues, noting that he couldn't understand why LGBTQ+ people were hated by most Ukrainians and that he wanted to start being an ally. Lyosha's interest was further piqued by this conversation about feminism, which he had previously not seen as a discourse that was open to him. Tonya described how radical right-wing people and neo-Nazis actively work against feminists and leftists in general, but that because of their ingrained sexism, they often do not use violence against activist women, who they perceive as weaker than men. Lyosha continued, asking Tonya about political intolerance and why it happens. Here, she reiterated what many leftists had described before:

> People respond negatively to leftist ideas because these ideas seem close to communism, even if they are not, in reality. These nationalist forces create the face of the enemy, and the face of the enemy is the Soviet Union, or Russia and the Russian people. They have been creating this image for a long time, and it makes people think that leftists support communist views that existed during the Soviet Union. And since nobody wants to return to this, or most people don't, then the leftists become the enemy because they represent a return to this, even though they actually don't.

Although the negative attitude of the club's French visitor put a damper on the evening, I found that this and other conversations with Lyosha represented precisely the goals of the Free School in action. Rather than Tonya's acting as a teacher telling him want to think, Lyosha used his participation in the club to educate himself about more tolerant ways of thinking and being in the world. The lack of hierarchy between Tonya and Lyosha made Lyosha more receptive to Tonya's otherwise radical ideas – recall Nastia's concerns that talking about anything to do with the left on Maidan was a risk she was not necessarily willing to take. Because of the equal playing field between Tonya and Lyosha, he changed his opinions on political issues and became invested in gender equality and supporting LGBTQ+ people in Ukraine.

In 2021 I read this story to Tonya, who did not remember the details but felt gratified by the Free School's positive effect on Lyosha. The theme of the Free School was a difficult one for Tonya, because she became completely burnt out by it: "When the Free School stopped working, I had so much burnout, I didn't even want to think about it. It was an enormous task and I had to do it all as a volunteer." The awareness that she had to leave the Free School behind is resonant of Tonya's current conceptualization that constantly working, even as an activist, is a capitalist paradigm. But the Free School does live on in other forms. Misha, the programmer who wanted to propose IT courses in 2014, did manage to contribute to an IT education program based on skill sharing that continued for several years. Ivan, the philosophy student from the chapter's opening anecdote, is now a programmer himself and is part of an IT workers' cooperative that itself was inspired by working with Misha and the Free School principles.

Fighting Back: Leftist Responses to Violence

Beyond the centrality of the principles of liberation pedagogy among leftists, another leftist initiative had a rather different goal: how to respond to the violence leftist activists faced from right-wing vigilantes. Leftists organized in various ways to resist their own marginalized position in the broader political sphere. Such practices of resistance became crucial experience for Maidan, where leftists remained marginalized but were committed to participating, even in the context of further threats from police as well as right-wing protesters. Although I never came across a circumstance in which a leftist activist targeted someone from the far right with violence, the continued attacks on leftists suggested that right-wing attackers assumed leftists would not fight back or were committed to non-violence. Leftists condemned the targeted attacks against their comrades as well as the ways radical right-wing activists justified their attacks, but many leftists were also willing to fight back.[8]

In October 2013, a group of leftist activists from various organizations created a self-defence class based on principles of *krav maga*, the Israeli street-fighting practice. These classes shifted focus over time, initially helping participants develop quick responses to possible attacks and ways to protect themselves and escape. Later, following the expansion of mobilizations on Maidan, the classes focused more on dealing with possibly dangerous crowd situations, with police officers, pepper spray, and attacks on journalists and photographers. The initial classes assumed a leftist would be attacked going home alone; the later ones responded to attacks on whole groups and the more real dangers of being present on Maidan.

Krav maga itself was an appropriate martial art to learn, as it fit within liberation pedagogy-based conceptualizations of how learning can be shared. As Einat Bar-on Cohen describes, "*Krav maga* draws its learning from 'natural,' 'instinctive' fighting body movements and tendencies, conditioning the fighter's brain to react automatically, and improving performance through closely scrutinising actual violent events. *Krav maga* is therefore very adaptable to a broad range of needs and situations ... Since *krav maga* movements are purportedly based on how children naturally grapple and fight, they can be taught at a basic level to anyone within a short period of time" (Bar-on Cohen 2010, 272). Indeed, our instructor, Kolia, explained to me that he hoped that the participants would all be able to learn enough from the classes that they could teach someone else at least basic techniques. Although he enjoyed teaching, he wanted to treat the practices as a skill share, which had leftist, egalitarian origins in his view. The need to organize self-defence classes was borne out of the threat of violence, but throughout my notes I describe the practices and spaces as largely positive and communal. *Krav maga* was an important site of team- and community-building for leftists, in addition to being a useful skill.

The first practice space was a gym far from a convenient metro stop, but it was large, containing a big mat, a carpeted area, and a fighting ring. There were around twenty men working out when our group of a dozen arrived. There was only one changing room, with no spaces for women to change separately from men, prompting the few female participants to wonder if women had ever used this space before. Rap music was blaring loudly throughout the gym. While watching the earlier group of men finish their workout, I noted that the group was very serious looking, doing group sit-ups and shouting together, and their instructor carried a riding crop that he kept snapping. These men were in sync, very muscular with stereotypically masculine bodies. Some leftist participants commented later that they noticed some of these men had the "look" of skinheads, and one was even wearing a shirt with a white power slogan.

In contrast, our group of leftists appeared different and presumably came to the gym with different intentions. The first group of men stayed to watch some of our practice, probably noting that many of our participants were not wearing typical exercise clothes or nice sneakers. Perhaps they were more interested in the four women who joined the group, or our very basic exercises. In this first lesson, we learned *krav maga* stances and some defence movements, as well as basic punching drills. While, for the most part, the women paired off to work together, in some instances male participants insisted on pairing with women so that we might experience a stronger assailant, imitating real-life risks. Throughout the time I participated in *krav maga*, male participants – who had often had experience in self-defence training – wanted to make sure that the women were gaining the same knowledge as everyone else.

Ultimately, the group ended up moving to two more spaces over the course of the months I practised with them. The first gym was deemed risky because of the presence of possible right-wing groups, and its distance from the metro and from the city centre was a point of contention. Our next practice was at an open space that usually housed yoga classes but that also contained floor mats and punching mats that we held to practise with partners. This space was more expensive – another area of discussion, as activists wanted the practice to be as inclusive as possible, and certain activists could not afford to contribute to the use of this space – but it was safer and more accessible from the centre of the city. We stayed at this location through most of the winter, trying a new space only in March 2014.

Our classes typically began with a warm-up, jogging in circles and doing strength exercises. Then we would review the basic techniques of punching and defending, and then Kolia would demonstrate a new skill. These skills ranged from breaking out of headlocks or breaking free from someone who grabbed your arm to bringing down your assailant by attacking his eyes, nose, and mouth. Typically, we partnered up in twos, with Kolia sometimes asking female participants to pair with men so that we would not be inclined to go easy on each other. In some classes, we did group exercises that were based on crowd scenarios, rather than on one-on-one attacks. Ultimately, the classes focused as much on being prepared to expect violence as on fighting techniques themselves. In one repeated task, everyone stood in a circle and slapped the person next to them in the face, and that person was expected not to blink or flinch. When participants practised defence tactics, we were required, at least sometimes, to push our partner as far as possible so that each person would know how such an attack might feel. Everyone was given tasks to increase vigilance of the situation around them – for example, counting the number of people wearing hats or the colour red on their journey home.

These basic tactics of vigilance and preparedness were, of course, enhanced by fighting and defence techniques, with varying levels of possible damage to the person who might be doing the attacking. Kolia often focused on keeping the classes relevant to actual possible attacks, rather than preparing participants only for controlled situations. Occasionally, a guest instructor would give us special sessions. In one special session on crowds, the instructor, Dima, lectured about how crowd situations can change people's mentality, and he explained that a person's position in a crowd would have a significant influence on how he or she must respond to violence: if a person is in the centre of a crowd, he or she cannot escape, but if one is on the periphery, he or she becomes the first line of defence. The group also simulated a situation that activists were likely to meet in reality. In this exercise, we divided into two teams called *Han'ba* (shame) and *Provokatsiia* (provocation), two of the most commonly used epithets against leftists at protests. Kolia turned off the lights, placed a pile of punching mats in the middle of the teams, and made everyone run around shouting *han'ba* or *provokatsiia* while a strobe light flickered. The exercise – in which we used the punching mats to push "enemies" from the other team and protect "friends" – attempted to prepare the group, both physically and mentally, for violent crowd situations. The use of *han'ba* and *provokatsiia* in this instance was in part a joke because of their common misapplication to leftist protest actions, but it also helped participants think about identifying an "in-group" in an overstimulated, dangerous environment.

Dima's lessons, while useful, were more serious than Kolia's. Dima was realistic about engaging with violence: he stated outright that it would be difficult to get out of a situation in which there are multiple assailants. He also included some gendered language that was typically not used by leftist practitioners. Dima recommended not to bring "your girlfriend" to a protest. By this, he meant not to bring someone who was unprepared to deal with violence and to protect themselves, because you want to be in a position to defend only yourself. But, Dima said, if you do bring your girlfriend, have her hold onto you and lead her to safety, and if there is an attack, you need her to get down so you can protect her. While probably good advice for any protester who needed to protect anyone less capable of defence, he could have used a different example to show us how to protect someone who knew less about defending themselves.

Most often, "the police" appeared in our classes as assailants.[9] Dima first brought police violence to life by teaching a lesson on engagement with a police officer who is trying to beat you with a baton: he recommended that the best thing to do is to move towards the police officer so that he does not have as much force with which to beat you; or, if you can, to move back and out of reach of the officer and his baton. He said that police typically are brought to a protest to clear people out, so they are less likely to stand there and beat you – a statement he made just days before police violence against protesters broke out in January 2014.

After this lesson, Kolia too began to evoke police more often in our classes. He explained that the police – specifically, riot police, pervasive around the protests in the city centre – are trained not to fear what is happening because they are prepared to respond to it, and they can predict what kind of violence will happen in what circumstance. However, people on the "other side" – non-police – are not prepared for violence, so they are frightened and can behave in ways that provoke more violence. Therefore, everyone must be prepared in the same way the police are prepared, but without an intent to do harm. Kolia recommended that participants should avoid fighting with a police officer, but, if necessary, there are ways to engage with him, such as asking strange questions if he tries to attack a protester – "What are the last four digits of your phone number?" – which can help one gain an advantage. He further taught us ways to attempt to control a police officer's baton to prevent an attack if the person could not otherwise run away, though he did not recommend doing this if running away was at all an option.

The significance of these exercises was that, even when partnered or in small groups, they used the rhetoric of "us" and "them" that was established by real-life attacks against leftist activists. There was a clear shift in our practices: in the fall of 2013, we focused on one-on-one violence; later practices, especially after January 2014, paid more attention to crowd situations and potential instances of police violence. As representatives of the governing regime, police were considered part of a "them" that did not support the right of radical leftist activists to organize and resist. Even if the police were fighting against *all* protesters, no matter their political affiliation, the classes never ceased to be organized around the principle of fear of right-wing violence.

These self-defence courses brought attention to the recurring attacks on activists and events in a way that mainstream media – in Ukraine and elsewhere – had thus far refused to do. It allowed leftists to see that their fears were legitimate and shared, but also that they were not powerless. Leftists who did not want to back down in their activism and views but wanted to be free of the constant fear of an attack decided to control some of the circumstances surrounding those attacks – namely, their own preparedness to respond to violence. These classes taught activists not only how to defend themselves if they were attacked, but also small techniques for anticipating such attacks in order to be able to respond in a way that could keep a person out of the hospital. After class, we stopped wearing hoods and listening to headphones on the way home so that we could not be taken by surprise. Although the *krav maga* classes were developed in response to the threat of right-wing violence against leftists, these tactics proved useful once Maidan began and the threat of violence became more widespread.

Attending these classes allowed me to access a site of leftist formation based on a response to increasingly systemic violence, but it also opened up a realm of internal dynamics in which left or radical ideas structured every interaction. As the classes included both women and men, these radical ideas affected how gender was enacted and reproduced in our classes. At the first gym, many suspected no women had ever breached such a masculinized space, contributing to the discomfort. The men working out before the leftist group arrived had a militarized, unified kind of organization, and appeared shocked and amused when they saw a co-ed group. In the practices, Kolia and the other organizers were committed to treating men and women equally in our group, both driving the women as hard as the men, but also rejecting the idea of "positive gender discrimination" that would assume women to be less likely to be attacked because of their status in mainstream Ukrainian society. Although women rarely have been targets of physical violence by ultra-nationalist men, except during LGBTQ+-rights and feminist demonstrations, the self-selected women who attended these practices were not excluded. Women (including myself) often paired off with other women during our training sessions, but they were also required to practise with men, who did not hold their strength back to protect women. Most of the women refused to be seen as a weaker sex, fighting as hard as the men in the class, although twice women came to participate but changed their minds once they realized we would actually be punching and kicking each other.

At the same time, these classes were a place for men to create and perform a radical leftist version of masculinity that does not gel with mainstream attitudes towards men. Most of the men in the class had not completed military service because of their student status,[10] so their presence in the first gym was nearly as strange as the women's. However, they were not training to achieve this kind of militarized masculinity; instead, they were creating a form of protective non-gendered behaviour towards which all of us could strive. In this mentality, men were not the automatic protectors of women; rather, those who know more should be the protectors of those who know less. Allowing this group to generate a protective camaraderie in the context of targeted violence meant rejecting gender norms that ordinarily put men in competition with each other. This space was an enactment of gender equality in the eyes of the participants, an equality that was based not just on accepting women but also on creating a non-militarized, well-prepared activist group that cared for and protected everyone involved.

Conclusion

This chapter's focus on leftist formations largely outside of Maidan elaborates how leftists in Ukraine work internally to build a movement and a community. The activists' profiles illustrate the diversity of viewpoints that make up the Ukrainian left, and the two examples of leftist practice – the Free School and *krav maga* – show that leftist space is a constant process of negotiation to becoming committed to principles of liberation pedagogy, mutual aid, and gender equality. Through these examples, we see that leftists want to change what it means to be part of the left in Ukraine. They are dedicated to detaching leftist ideas from their communist associations by building up spaces in which theory and practice go hand in hand to make a safer world in which to advocate for ideas of equality and tolerance. In the next chapter, I turn to the dominant national ideology in Ukraine, which continues to make such advocacy work a challenge to the contemporary left.

Chapter Three

Decommunization and National Ideology

On a cold night in December, crowds gathered at the bottom of Shev-chenko Boulevard in Kyiv. With a contraption of ropes, protesters had managed to climb the ten-foot-high marble plinth to snag the statue of Vladimir Lenin that had stood in that spot for almost seventy years. As the crowds cheered *Komuniaky – na hilliaku* (Hang the communists), Lenin teetered back until, ultimately, crashing headfirst to the ground behind the plinth. Flares flashed and sound grenades banged, and the crowd chanted *Re-vo-liu-tsi-ia!* before breaking into the national anthem. Other slogans circulated as protesters took photos of the fallen statue, its head broken off, and began chipping away small shards of the marble body. After rounds of *Slava natsiï – smert' voroham* (Glory to the nation – death to enemies) and *Ukraïna ponad use* (Ukraine above all), protesters began to chant *Razom – i do kintsia* (Together to the end) and encouraging those still present on Shevchenko Boulevard to move towards Maidan. The Svoboda Party, a right-wing party, claimed credit for the action.[1]

The next day, I went to see Lenin's body. There was still quite a crowd, largely male, using small hammers to break apart the main part of the statue. The hands and head – which had been replaced in the 1980s – had disappeared by then. Most people took turns taking photos with Lenin's body, sometimes perching on top, while others took photos and videos of their part in the dismantling of the body (figure 3.1). The marble plinth had already been defaced with Nazi symbols and a "White Pride" tag; on top, where the Lenin statue had been just hours earlier, was a sign reading *Ukraïntsi – vy naikrashchi* ("Ukrainians – you are the best!") and two flags: that of the European Union and the red and black flag of the Ukrainian Insurgent Army.

Later that evening, as it started to snow, I ran into Andriy, who was a friend of a friend I had met in L'viv who'd come to Kyiv to spend

Figure 3.1. Crowd in Kyiv demolishing the body of Lenin's statue after it was pulled down
Source: Author's photograph.

the night. Amid the uncertainty and atmosphere of violence, with riot police officers setting up lines near the former Lenin statue, Andriy told me about staying up all night and dancing to music, assessing his evening as "cold, but fun (*veselo*)." Andriy pointed out several times that no one knew what would happen next, and that all night, even though it was calm (*spokiino*), he knew that at any second something could happen. But, he said, we can't go back from here (*my ne mozhemo povernuty nazad*), because even without a clear plan, he knew it would be much worse. Andriy said he supported what was happening on Maidan, but not 100 per cent. He surprised me by saying that he thought it was a bad idea to destroy the Lenin monument. He felt that it looked like a provocation, either by the far right or by Yanukovych's infiltrators, to incite violence. It didn't help anything on Maidan, and it wouldn't get anyone to support what was happening on Maidan if they didn't already.

Bringing down the Lenin statue was a key turning point in the Euromaidan protests. It reinforced the notion that decommunization was central to Ukraine's post-Soviet national ideology, which had been building up until the Maidan protests began and was strengthened throughout the mobilizations. In this chapter, I explore anti-communism and decommunization policies in Ukraine and the role of Euromaidan in bringing anti-communist positions into the mainstream of Ukrainian politics. Because the Maidan protests created the space for a contestation of national narratives, as I show, the protests enabled the development of a specifically anti-communist national ideology to permeate post-Maidan politics and encouraged the continued marginalization of leftist voices during and after the protests.

Anti-communist Protest and Decommunization-as-Politics

Maidan elevated discussions of decommunization into the mainstream political sphere. This point was not lost on leftist activists whose continual attempts to participate on Maidan were rejected and met with violence. The notion that Ukraine needed to go through a process of political decommunization became popular on Maidan. To many, Ukraine needed to be further distant from its communist past in order to move forward on the path to Europe. Journalist and leftist activist Andriy Movchan pointed out the centrality of decommunization for the mobilizations at a conference, "The Left and Maidan," held in Kyiv in April 2014. When asked to present about his views and interpretations of leftists' roles on Maidan, Movchan replied:

> Leftist groups' attempt at intervention into the movements of Maidan happened regularly. Each attempt that appeared on Maidan, as a separate group, separate block, with its own subjectivity, each ended either with some misunderstanding or with violence from the side of the right and ultra-right. It seems to me that the question that stands before us is this situation and the reason for it. And the reason, it seems to me, doesn't have to do with the weakness of leftist groups, which is factional to today. The reason has to do with the exact character of these protests under the name "Maidan." … There was one unifying idea – the idea of anti-communism. In other words, the idea that unified absolutely different groups, different political views, different social projects, wasn't nationalism, or fascism, or patriotism, or even Euro-integration, but precisely anti-communism united these groups.

Movchan suggested that, instead of a view in which European integration and anti-Yanukovych activism brought people together, anti-communist attitudes informed protesters' desires to be part of Europe as well as their adherence to certain national narratives that became prominent in the protests. Movchan's claims incensed many of the conference's attendees, but it is important to take them seriously, as decommunization through legislation became a crucial political platform of the Poroshenko government elected after Maidan.

Decommunization and anti-communist positions have played a complex role in countries in the former Soviet sphere – Poland, the Czech Republic, Slovakia, Hungary, Romania, and Bulgaria – that have gained membership in the European Union. I consider that "anti-communism" refers to the positions and attitudes of participants in political society, ranging from party leaders to voters and ordinary citizens. Anti-communist positions evaluate the "legitimacy of the past political and economic system" and "reject the moral authority of the past regime" at the same time that they "imply a duty for anti-communist leaders not only to condemn but also to redress the injustices perpetuated under the past system" (Appel 2005, 380). Decommunization, then, is the process of implementing anti-communism as a political platform, the combination of the condemnation and rectification of wrongs committed by communist regimes.

What exactly has decommunization entailed? Is it simply a government's "dealing with the communist past" (Kopeček 2010, 200)? Or is it more: the active effort to reject and erase communism and its perceived influence on society, politics, and economics from the contemporary landscape? In Ukraine, decommunization has included a complete condemnation of the communist regime and everything associated with it, from street names to symbols to the Communist Party itself. It has also incorporated the rejuvenation of historical anti-communists, such as Stepan Bandera and other members of controversial Ukrainian organizations of the twentieth century. In 2015 decommunization resulted in the full ban of the Ukrainian Communist Party from standing for elections, a ban which the party has appealed through the European Court of Human Rights.

Many scholars have considered the role of decommunization in encouraging burgeoning democracies in eastern and central Europe (González-Enríquez 2001; Halmai and Scheppele 1997; Kopeček 2010; Mungiu-Pippidi 2006; Sadurski 2003). In particular, the use and effects of "lustration" laws to "cleanse" new democracies of former communists and their collaborators has provided a complex view of the possible paths of decommunization (Appel 2005; Calhoun 2002). Ukraine never pursued lustration, although the term became common on Maidan in the spring of 2014. In March that year, I asked some men standing around a tent on Maidan what lustration meant to them. One major concern for these men was control over the budget: one told me that only deputies, those in the Rada, have control over how the budget was decided, while those who voted for the deputies had none. He was concerned that former politicians such as Leonid Kuchma, Ukraine's second president, still had influence on the budget. According to this activist, the community did not have any influence on the budget, but next year, when lustration would have taken place, there would be civic control of the state and city budgets. He saw lustration as part of the process of taking back control from inept politicians.

To me, it was unclear how budgets and lustration were directly connected, outside of the assumption that lustrated politicians such as Kuchma would no longer have control over the budget.[2] Another activist defined lustration in much simpler terms: "Responsibility." Another looked at Ukraine's short period of independence as an explanation for the lack of lustration: "Ukraine is not an old country," he told me in Russian. "That is why we have such a problem with corruption, and corruption is why we need lustration." In my field notes, I concluded that there was not a clear definition of lustration among Maidan activists, and it seemed that most people did not know how to move forward with the process itself, even if they knew they wanted politicians such as Kuchma and Yanukovych to be held accountable (figure 3.2).

Perhaps politicians did not see a way to move the lustration process forward either. After his election, Poroshenko focused much more earnestly on the aesthetic elements of decommunization, rather than on cleansing the ranks of government workers who might have had connections with the previous administration. In May 2015, he signed into law a package of legislation known as the "Decommunization Laws." Two of the elements of this legislation were, first, to make denial of the criminality of the Soviet and Nazi regimes a crime in itself and, second, to change the legal status of "fighters for Ukraine's independence," or members of Ukrainian nationalist organizations in the twentieth century, to provide their families recognition and social guarantees (Channell-Justice 2015; Shevel 2016; see also the multifaceted discussion on the *Krytyka* blog.)[3]

Decommunization-as-politics is a useful tool for a new governing elite to secure its power. For new governments, displaying an anti-communist position serves as proof of an authentic break with a communist past, even if members of the governing regime remain the same (González-Enríquez 2001). In other words, even in the case of governments whose members did not change substantially following the end of state socialism (the case of Ukraine, for instance), decommunization and even lustration can still be mobilized as tactics to gain legitimacy among newly democratic constituents.

Decommunization – and, similarly, the rhetoric of post-socialism – also plays a crucial role in the creation of new democratic subjects (Chelcea

Figure 3.2. Protesters destroying flags of the USSR and the Party of Regions on Maidan
Source: Author's photograph.

and Druta 2016; Eyal 2000). In order to integrate them fully into the Euro-American global capitalist system, the residents of these countries must be "decommunized," as deemed by political leaders convinced that capitalism is the only way to survive the initial post-socialism. The lingering legacies of state socialism are so entrenched in the bodies of post-socialist citizens, it is claimed, that these people prevent post-socialist states from joining Western capitalist modernity (Ozolina 2019; Ţichinde-leanu 2010; Todorova 2005). Only active policies of decommunization – and their support by the populace – can bring eastern and central Europe into the modern sphere. Certainly, these political manoeuvres have not prevented scholars and activists from generating stringent critiques of the effects of neoliberalizing policies on the citizens of these newly independent regimes, especially as these policies have created greater ethnic, social, and economic inequalities than existed or were perceived to have existed under socialism (Ban 2015; Cervinkova 2016; Gökarıksel 2017).

To secure this shift in precarious economic and political contexts, then, communism and its effects must be soundly condemned. Although perhaps an understandable, if contestable and contested, step in the early and mid-1990s, the question of how to decommunize a country like Ukraine that had not been communist for twenty-five years presents a different challenge. As Oividiu Țichindeleanu describes, "the postcommunist culture industries excelled in the fetishistic production of *accursed symbols* linked with communism, left thought, and the common man, and the converse import of works and figures of the *masters of thought* from the right side of the political spectrum, a cultural tradition forbidden and censored by communism" (2010, 27, emphasis in original). I find this description apt for Ukraine: the project of decommunization consists of demonizing *anything* related to Ukraine's communist past – up to and including the Communist Party and any other leftist political configurations – and of valorizing those parts of history that were hidden or rejected during communism.

The far reaches and fuzzy definitions of the Decommunization Laws make current non-party leftist organizations easy targets of the legislation. These organizations' interest in Marxism and class-based analyses of social problems, while completely unrelated to the Communist Party of Ukraine of the Soviet or post-independence period, is regularly collapsed into the goals of decommunization, making non-party leftists targets of anti-communist activism. Returning to Andriy Movchan's conclusions, we can see that both decommunization and anti-communism underlay the multiplicity of voices on Maidan and were used to justify a broad rejection of leftists' presence during the protests.

Important for Ukraine are links between processes of decommunization and the re-creation of national and political identities (Appel 2005). Specifically, a functional national identity is a crucial aspect of European-ness, but this national identity is perceived to be non-existent when communist influence continues to permeate the country. Thus, decommunization of politics, economics, and national culture must be part of establishing a Europeanized national identity. This helps explain why national narratives were so crucial to establishing Ukraine as European during the Euromaidan mobilizations, as well as what those narratives contained. Further, they help explain why these national narratives took precedence over other issues of Europeanization, including economic development requirements and non-discrimination legislation, both of which have proven to be problematic since Ukraine's Association Agreement was signed in June 2014.

Rupture and Reintegration: Citizens, State, and Nation

The mass mobilizations in Ukraine resulted in President Yanukovych and his cabinet fleeing the country (mostly for Russia), even though Yanukovych had become president following what is generally agreed to have been a fair election in 2010.[4] Yanukovych was the legitimate leader of a democratic Ukraine. Since Ukraine's independence in 1991, though, citizens' distrust of the state had grown with each regime. The protests on Maidan were a manifestation of the growing rupture between citizens and the state, in which the regime no longer could be trusted to represent people's best interests. This rupture culminated in the overthrow of the state, a state represented by the Yanukovych regime.

I do not suggest that Maidan represented an idealized idea of a unified nation fighting against a corrupt state, however; the "nation" has been such a contested concept in Ukraine that the protests were easily filled with people all protesting the state without embodying the same nation. Thus "Maidan" is not an ersatz "Ukrainian nation" but represents the varied and contentious claims that ordinary Ukrainians tried to make – some successfully – on the state and its representatives. For this reason, leftist and other politically marginal groups felt it was important and necessary to be part of the mobilizations because they were perceived as an extraordinary moment in which extraordinary claims could be made. But leftists were critical of the view that the goal of the protests should be about remaking a state to be more representative of Ukrainians – as we saw in the flyer that opened the Introduction, leftists are largely critical of nation-states as the world's primary political actors.

For many protesters, however, participating in Maidan was a way to reintegrate the state and its citizens. They rejected the state as anti-Ukrainian, and hoped to replace it with one that would actually be accountable to its citizens, ensured through the practice of new democratic presidential elections. These protesters relied on the reproduction of specific national narratives in order to validate their claims of being representative of a unified version of Ukraine. By framing this as a national ideology, I move away from defining and evaluating the idea of "the nation" and "nationalism" in contemporary Ukraine. Instead, I trace how Maidan provided the opportunity for this particular ideology, rather than some other one, to gain traction among more people than would ordinarily be seen as part of the right wing.

I employ Katherine Verdery's (1991) concept of "national ideology" to help better understand the political concepts mobilized by those who were attempting to use national narratives to encourage this reintegration. In her discussion of socialist-era Romanian national ideology, "the nation" and its existence were taken as a given, allowing a national idea to permeate Romanian state socialism. Thus, *nationalism* – a political ideology in which the definition of an independent nation must be the primary goal of political action – is based not only on establishing *who* and *what* constitute the Ukrainian nation, but also on the assumption that the Ukrainian nation is more important than other political issues. In other words, Ukrainian nationalism should be seen as a political ideology that assumes the primacy of the nation even as various groups might have different ideas about what that nation should look like.

There are certainly many people in Ukraine who believe that the territory on which they live is indeed a nation that should have political institutions in the form of a "state." There are leftists who support this idea, even if they are critical of the forms that "nation" and "state" historically have taken. There are also leftists who consider themselves anarcho-nationalists: they are supporters of the Ukrainian national community but inherently critical of the form the "state" can take. These different groups – dispersed geographically, with anarcho-nationalists being most active in western Ukraine – show the ways political visions of nation and state can differ, making a unified national position extremely unlikely.

The radical right, in opposition to the radical left, however, often promotes the position that Ukraine should be home only to Ukrainians and Ukrainian speakers, and their national ideas dovetail with exclusionary attitudes towards LGBTQ+-identified people, as well as immigrants and ethnic minorities – see, for example, Bustikova (2019) for more on how right-wing political parties respond to the inclusion of various minority groups. Rightists enact these beliefs in various ways. First, they often target leftist-organized demonstrations and actions because leftists support these minority groups' rights. But they also mobilize versions of Ukrainian history that were suppressed during the country's years of state socialism, suggesting that these historical elements constitute an "authentic" Ukraine. Therefore, because leftist ideas and practices are still being linked to socialism and communism, and because leftists are critical of the nation-state form, they become fair targets for the radical right as part of the right's attempts to rejuvenate Ukraine's repressed, authentic past.

National Ideology on Maidan

As I described earlier, the increasingly hegemonic national ideology in Ukraine holds that the development of the nation is a primary political objective, even as the content of that national ideology can be manipulated. It is necessary to recognize that the idea of a Ukrainian nation is itself contested, as we have seen in Russian political discourses that question Ukrainian national sovereignty because of centuries of Russian domination over this territory. Because of the threat – perceived and real – to Ukrainian sovereignty, the promotion of a national ideology grounded in Ukraine's history of oppression is an important political project, made more prominent during Maidan.

My ethnographic observations from 2013–14 showed that the national ideology promoted during Euromaidan was largely grounded in a glorification of certain historical figures and groups that were definitively anti-communist. Some of these figures and groups were also known to collaborate with the Nazi regime against the Soviets, and some were also sympathetic to Nazi ideology. I concluded in 2014 that the attention given these figures and groups reinforced discord in Ukraine, rather than uniting the diverse regions of the country. Because of the popularity of valorizing Ukrainian anti-communist mobilization in the 1940s and 1950s across western Ukraine, I determined that a national ideology that was so closely linked to those figures and groups would be alienating to others in Ukraine – namely, those in eastern Ukraine who were more likely to speak Russian as their first language and who had been incorporated into the Soviet Union much earlier than those in western regions.

This conclusion, however, relies rather heavily on the idea of the "two Ukraines" proposed by Mykola Riabchuk (2002), which assumes that Ukraine can be divided somewhat cleanly into two regions: West/Europeanized, and East/"Creolized" and anti-Ukrainian. This thesis has been countered many times since Ukraine's independence (Barrington and Herron 2004; Hrytsak 2004, 2019), but most recently and most thoroughly in the volume *Regionalism without Regions*, which takes a more nuanced approach to memory politics and national ideology. The authors of the introduction establish that historical memory is contested across Ukraine, not just at the national level, but also as it unfolds in each of Ukraine's twenty-four oblasts (Myshlovska, Schmid, and Hofmann 2019, 5). Researchers' survey of people's attitudes towards specific historical figures – including Stalin, Catherine II, and Stepan Bandera – in 2013, before Euromaidan began, showed great regional variation of how people evaluated history, not distinctly visible in terms of an east-west divide. As the authors rightly conclude, "the nationalist, Soviet, and other versions of the past continue to coexist in many different forms in independent Ukraine and are constantly being challenged and transformed by new narratives" (Liebich et al. 2019, 115). Furthermore, external factors, such as local, national, and international media, influence which narratives of the past take hold in a given place at a given time. With this in mind, we can see more easily why and how Euromaidan created space for the contestation of national narratives of historical memory.

To illustrate how Maidan promoted certain national narratives, specifically those organized around anti-communism, I explore two components of this national ideology: a demonization of communism and a veneration of controversial nationalist organizations. I examine these elements of national ideology through examples that incorporate events from before and during the Maidan protests. Because of my ethnographic positioning among leftists, I begin by describing a violent reaction to a presentation of a book about Leon Trotsky's writings about Ukraine, which presents a common way that right-wing groups respond to leftist efforts to discuss Ukraine's communist past. This event shows some of the tensions, described earlier, that contribute to leftists' perceived affiliations with communism and their exclusion from discussions about the nation. Then, I consider the destruction of Kyiv's Lenin monument, and what followed, to show how anti-communist sentiment spread widely across Ukraine.

Next, I turn to the "heroes" who were mobilized to replace the communist figures in Ukraine's history. Although their importance remains contested, the groups, figures, and slogans of mid-twentieth-century Ukrainian nationalism were ubiquitous on Maidan. The post-Maidan decommunization processes reinforced the state-supported efforts to rehabilitate these groups in Ukraine's national narratives. As the 2019 election of Volodymyr Zelensky shows, however, the cosmetic reinterpretation of the past cannot rebuild a struggling economy or erase years of corrupt practices that have marred Ukraine's democracy. History and memory will continue to be politicized as government figures see fit, but these efforts must always be contextualized in the real lives and real priorities of everyday Ukrainians, including all of those who stood on Maidan.

"For a free, united, independent Soviet Ukraine": Rehabilitating Trotsky

As described in the previous chapter, many leftist activists were interested in open discussions of historical figures associated with Soviet socialism and thus easily rejected from Ukrainian historiography. One group, Left Opposition (*Liva Opozytsiia*, LO), has focused its interest in this regard on Leon Trotsky. Described on its Facebook page as a "contemporary socialist, feminist, anti-fascist, and ecological initiative," the group's main efforts in the past several years have been organized around workers' rights. In 2013, when I began my fieldwork, I met one LO activist in Odesa and several others in Kyiv. Around that time, the group released a small volume of collected essays and speeches about Ukraine by Trotsky, entitled *Ukrainian Trotsky: Texts by Lev Trotsky on*

Ukraine. The volume included essays about Trotsky's relationship with Ukraine – he was born in the Kherson governate (southern Ukraine) in 1879 – and his politics in the early Soviet period, as well as Trotsky's own words, translated from Russian.

Trotsky's legacy in the Soviet canon is complex, and he is perhaps not an obvious choice for leftists in Ukraine to take up as a hero of Ukraine. The editors of the volume intended to reinsert Trotsky into Ukrainian historiography because of his use of concepts such as independence, unity, and freedom in his vision of how Ukraine fit into the Soviet Union. In their foreword to the volume, the editors write,

> Certainly, Trotsky was not the first who posited the indivisibility of the social and the national in the struggle for Ukrainian revival, but he was the last of the leaders of the October Revolution whose voice was further heard in favor of the freedom of Ukraine up until his death at the hands of an agent of the Stalinist regime in 1940. Even before the Second World War, Trotsky concluded that the independence of Ukraine, its right to self-governance, solemnly proclaimed in Stalin's constitutions, turned into a fiction. Is this not the same thing we see today? Are not freedom, unity, independence – all these favorite concepts of patriots – just fickle phantoms? (Liva Opozytsiia 2013, 6, author's translation)

The editors contextualize Trotsky's own unfulfilled desires for Ukraine in the context of 2013. They claim that freedom, unity, and independence had not yet been achieved in contemporary Ukraine and that the trajectory of its capitalist development was limiting Ukraine's potential. Citing a survey from the Razumkov Centre, then one of the few independent polling organizations in Ukraine, the editors add,

> A survey of social opinions convincingly shows that the majority of the citizens are sure that after the achievement of formal independence in 1991, the situation in the country has still not improved – in any area. In their view, the level of culture, quality of life and social protections decreased and continue to decrease, the economic situation worsened and continues to worsen; while crime and corruption relentlessly increase. Thus, at the dawn of independence, many spoke about democracy (they said, yes, we're poor, but we're free!) – and today, after twenty years, even the dynamic of the level of democracy after the declaration of independence is assessed negatively. (Liva Opozytsiia 2013, 6, author's translation)

In the volume and through its activism, Left Opposition promotes an anti-capitalist agenda as the way forward to true freedom and independence, and implores readers to draw from Trotsky in this regard, bringing him back into Ukrainian history as a valid revolutionary figure. The editors conclude: "At the beginning of the 1930s, Trotsky put forward the slogan, 'For a free, united, and independent Soviet Ukraine!' This slogan remains unfulfilled until now. Hence, it is our current slogan" (7, author's translation).

The editors attempt to draw from opinion polls to show that most people in Ukraine at the time were not satisfied with the quality of Ukraine's democracy. The events of later that fall proved the polling data correct – that many people felt it was time to hold politicians accountable for building better democratic institutions. In this sense, leftists' ideals fell directly in line with others' criticisms of Ukrainian governance. However, their efforts to infuse democratic activism with Marxist ideals through this volume were not welcome. Alternatively, it shows how purportedly democratic activists in Ukraine, especially those representing the far right, have a particular vision of Ukrainian independence that is not based on pluralism or a civic idea of the nation (Shulman 2004). The release of the volume and its attempted presentation in Kyiv illustrates this diversion among pro-independence activists in Ukraine.

Ukrainian Trotsky was to be presented in mid-November 2013 at a prominent bookstore in the centre of Kyiv. The five presenters included two members of LO and three academics, including one who came from London for the event.[5] As I arrived, the presenters were taking their seats, and I looked around for some familiar faces. Instead, I found many attendees dressed in full-body camouflage and combat boots, a style I later learned is usually associated with right-wing activists and neo-Nazi groups. Joining a group of LO associates in a corner, I noticed the presenters looking anxious as they began to introduce themselves. Before they could begin discussing the book, a man in a baseball cap in the front row stood up and began ranting at the presenters that Trotsky – and, by extension, the presenters themselves – had perpetrated the Ukrainian famine of 1932–3 (*Holodomor*),[6] was homosexual,[7] and supported Satanism.[8] The man in the baseball cap – Artem Skoropadskyi, a Russian-born journalist and self-identified Ukrainian nationalist, who became a constant presence on Maidan – was soon joined by others yelling slurs about Trotsky, the presenters, and the book, and they refused to let the presenters speak about the book, saying it was a political project for leftists and communists, despite the organizers' claims that they were attempting to lead an academic discussion.

Before long, about half the audience was on its feet, chanting loudly[9] – *han'ba* (shame), which is a common way to show anger and displeasure;

smert' voroham (death to enemies), the enemy being Trotsky and his current supporters; and *komuniaky – na hilliaku* (hang the communists). The presenters, their supporters, and the bookstore employees tried to calm these instigators, but to no avail. After a quarter of an hour of this disruption, the police arrived and attempted to clear the space. They forced everyone out of the bookstore, but many of the ultra-nationalists waited outside for the presenters to leave, going so far as to slash the tires of the LO members' van. The presenters remained in a back room until an escort arrived to take them home safely; I tried to wait for the presenters with a group of women from various leftist organizations, but we were forced to leave through a back door so as not to draw attention to the presenters.[10]

Why did the book presentation of Trotsky's ideas about Ukraine create such an antagonistic atmosphere between left and right activists? If, as described earlier, both groups theoretically support Ukraine's sovereignty and freedom, why is it impossible to bring Soviet leaders into the discussion of Ukrainian independence? Right-wing activists such as Skoropadskyi draw from a national ideology that presents a singular narrative about Ukraine's relationship with the Soviet Union: that it was bad, and that Ukrainians were always the victims of Soviet policies. Certainly, the inhabitants of the territory of contemporary Ukraine *were* often the targets of Soviet policies with negative consequences. *Holodomor*, the manmade famine, killed at least three million people in the eastern regions of Ukraine and replaced many of them with Soviet Russian inhabitants, completely transforming the ethnic and linguistic makeup of this territory (Appelbaum 2017; Snyder 2010).[11] Kate Brown (2004) has documented a different policy of deportation and relocation of Ukrainians in the western territories in the Polish borderlands, which removed the Ukrainian, Polish, and Jewish populations of the region and repopulated it with Sovietized citizens. Ukraine experienced a multitude of repressions at the hands of the Soviet regime, and to be clear, leftist activists are not denying these crimes in their efforts to rehabilitate Trotsky.

Joseph Stalin is the most clearly anti-Ukrainian of the main early Soviet leaders, but Lenin also supported policies that ultimately harmed Ukraine and Ukrainians, and Trotsky remains linked to both of these figures. According to the LO volume and his own written works, Trotsky was a vocal supporter of the existence of a united, independent Ukraine within the Soviet Union. In the 1920s, Stalin was the architect of the Soviet nationalities policy in which both Lenin and Stalin agreed that nations – based largely on a shared language, history, and, to some extent, territory – have rights, including the right to self-determination

(Slezkine 1994, 417). This definition meant, in theory, that no nation was superior to another, and that any nation could be modernized with the right economic and social development. The call for national self-determination was a mechanism to condemn the exploitation of colonization; as Francine Hirsch puts it, "[i]n an effort to reconcile their anti-imperialist position with their strong desire to hold on to all of the lands of the former Russian Empire, the Bolsheviks integrated the national idea into the administrative-territorial structure of the new Soviet Union" (Hirsch 2005, 5). The policy born from this integration, indigenization (Rus. *korenizatsiia*), envisioned representatives from each national ethnic group being in control of that nation's affairs within the Soviet Union, thus encouraging support for the Bolshevik regime from within, rather than colonizing the Union's regions and forcing them to submit to the revolution (Slezkine 1994, 433).

The reality, of course, was not so simple. First, the Soviets were not the first to attempt to build a strong centre while dealing with the diverse nationalities and ethnicities of peoples from Europe to the Far East (see Hillis 2013). Second, Lenin and Stalin both rejected any kind of "bourgeois nationalism," which was a distraction from the ultimate goal of class revolution. This distinction made it easy to target certain national groups that had a history of nationalist activity, including Ukrainians. Thus, Soviet nationalities policy was meant to use the category of "nationalities" to bring diverse people into the same political entity, ostensibly to modernize and to move past capitalism into socialism and communism, but the policy grew to be a hierarchical mechanism, with the Russian nation as its centre. And, as Hirsch argues, "[e]ven as the Soviet regime was amalgamating clans and tribes into nationalities, it reneged on (or 'reinterpreted') its earlier promise of national self-determination and condemned all attempts to separate from the Soviet state as 'bourgeois nationalist'" (Hirsch 2005, 8). As this policy morphed, Lenin's original ideas, and Trotsky's support for national sovereignty within the Union, were marginalized.

Thus, attempts to rehabilitate Trotsky in this way might be unwelcome to the average person in Ukraine, who either grew up under a repressive, single-party surveillance state, or, for those born near and after independence, who were raised with a clear idea of just how bad that state was. Catherine Wanner has further suggested that the development of a shared national sentiment of being "Ukrainian" was based not on a shared territory or language, necessarily, but on shared experiences of victimization, especially in the Soviet period. In particular, Wanner uses the examples of the *Holodomor* and the Chernobyl disaster of 1986 as events that galvanized *glasnost*-era Ukrainians to begin to view their state system as exploitative and repressive. Wanner argues that these events became part of the foundation of a Ukrainian national consciousness that was mobilized in 1991 towards independence from the Soviet Union. It is particularly because these events are so vivid in individual memories of people living in Ukraine that they resonate when interpreted as elements of a shared national sentiment (Wanner 1998, 36–7).

The current dominant national ideology promoted by radical right-wing groups insists on narratives of Ukrainian repression and victimization during the Soviet period. This is linked to the broader process of decommunization. To these groups, contemporary leftists continue Soviet narratives of socialism and must be rooted out if Ukraine is to be completely free of communist influences. They cannot, then, support any discussion of the complex roles of Soviet historical figures, because their national ideology cannot integrate the idea that someone like Trotsky could have promoted Ukrainian independence. For right-wing national ideology, the Soviets *only* repressed Ukrainians and their claim for territorial integrity, even killing them in order to homogenize the Soviet Union. Because even new leftists are perceived as being associated with the Communist Party, this element of decommunization – the destruction of the new left, as well as any remaining aspects of the historical left – is generally accepted in society at large. This also helps explain why Lenin monuments around Ukraine were such clear targets for national activists during the Maidan protests, resulting in the phenomenon of *Leninopad* as it unfolded over the winter of 2013–14.

Monumental Propaganda: Lenin in Kyiv

Kyiv's "Bessarabian Lenin," the monument that was brought down in 2013, was erected as part of the Soviet Union's broader efforts to use monuments to establish and reinforce a specific historical narrative. Oleksandra Haidai writes that Lenin statues began appearing in the second half of the 1920s, stating that, "during Soviet times, they overwhelmed the territory of the state, and the figure of Lenin was turned into the object of nationwide worship" (Haidai 2018, 44, author's translation). Kyiv became the capital of Soviet Ukraine in 1934, so "monumental propaganda" (*monumental'na propahanda*) became significantly more important in the city (*Istorychna Pravda* 2013). In 1944, Khrushchev signed an order to develop Khreshchatyk, Kyiv's main street, including incorporating a monument to Stalin at one end (now European Square) and Lenin at the other, across from Bessarabs'ky Market. But this exact spot was contested by locals, particularly because it had held a German gallows during the Nazi occupation of the city, where public executions had taken place. However, because the area came out of the war largely unscathed (untrue for other parts of the city) and construction could begin immediately, the monument was placed at the bottom of Shevchenko Boulevard. The statue, over ten feet high, by Serhiy Merkurov, was unveiled in New York City at the World's Fair in 1939 and brought to Kyiv in 1946.

A second major monument featuring Lenin was erected in Kyiv on what is now Independence Square in 1977. This monument was removed following a decision of the Kyiv City Council in 1991, and the Globus shopping mall built to replace it. The Bessarabian Lenin, however, remained where it was, and the Communist Party continued to use it as a site for mass actions (*Istorychna Pravda* 2013). Debates over the monument's status included whether to designate it a "monument of national importance" or remove it completely, a decision that could legally be made only by Kyiv's City Council or by the Regional State Administration. Activists had attempted to destroy it before: Ukrainian nationalists from the Tryzub (Trident) organization managed to damage the monument in 2009, but it was restored soon after (*BBC Ukrainian* 2009; Cybriwsky 2014; Plokhy 2021).

That the Lenin monument was such a site of struggle among groups illustrates Haidai's argument that the Soviet state used monuments to mark public space as "its own" (*svoie*): a manifestation of "the similarity between communist and nationalist ideologies. They both have a unitary perspective and have a metanarrative with a unique pantheon of heroes as a foundation, which is projected on the territory of the state" (Haidai 2018, 46). Statues and monuments were used to unite the territory's diverse ethnic populations and traditions through a unified narrative in public space, as well as to show the superiority and power of the Soviet government itself. Thus, the contestation over Soviet monuments, and what to do with them afterward, is also an important aspect of building national ideology.

The removal of Soviet-era statues, as several scholars have recognized, was an important step in many former republics in visualizing a break with the Soviet Union (Verdery 1999). In 1990, Chervonohrad, a city in western Ukraine, was the first in the Soviet Union to dismantle a Lenin monument (Haidai 2018, 172). Other cities in western Ukraine removed their Lenin statues as early as possible in the 1990s (Cybriwsky 2014; Wanner 1998), but the particular statue that remained standing in Kyiv grew as a symbol of the "old" regime over its continued existence during Ukraine's independence. Gaining that representational power, it became even more important to destroy it – and violently – almost twenty-five years after the end of Soviet rule. Lenin had come to signify not only the period of Soviet rule in Ukraine, but also, and perhaps more important, the Yanukovych regime's commitment to Putin's vision of the Ukraine-Russia relationship. Thus, destroying Lenin in 2013 was not simply a statement that protesters were ready for a real break between Ukraine and communism; it was also a stance against continued Russian domination in Ukraine. The generally positive response to the violent destruction of the statue shows that Kyiv residents in general were largely ready for the statue to be gone, especially because it signified the direction of the protests.

Importantly, Lenin's destruction in Kyiv led to an expansion of the practice across Ukraine, called *Leninopad*, from the word *snihopad*, or "snowfall." Particularly in response to the mass violence used against protesters during 18–20 February 2014, more than 100 Lenin statues were brought down, particularly in the central oblasts of Ukraine (Haidai 2018, 178; Liebich et al. 2019, 82–3). Altogether, in February 2014, 320 Lenin statues were demolished (figure 3.3). *Leninopad* continued through the rest of the year, until more than 550 monuments had been forcibly removed or taken down following decisions by local governments (Plokhy 2021). The implementation of the Decommunization Laws that followed in 2015 brought down the remaining monuments, as well as implementing changes to street, town, and city names.

Participating in *Leninopad* became an important way for the populations of various cities and towns to mark themselves as authentically Ukrainian.[12] As Haidai argues, the protests in Kyiv activated otherwise marginal nationalist groups in central regions, but, following the violence in February 2014, "participants in regional actions followed the methods of their own Kyiv predecessors" (Haidai 2018, 178; see also Channell-Justice 2019c on regional replication of protest tactics). Lenin statues in the main population centres became the most obvious choice to mobilize against, but smaller towns and villages across central Ukraine took part in the dismantling of monuments as well. Although cities and towns in eastern and southern Ukraine were slower to take up the destruction, Lenin statues came down in Mariupol, Kharkiv, and Dnipropetrovs'k (now Dnipro, following decommunization).[13] Liebich et al. (2019, 84) argue that "a common national memory has been constructed by condemning, ousting, and delegitimizing the Soviet narrative and replacing it with memory and narratives about the heroism and suffering of the Ukrainian nation." But these authors, as well as Haidai, also recognize the significant challenges to establishing which heroes and heroic narratives might take the place of Lenin. In other words, the generation of a new national ideology is just as difficult as destroying the old one.

Figure 3.3. Plinth of the former Lenin monument after the statue was pulled down

Notes: The sign in front of the plinth reads "There must be a monument to the Heaven's Hundred here." An elderly woman leaves flower petals around the plinth; whether the petals are to memorialize Lenin or the Heaven's Hundred is unclear.

Source: Author's photograph.

Eventually, the decommunization of public spaces became a government mandate. Streets, cities, and towns changed their names, statues of Soviet figures were removed, and even Soviet-era murals and other public art were targeted by Decommunization Laws. Scholars, both in and of Ukraine, have debated this focus on monuments and names (see Hrytsak 2015). For example, *Krytyka*'s online forum ran multiple pieces considering this problem in relation to the decommunization laws, instead of what it considered to be more substantial reforms for Ukraine (see also Kozyrska 2016). As Verdery and others have noted, however, statues and monuments are the representations of those regimes and narratives, and the practice of creating new symbols and destroying old ones also creates the symbols of new, "authentically" Ukrainian values.[14] Whereas other post-independence regimes in Ukraine never put forward decommunizing policies, as did many other eastern European countries, a key component of the post-Maidan era has been the active efforts to link political legitimacy with anti-communism. This shift has placed leftists in a precarious position because they were already targets of violence due to perceived sympathies to communism.

Yet this clear commitment to a specific, post-Maidan national ideology has not necessarily developed as its early leaders hoped. Under President Poroshenko, the government supported a dominant national ideology that gave little ground to other dissenting political voices. It limited leftists' political possibilities and reinforced their marginalization. In 2019 Poroshenko ran for his second presidential term under the slogan "Language-Army-Faith" (Ukr. *Mova-Armiia-Vira*), and his continued alliances with alleged right-wing figures alienated him from much of the population. When his opponent, TV comedian Volodymyr Zelensky, shifted the focus away from aesthetic concerns such as street names, he reopened the contestation of national ideology. Coming from eastern Ukraine and a Russian-speaking family with a Jewish background, Zelensky represented a possible political pluralism that Poroshenko had been seen to try to smother. Without assessing his suitability for the job, it is important to note here that Zelensky represents a development in recent years that the seemingly clear direction of the national ideology of Euromaidan has become more muddled.

The Political Lives of Historical Figures

Thus far, I have established the centrality of anti-communist and decommunizing positions in contemporary Ukrainian politics. I now turn to the issue of those historical figures that have become dominant in Ukraine's national ideology since its independence. Verdery (1991) argues that the idea of "national ideology" is a discursive struggle in which the concept of what makes the nation itself is the central issue. The debates around what constitutes a nation at a given time and in a given place reinforce the fact that the nation is a contested notion in the political system at hand. The fact of the government's intervention in the decommunization of street, town, and city names shows that institutions that make up "the state" care deeply about what makes up "the nation." Especially because of Russia's strong influence on Ukraine, from infiltration of political figures to economic agreements to pervasive media presence, establishing what "the nation" is has been an important project since 1991. In the years since independence, Ukrainian nationalism has pushed back on this Russian influence by consolidating the idea of who and what makes contemporary Ukraine. Yet, even as the various groups and actors participating in this nationalist project agree on the primary importance of the nation over other political issues, the idea of the nation itself continues to be contested. This contestation ensures that nationalism – and the national ideology built from it – is a powerful political force.

The idea of the nation itself is ideologically neutral. Why, then, does nationalism so often become associated with right-leaning political stances? In the context of Ukraine, where the left has been associated with communism and state socialist institutions, it follows that the right would be associated with political ideologies diametrically opposed to communism (see Bustikova 2019 on the mutual effects of right and left parties on one another in the post-socialist space). The Soviet regime's repression of Ukrainian national positions and politics, some of which I have already discussed in this chapter, led to nationalism's becoming a force to counter communism in Ukraine. Nationalism became the property of the right because it opposed communism, the property of the left; therefore, tensions between right and left in contemporary Ukraine often play out around problems of national identity. The left has little power or input in discussions of the nation, as I showed in the negative ramifications of the *Ukrainian Trotsky* event. Here, I argue that the national ideology at work today actively marginalizes leftists in order to encourage the legitimacy of certain national narratives that draw especially on anti-communist heroic figures.

In recent years, radical right-wing activists have worked to link leftists' criticism of the nation with a pro-communist agenda. Because leftists are critical of the increasingly dominant national ideology, and because that ideology is anti-communist, right-wing activists portray leftists as desiring a return to communism to the detriment of the Ukrainian nation. As a result, right-wing activists can easily justify attacks on leftists, often shouting "Communist!" as they assault them. These attacks contribute to the narrative that leftists can and should be targets of grassroots decommunization activism, the threat of which helps silence leftist activists. Ivan's suggestion in the previous chapter that the Soviets wrote the entire "vocabulary" of the left – meaning that all leftism is to be associated with communism – shows the perceived continuity of communist politics and contemporary leftist activism. Young leftists, however, reject this connection, and see their role as creating a new rhetoric about leftist activism after the end of communism.

Rehabilitating figures such as Trotsky, then, might not be a wise strategy if leftists wish to influence the direction of Ukrainian national ideology. The contemporary leftists I worked with are not affiliated with the current or former iterations of the Ukrainian Communist Party, and many do not associate with communism at all. But they take a major risk when they attempt to spark a conversation about Ukrainian politics that suggests that the political sphere should be amenable to a leftist presence. At the party level, leftists have faced difficulties in breaking into representative and institutional politics, although this might be due more to the structure of the electoral system than to political ideas.

On the other hand, right-wing political parties have gained some presence and strength since independence. The right-wing Svoboda Party reached its peak in popularity before the 2012 parliamentary elections when it received 10 per cent of the vote (Shekhovtsov 2014), which was a reactionary response to Yanukovych's election to the presidency two years earlier. The role of right-wing parties and groups in Euromaidan is contested: leftist scholar Volodymyr Ishchenko argues that "the dominant position established among experts on the Ukrainian far right has been that both the Svoboda Party and the Right Sector were not dominant in the Maidan protests and did not play any crucial, not even a significant role" (Ishchenko 2016, 454). Ishchenko also documents that these same scholars have concluded that this low level of influence on Maidan led to a low level of support in post-Maidan elections, as both Oleh Tyahnybok and Dmytro Yarosh, two major right-wing leaders, drew less than 2 per cent of the votes in the 2014 presidential elections, and their parties – Svoboda and Right Sector, respectively – did not meet the threshold to enter the Rada.

Ishchenko claims, however, that analysing electoral competition alone does not accurately reflect the influence of the far right in, for instance, mass protests. He argues that "small organized minorities may play a role in the protest movements disproportionate to their percentage among the protesters, or support among the population in general (Ishchenko 2016, 454; see also Ishchenko and Varga 2021). The way that right-wing historical groups and figures were mobilized on Maidan reflects Ishchenko's conclusions, because right-wing visions of Ukraine's past influenced the national ideology that was promoted during the protests. Although I do not argue that radical right-wing activists determined the trajectory of events on Maidan, right-wing politics were much more dominant in this national ideology than any leftist political agenda (for a discussion of the mobilization of different nationalisms on Maidan, see Carroll 2014; Kulyk 2014; Kuzio 2015; Risch 2015).

These groups included the Organization of Ukrainian Nationalists (OUN) and Ukraïns'ka povstans'ka armiia (UPA, or Ukrainian Insurgent Army), known for fighting against the Soviets in western Ukraine throughout their rule. These two groups were led by multiple figures but are often represented by Stepan Bandera, the leader of one of the branches of OUN from 1938. Bandera's arm of the group integrated UPA into OUN in the 1940s, pursuing an insurgency against the Soviets throughout that decade (see Risch 2011; Subtelny 2000; Wilson 1997). These groups historically have been extremely polarizing in Ukraine, largely because they were formed in the western regions of Galicia and Volhynia – which Magocsi (2002) has referred to as Ukraine's Piedmont, in reference to the Italian region that is seen as essential to Italy's unification – the last territories to be incorporated into Soviet Ukraine. These groups also entered into various associations with Nazi Germany, through alliances with local governments or through volunteering in the German Army in special brigades (Khromeychuk 2013);[15] their members also contributed to the decimation of Volhynia's Polish population after the Second World War (Risch 2011).

The appearance of references to OUN and UPA was perhaps inevitable on Maidan. From early on, protesters embraced the moniker "Banderites" (*Banderivtsi* – supporters of Bandera), previously used in a derogatory way to designate a nationalist, especially in Russian media. In 2012, I saw homages to Stepan Bandera in various western Ukrainian cities. During and after Maidan, Bandera became prominent in Kyiv. The Congress of Ukrainian Nationalists placed a large banner honouring Bandera right next to the central stage. UPA slogans – in particular, *"Slava Ukraïni"* – "Glory to Ukraine" – began to be used as a greeting. To mark oneself as having sympathetic views – as was the case when marking oneself as a UPA sympathizer or member in the twentieth century – one simply had to respond *"Heroiam slava"* – "Glory to the heroes." Leftists began to tell stories of people in crowds chanting the slogan (as a call and response) and then being harassed when they did not respond with "Glory to the heroes." Not only were the nationalist slogans marking participants off as the "right" kind of participants on

Figure 3.4. Banner honouring Stepan Bandera by the main stage on Maidan, sponsored by the Ukrainian Congress of Nationalists
Source: Author's photograph.

Maidan, they were a way to allow the most active nationalists to police others into behaving "appropriately" as patriots of Ukraine (figure 3.4).

The usage of these slogans was a marker of the increasing hegemony of a particular national ideology that was then used to designate the patriots and fighters for Ukraine who were on Maidan. I found inklings of what would become a prominent part of the tent camp and occupied buildings on Maidan: the organization known as Right Sector (*Pravyi Sektor*), at an 8 December protest. A small tent across the street from the Trade Unions building with a banner reading Right Sector and a UPA flag were all that marked the group's presence. The Right Sector united three major groups of radical nationalist views in November 2013 after the Maidan protests began: Tryzub, the Ukrainian National Assembly-Ukrainian People's Self Defense (UNA-UNSO), and Patriot of Ukraine (PU). Right Sector became a prominent feature of Maidan through the winter. It continually occupied various buildings – sometimes storefronts near Maidan – from which to stage its actions, and its members dressed in camouflage, giving the group the militaristic, threatening look it was trying to achieve. Further, through the winter, its members nearly always covered their faces with black cloths or balaclavas, obscuring their identities. They also refused to speak to the press, using a media liaison – Artem Skoropadskyi, the man in the baseball cap who started the provocation at the *Ukrainian Trotsky* event – who spoke openly to journalists about the possibility of an armed uprising led by Right Sector, even before the government used force against protesters. Right Sector did indeed gain access to a large number of weapons and became a group of armed militants, beginning in January and February.

The national ideology promoted by groups like Right Sector was, somewhat surprisingly, not based on a linguistically exclusive position. Many Right Sector activists spoke Russian, and speaking exclusively Ukrainian was not a prerequisite for participation. This contradicts what many would assume to be a necessary connection between language use and national ideology, but what was more important for Right Sector was connections to nationalist imagery from mid-twentieth-century anti-Soviet organizations such as OUN and UPA. Many images relating to OUN and UPA and connecting these groups with freedom and anti-communism continued to appear throughout the Maidan period, particularly as militarized groups attempted to gain larger membership. The "Glory to Ukraine – Glory to the Heroes" slogan was constantly used. The people killed on Maidan were referred to as "heroes," incorporating them into a contemporary version of UPA-era slogans. Ultimately this ideology included a commitment to Ukraine's territorial integrity, which its promoters felt echoed the goals of twentieth-century anti-Soviet militants. Thus, anti-communism was an essential element of the stances of Right Sector and others, which helped anti-communist attitudes become such a central unifying factor on Maidan.[16]

Groups like Right Sector are one example of how self-organization permeated the Maidan protests. When Right Sector appeared on Maidan, it was not a political party and had no affiliation with existing political parties. This helped legitimize its position in the protests, which it parlayed into a relatively unsuccessful bid to enter party politics in the elections that followed the end of the mobilizations. But Right Sector's fate as a political party is less important than the way the group promoted a particular national ideology that marginalized alternative political voices and focused on militarized anti-government protest, which I argue later on also led to a reinforcement of traditional gender roles based on an ideal of military masculinity.

Conclusion

Only since Maidan has decommunization become a practicable political issue in Ukraine, but the presence of right-wing groups shows that the links between anti-communist and pro-national positions can be fluid and contested. Maidan allowed one particular national ideology to permeate official politics when the protests ended, but even this national ideology seems to have had an expiration date. Poroshenko's political platform for the 2019 presidential elections, "Language-Army-Faith," assumed that he could get elected based on his work for the idea of Ukraine that came out of just such a national ideology. He supported laws protecting Ukrainian as the sole state language, laws that are always contested by Russian speakers who fear encroachment on their rights, a fear stoked by Russian disinformation and propaganda. Poroshenko also supported legislation that integrated all volunteer battalions into the Ukrainian military, and advocated for further military aid from major allies, including the United States. Finally, he lobbied for recognition of the autocephaly of the Orthodox Church of Ukraine, separate from the Russian Orthodox Church. In 2019, Patriarch Bartholomew I of Constantinople signed the *tomos* (decree) granting the church autocephaly.

But these achievements were not enough in the face of accusations that Poroshenko profited from military agreements and that he was using his position as president to control the appointments of anti-corruption officials. Voters perceived Poroshenko as corrupt, and his commitment to Maidan's national ideology could not prevent his loss in the presidential elections to Volodymyr Zelensky, a TV comedian with no previous experience. Zelensky's neutral policy and lack of connection to right-wing military battalions, such as those that Poroshenko had legitimized in consolidating the army, made him appealing to a wide swath of voters, including many leftists, who perceived the possibility for a renewed political pluralism with Zelensky.

Leftists' fight against their own political marginalization remains salient, and their activism on Maidan – despite Andriy Movchan's pessimistic conclusions – was essential to framing their current political commitments. The next several chapters explore how different groups of leftist activists found ways to be present on Maidan, despite their ideological differences with many protesters.

Chapter Four

#LeftMaidan: Violence, Repression, and Re-creation

It was a gray, rainy day on Friday, 22 November 2013. Across Maidan Nezalezhnosti, beneath the independence monument, was a sea of umbrellas. A few bright blue and yellow Ukrainian flags broke through the largely drab colours of the square, people's winter coats, and the cloudy sky. In front of the Kyiv Conservatory's white columns, a small stage that could fit no more than two people had been erected, and two men in ponchos were at the microphone. Trying to excite the small crowd, the men on the stage made speeches about how Ukraine is part of Europe, and they urged the crowd to join them in the call and response chant: "*Slava Ukraïni! Heroiam slava!*" ("Glory to Ukraine!" "Glory to the heroes!"; figure 4.1).

The night before, some people had gathered in the square to protest the decision of President Viktor Yanukovych not to sign the Association Agreement with the European Union. Friday morning, I met up with a student activist named Havryil, and we started talking about the events of the night before. Havryil was excited. He thought it might be the spark that would set off the next big revolution, as in 2004. He wanted to convince other student and leftist activists to write some materials, not against the protests, but encouraging people to be critical of the EU while they were also protesting against the influence of Russia. We discussed our hopes that the protests might explore the challenges of European accession, even as they did not advocate returning Ukraine to the Russian sphere of influence. But as soon as we were in the shadow of the independence monument, Havryil's enthusiasm dissipated. We began to hear the slogans from the stage, which also included "*Slava natsii*" (Glory to the nation!), "*Smert' voroham*" (Death to enemies); and "*Ukraïna ponad use*" (Ukraine above all), reminiscent of the Nazi slogan *Deutschland über alles*. These slogans, linked to the Ukrainian Insurgent Army (UPA) of the mid-twentieth century, marked the protests with a distinct dynamic that continued throughout their entire existence.

Figure 4.1. Maidan Nezalezhnosti, 23 November 2013
Source: Author's photograph.

When he heard the nationalistic slogans from the small gathering, Havryil was disappointed. But he somehow managed to put his concerns aside. As Havryil described to me then, even though the masses of people who gathered in late November seemed inclined towards nationalist slogans, he felt that leftists should try to intervene in the protests as early as possible. He thought it might be possible that leftists could direct people towards social issues, like economic inequality, if they mobilized early and often. At the same time, he wanted to find a way to clarify that leftists were sympathetic to the protesters' anti-Russian sentiments. He wanted other leftist activists to help promote the idea that Ukrainians do not have to choose only between Europe or Russia, a challenge in a context where many people viewed the EU and the Association Agreement its leaders were offering as Ukraine's only saviour from Russian dominance.

Havryil's attitude became common among leftist activists: while many disagreed with much of what was going on, they still felt it was essential to participate and to influence the direction of the protests as much as possible. By tracing leftists' shifting attitudes and actions from November 2013 through February 2014 and beyond, it is possible to establish a typology of the Maidan protests that helps explain people's drastic responses to events throughout the winter – specifically, it helps explain the different attitudes towards violence that protesters, including leftists, adopted as the stakes shifted over time. This typology also helps elucidate why leftists changed strategies in order to continue to participate in the protests, and it considers how self-organization became a widespread response to the state-based violence that became increasingly drastic over the course of the protests. I illustrate this typology with ethnographic descriptions, particularly focusing on leftist initiatives that developed in response to broader shifts in the protests and the protester-state relationship.

Most participants, including leftist activists I interviewed, agreed that Maidan went through three significant shifts over its lifespan, which I use to frame the typology that follows. The first stage, which lasted from 21 November 2013 to 30 November, when students sleeping on the square were brutally beaten by the *Berkut* (riot police), was a *reactionary* stage that was extremely dangerous for leftist activists. At this stage, leftist activists negotiated for space on Maidan using shifting discourses until they found frames that other protesters accepted and could adapt to their own demands. From 30 November through 16 January 2014, when the so-called Dictatorship Laws passed in the Rada, Maidan was a space of *uncertainty* in which leftist activists had, to some extent, discovered ways to participate in protests while protecting themselves from violence, but they lacked long-term goals for their participation. Finally, from 16 January, between the passage of the Dictatorship Laws and the first protester death, until the end of February, following the greatest violence against Ukrainians since the country's independence, Maidan became a space of *possibility*. For leftists as well as other protesters, the sense that ordinary people could change the course of Ukrainian history became a predominant sentiment, and these activists followed targeted initiatives against the Yanukovych regime through to a resolution. Through the spring of 2014, which began the "post-Maidan" period, many of the successful leftist initiatives dissolved while other creative efforts to penetrate the new regime appeared.

Leftist activists' attitudes towards Maidan shifted over time. Leftists had diverging perspectives about whether or not to support Maidan in the name of whole organizations (such as the student union Priama Diia), up until the passage of the Dictatorship Laws. As several activists mentioned to me, this was the turning point when it became clear that the protests had very little to do with Europe and everything to do with police violence and state repression. Leftists took advantage of this shift to become more united in their response to the repressions, even as their political orientation became less prominent in their self-representation.

Leftists attempted to encourage non-party mobilization and self-organization from the very first days of the protests. However, their interventions during the first stage often used radical leftist and anti-national rhetoric, which was extremely unwelcome on Maidan and was met with violence by other protesters. After 30 November, when the Berkut cleared the square of sleeping protesters, leftists played a crucial role in the direction of protest discourses by using the language of the "state" in their interventions. Stage two was marked by the circulation of discourses among protesters – including, but not exclusively, leftists – of the *politseis'ka derzhava* (police state). Finally, learning from their positive impact in stage two, leftists continued to move away from identifiably leftist projects during stage three and instead responded to growing violence between police and protesters with non-ideological initiatives that embodied leftist principles without requiring visible (and dangerous) leftist words and slogans that would mark them as targets for continued right-wing violence. By stage three, Maidan had achieved an equilibrium in which both radical right and left activists could engage with the mobilizations without feeling threatened by each other; indeed, by then, it was clear that the real threat was the state and its armed police.

Reactionary Maidan: Nationalist Rhetoric and Leftist Missteps

A few days after my initial discussion of the protests with Havryil, I walked to Baseina Street, where leftists had a shared space they sometimes used for events and meetings. There was supposed to be a lecture that evening, but everyone had become distracted by the protests and decided to get together and paint signs for a protest that evening – although every now and then, I would hear someone ask, *U nas bude lektsiia?* (Are we going to have a lecture?). I was working with Dasha, a leftist activist whom I had gotten to know in our self-defence classes. We were struggling to come up with a clever slogan as we watched those around us painting large banners and colourful signs. She showed me a flyer from the right-wing group Tryzub advocating for a potentially violent national revolution to preserve the Ukrainian state (*ukraïns'ka derzhava*; see figure 4.2). My translation of the flyer follows:

Figure 4.2. "We are Banderites! We are going!"
Source: Author's photograph.

We are Banderites! We are going!

From our glorious people we go into the wide world with God in our hearts and a sword at our side.

We go to the village houses, to our brothers, that plough the land with calloused hands, crossed with the blood of their ancestors, the land, the fruits of which are sold by strangers at the thieves' crossroads of East and West, and we proclaim that the land must belong to the one who cultivates it, and that there are moments when the plough should not be driven into the ground, but into the body of the enemy, protecting the right to be the master of one's own land.

Let's go to the factories where the Ukrainian worker, hiring themselves out, forging gold for their oppressors, begging for meagre earnings, and we will teach him that only in a real Ukrainian state will he have the opportunity to arrange his own destiny on his own land.

Let's go to the underground mines, where the parasite of the Ukrainian miner extracts the treasures of the Ukrainian earth, which belongs to the Ukrainian people, and thus to the miner, as a son of that people.

Let's go at midnight, and we will go to those who drink the blood of Ukrainians and we will remind them that nothing in the world is more expensive than a tear shed by Mother Ukraine in solitude, and there will be no such payment that will dull our pain. It must be paid in full!

Let's go to the school between young children, where the enemy will try to fill their hearts with poison from Moscow and Washington, and we will teach them love and dedication to their native land.

We will reach the noble Cossack heart, in the depths of which is the understanding of the sacred truths: Faith and Honour stand above life.

And we have but one target:

A Ukrainian National State, and the path towards It: The Ukrainian National Revolution!

We will get the Ukrainian State or we will perish in the struggle for It!
GLORY TO UKRAINE! GLORY TO THE HEROES!

Dasha was upset by the flyer, which advocated the use of violence to preserve a very particular idea of Ukrainian nationhood. In a critical response to this material, she suggested a play on the nationalist slogans "Glory to the heroes – Death to enemies!" that would read "Glory to enemies!" (*Slava voroham!*). She drew the outline of the slogan in big, black bubble letters, and I helped her colour in neon stripes.

Although they knew their ideas might be somewhat unwelcome on Maidan, leftists felt it was important to speak directly to protesters about how their ideas of Europe might be unrealistic or that the conditions of the EU deal were not going to be directly beneficial to regular people. While some of the banners and signs reflected these criticisms of Europe, there was no cohesive theme to the leftist presence. Some activists made red (socialist) EU flags; others wrote that Europe means "tolerance" (in English, written in rainbow colours) and "equality" (*rivnist'*), references to LGBTQ+ rights required by EU accession laws. Some more labour-oriented slogans tried to be more provocative and creative: "Solidarity with EuroPeople = Struggle with EuroBosses" (*Solidarnist' z yevronarodom = borot'ba z yevrobosamy*) and "Organize a trade union, don't pray for the EuroUnion" (*Orhanizui profspilku, a ne molys' na Yevrospilku*; the letter *ye* in the word Euro was stylized as €, like the euro currency, and the slogan also plays on the word *spilka*, the Ukrainian word for union that is not usually used to refer to the European Union; the word *soiuz* is usually used instead). Another sign read "Freedom/Equality/Sisterhood" (figure 4.3).

The space on Baseina was only another fifteen-minute walk back to the centre of Maidan, so a group of leftists walked there together. My field notes capture some of the energy from the moment the group of leftists entered the square for the protest:

> They all stood together (maybe 20–30 folks?) on the steps in front of the [independence] statue but people got really mad really fast. Mostly they called them *provokatory* and shouted *han'ba* ("shame"), but there was lots of shoving as well and people ripped and broke all the signs we had made. Lots of instigators came to surround our people. There were some people who came to stand in solidarity, some Maidan security people, and then instigators. Someone attacked Roman (he told me that *krav maga* techniques got him out of the attack without having to hit anyone), but then they ended up making a space through people and kind of forced our people down the stairs. Then they were surrounded there for about a half hour. The people on the edges were basically trying to figure out who was there supporting us, who was there against us, and so on. Maria had me go around and take photos of everyone in the vicinity to document who was there, who are recurring people, identifying who was instigating, etc. Interesting that a lot of the mad people were older, but some young nationalists, like the first girl who started it off – but she was drunk, too. At the end, everyone said this is completely normal. Maria said that at their last LGBT march the same exact thing happened, destroying banners, surrounding them, shouting at them, etc. I said it sucks that this is what they have to consider normal.

Figure 4.3. Leftist protest sign reading "Freedom, Equality, Sisterhood"
Source: Author's photograph.

My photos from that night show a variety of people, including the young, drunk woman attacking the woman holding the "Europe is Tolerance" sign. Other people in the photos are mostly men, with Ukrainian flags or blue and yellow ribbons pinned to their coats. Others wear the red and black colours of twentieth-century Ukrainian nationalist organizations, and some prominently displayed the *tryzub*, or trident, another Ukrainian national symbol. Some cover their faces, while others snarl or smile at my camera. The leftists attempted to break off the main instigators of the attack and talk to them one-on-one, which appeared to be a relatively successful tactic to stave off further violence. Other activists distributed leftist materials to try to help explain their presence. In the end, though, the only banner that survived the night was a long, large, silky, red banner that read "Glory to Reason!" (*Slava ratsio!*).

When it finally appeared that enough people had calmed down and the group could leave without being followed, the participants of the action, myself included, sat together in a cheap cafeteria to discuss what had happened and what went wrong. As they saw it, there was no message to the action and everyone was saying something different, so no one observing their protest could get anything out of it. In particular, the "Glory to the Enemies" banner prompted a lot of sighing and eye-rolling –

they could not believe that this had seemed funny just a few hours before. While they understood it was *stiob* – a form of sarcasm or irony that articulates complicated attitudes towards authorities and dominant discourses that are otherwise often unspoken (Yurchak 2006) – they now assessed that this type of *stiob*, which commented *both* on the problem of the nationalist slogans *and* on the lack of clarity in who "enemies" means in any given situation, was either too "individualized" or too "intellectual," as they put it. Because their *stiob* was lost on observers, plenty of whom might have been paid to stand there,[1] it was just read as offensive. On the other hand, the leftists agreed that the banner reading "Glory to Reason!" was funny to everyone because the agreed-upon sentiment on Maidan was that the Yanukovych regime had lost any reason or logic. That was a successful example of *stiob* in part because it did not invoke any other political ideology and was not an overtly leftist banner.[2]

I asked some activists who participated in the action about it much later, and it had become infamous. I only had to mention "that night," and people who had participated knew which night I meant. As one activist, Zhenia, put it, "It was pretty clear that the stuff written on our posters would insult many people." The group had not planned any unified message, and so each person wanted to be as creative as possible – "We just got so encouraged suddenly!" she explained. I asked Zhenia if she had learned anything. "I guess it was a useful experience," she said. "Like, open your eyes, put your feet on the ground. It was bad, but … I don't consider it the worst moment." Masha, another activist who had been present that night, reflected that she had never felt really comfortable on Maidan because of these violent early experiences. But at the same time, she said, "I was always sure that there is a strong reason to be at Maidan." Although these responses might seem counterintuitive, they were common among leftist participants. The very next day, Havryil, with whom I first went to Maidan, was pepper sprayed in the face by a right-wing thug for being part of an anarcho-feminist group. The day after that, I helped him and several other activists plan a leftist presence for that night on Maidan. Clearly, the very apparent dangers of being on Maidan could not overcome leftists' sentiment that they must be present and active at the protests.

I use the term "reactionary" to describe these early days because leftists in particular faced a potentially hostile crowd that did not yet have adequate language to articulate their criticisms against the Yanukovych regime. Even as Dasha and I were colouring the sign, we didn't know if it was a good idea; however, the violent, right-wing flyer she had seen encouraged her to be present, even if she was not exactly clear in her criticism of that rhetoric. But it is essential to keep in mind that, in late November, likely not a single person who was on Independence Square had any idea what was coming – each group felt it was important to be present and share ideas, but no one knew how to respond to those whose opinions differed.

As Zhenia's and others' comments relate, most leftists who were on Maidan that night learned a great deal from the experience. Not only that, they applied what they learned to their future engagements. Just a few days after that particular evening, however, the Berkut violently removed sleeping protesters from Maidan. Leftists used this opportunity in two ways. First, they began to use language of the "police state" to help other protesters name their enemy more clearly. Second, and relatedly, they took advantage of the presence of this new and clearly more dangerous enemy. I suggest that violence among protesters (particularly between left- and right-wing protesters) on Maidan decreased precisely because the forces available to state power were a much greater threat to the lives of the protests and, eventually, of the protesters themselves.

"Against a police state": Shifting Targets and Tactics

Two concomitant shifts changed protesters' attitudes to leftists' presence on Maidan. First, leftists used their experience of "that night" to implement major changes in how they interacted with other protests. After their negative early experiences on Maidan, leftists tried to find ways to avoid being designated as *provokatory*," as this would encourage other protesters to try to get the leftists to leave the square. They also wanted to find a more organized message to present on Maidan so that their observers' confusion could not manifest itself with violence. They discussed both issues extensively during planning meetings they held over the last week of November.

The night of 30 November, when sleeping students were beaten on the square, gave them a unified theme around which to organize themselves and for which they had ready-made critical discourses available. On Sunday, 1 December, a massive demonstration on Khreshchatyk took place, directly in response to the police clearing of Maidan. I wrote in my notes that I felt that the atmosphere was different, not as fast, and that people were more cheerful. I noted that perhaps this was because they were no longer waiting for "Europe." Indeed, over the course of the day, I saw that most protesters were targeting their energy towards President Yanukovych, as they assumed he had approved the attack on the sleeping protesters. They also felt the excuse for clearing the square – the upcoming New Year's celebrations – was absurd. Observing this shift to focus on Yanukovych, leftist activists began employing rhetoric about "the state" (*derzhava*).[3] The violence against students played a necessary role both in motivating more people (including leftists) to participate on Maidan and in bringing leftists' ideas to the forefront of the protests, where they were accepted and even embraced by a significant majority of protesters. As one leftist activist described to me, these ideas included being "anti-police, against repressions, for the freedom of peaceful gathering, for the freedom of perspectives." These ideas are not inherently leftist, but leftists were the first people present on Maidan who used this type of language to describe the attitudes of protesters.

Furthermore, leftists became more perceptive concerning reactions to their protest banners and their presence on Maidan. I attended several longer meetings before various mass protests where activists had lengthy conversations about what to put on banners, now asking for consensus before the banners would be made. Their goal was to make their messages clear, and they also hoped to gain support from other protesters with these slogans. For example, in a meeting to decide what to write on large banners that would be dropped from strategic points around Maidan, the slogan "Better anarchy than oligarchs" (*luchshe anarkhiia nizh oligarky*; my transliteration reflects a mixture of Ukrainian and Russian words in the structure of the proposed slogan) was deemed too "provocative" because of the word "anarchy." Even "death to oligarchs" (*smert' oliharkam*) was rejected because the use of the word "death" not only evoked the nationalist slogan "death to enemies" but also promoted a generally negative and violent attitude. In the end, one slogan that was used was the rhyming "Government changes, problems remain" (*vlada zminiuiet'sia, problemy zalyshaiut'sia*); another was the simpler "We are against a police state" (*my proty politseis'koi derzhavy*).

Many leftists realized the significance of the police action on 30 November in shifting the protests' focus and in their ability to challenge the state itself through their own actions on Maidan. The "We are against a police state" banner remained on Maidan throughout the rest of the tent camp's existence (figure 4.4). The occupants of the city hall building moved it from Khreshchatyk, the main street along which the banner was first hung, to the main room of the city hall, where protesters slept. Later, I photographed it hanging above the building's main entrance.[4] It is unlikely that the occupants of the city hall knew of the origins of the banner, which was part of its success: leftist language became unrelated to political affiliation after the students were beaten, and this was part of leftists' shift to gain a broader audience on the square while avoiding violence.

The first week in December was an extremely significant moment for the development and continuation of the protests. Many people suspected that Yanukovych thought the crackdown on the sleeping protesters would scare people away, especially if they would not be allowed to amass on Maidan the next day. Instead, it simply made the

Figure 4.4. Leftist banner "We are against a police state," occupied city hall, Kyiv
Source: Author's photograph.

protests seem more necessary. The target of the protests became the
state and its representatives – namely, the police, Yanukovych, and his
cabinet of ministers. I gathered stickers that read "I'm not here for the
money" and "I'm not leaving until Yanukovych resigns!" These signified a shift, another indication of the second stage of Maidan, from earlier protests – in which the assumption was that people would be paid,
and that they would leave when the money ran out – and an intention-
ality that had not existed before when the protests were focused on
Europe. More and more tents appeared on Khreshchatyk and around
Maidan, even as snow began to cover the streets. People on Maidan did
not seem to have any intention of leaving.

Leftists who had described themselves as "sceptical" at the beginning
of the protests began to feel more strongly that it was important and necessary to be present there. One activist from Kyiv, Heorhiy, specifically
mentioned 30 November as the point at which he began to fully support
Maidan precisely because it became "anti-government" and "anti-police
violence." Another longtime student activist said that the choice was
clearer for leftists to take a stand at that moment because "the question
was different. It was not about Association with the European Union,
it was about police brutality. So it was different for the left because of

course we were against police brutality." At the same time, it became very unclear what protesters – both leftist and otherwise – actually expected to happen. The key demand, as proclaimed by many banners and signs around Maidan, was the resignation of Yanukovych. However, as the main leaders of the Opposition were proving unable to secure this demand, it was unclear how the protesters envisioned its being met.

I began asking people around me what they thought might happen next and how long they thought the protests would continue. Most had no idea. Heorhiy felt that it was inevitable that people eventually would decide they had had enough of this government. In some sense, he said, it was better that these mobilizations happened sooner rather than later, because the status quo established during Yanukovych's tenure as president had become detrimental to ordinary people. But, like many around him, he couldn't predict what might happen. He made a statement that resonated deeply with me during a conversation in May, after the protests had mostly concluded: "I lost my sense of prediction somewhere in the middle of Maidan. I thought that, well, they're gonna stand for two weeks and then they're gonna leave. If somebody told me that 100 people will be killed in the streets ... I couldn't believe it." While I suspect Heorhiy meant over the course of the mobilizations when he said "the middle," his words also provide a spatial reference for the sense of uncertainty and unpredictability that was palpable on the square itself. His words captured my feelings exactly when I stood on Maidan throughout the winter, watching people of various ideological and political views committed to an idea of a better Ukraine that had no clear path for its realization. Yet people continued to stay in that square.

As winter encroached on the city, I found the protest camp becoming increasingly less friendly. Police presence around the square was at a peak, even if more and more events were set up to keep people entertained during their long days of occupation. At an "Open University," speakers discussed current economic trends, good versus bad oligarchs, earlier protest movements in Ukraine, and they even screened films, including a leftist-promoted one about a workers' uprising in Zhanaozen, Kazakhstan, in which protesters were killed by government forces. But I found that people – ordinary protesters, not tourists – were taking photos and videos constantly (myself included), but my and others' inability to tell who was a protester and who was a *provokator* seemed ominous. I collected a leaflet featuring a drawing of three hooded faces that provided tips on identifying *titushky* or a *provokator*. It read, "Don't yield to the criminal regime's provocations! Ten people can discredit 500,000! And remember, if you yield to provocation, you help the regime!"

Around the protester-occupied main square, anti-protest developments were also taking place. An "Anti-Maidan" had appeared in the neighbouring Marins'kyi Park, though many suspected that the pro–Party of Regions population was largely paid to be there. All throughout the immediate area around Maidan, a region of the city known as Lypky, fully dressed riot police barricaded every intersection and sometimes the streets themselves. These police made many people afraid to go to Maidan at all, as it was obviously unclear what they might do to protesters and even bystanders. It became impossible to get around the city centre normally, which, in conjunction with closed metro stations and regular rumours of bomb threats, created an atmosphere of fear and uncertainty that made protests seem riskier than ever before.

These experiences characterized the second stage of Maidan, what I call the "space of uncertainty," which continued until mid-January 2014. Leftists used this space to attempt to integrate themselves into the fabric of Maidan, to varying degrees of success. Stage two for leftists was marked by a shift in their increasingly more coded uses of leftist ideologies. In other words, they learned from the "reactionary space" of Maidan during the first stage, in which their overtly leftist presence was dangerous, to find alternative ways to be more engaged with the protests. This was aided by the more repressive responses of state organizations such as the Berkut, for which leftists readily provided criticisms that evoked their stance against a police state but without mentioning leftist ideologies. Not only did their ability to be flexible encourage leftists to keep participating, but the positive reception of their anti-state language made them more sympathetic to the protests as a whole, even if some participants' political ideologies remained at odds with those of leftists.

Black Thursday and the Dictatorship Laws: Shifting Possibilities for Political Action

I was returning from L'viv on an overnight train in mid-January when I received news of the Yanukovych government's most recent repressions of the protesters, making 16 January 2014 become known as *Chornyi Chetver*, or "Black Thursday." The Rada had passed a set of laws with just over half the lawmakers voting in favour – by a show of hands rather than the usual electronic voting system – of what they called the "Anti-Protest Laws" and what protesters and their supporters called the "Dictatorship Laws." The package of laws – which included amendments to various existing laws and codes – basically made all actions taking place on Maidan illegal, criminal, and punishable.[5]

Despite the unconstitutionality of the laws, most protesters considered them a threat. The legislation made many Maidan-based actions illegal, including the use of tents, stages, and sound equipment; the occupation or "blocking" of administrative and other buildings; wearing masks and helmets to obscure one's identifying features; and wearing clothing that resembles a uniform of a law enforcement agent.[6] The distribution of "extremist" material – both in paper form and online – was made illegal, although the laws did not establish what would make material or information "extremist." Among leftists, it was assumed that the material they distributed on Maidan, as well as what they exchanged online, would fall under the purview of "extremist." Major legislative changes included the recriminalization of slander and defamation (moving them from the jurisdiction of civil law to criminal law), and the protection of law enforcement officers, executives, and judges from the publication or distribution of any "offensive" information about them or their families. Any material circulating on Maidan or on the internet that condemned the president or any of his allies was now considered a criminal act.

Opposition leaders, including Vitaliy Klitschko and Oleh Tyahnybok, spoke out against the laws, describing them as without legal basis and "simply a usurping of power" (Balmforth and Polityuk 2014). Neither leader, however, was present in the Rada to vote against the laws. A large number of parliamentarians, particularly from Opposition parties, decided not to take part in the vote so that it would not be seen as legitimate. But their lack of contestation of the laws prevented Opposition parties from later being able to come together to present either a challenge to the laws or a package of laws that would protect protesters or grant them amnesty. Instead of organizing a political response to the 16 January laws, Opposition leaders tried not to engage with them, but the pro-Yanukovych parliamentarians took this as a chance to implement the laws. Because of this unwillingness or inability to organize a response to the Yanukovych regime, protesters on Maidan began to question their faith in these Opposition political leaders. Unable to take a credible stance against the laws, the Opposition leaders showed they had little power against the president and his party.

The Dictatorship Laws significantly changed the possibilities for political action for Maidan protesters. First, they were proof that whatever independent centres of power had existed earlier no longer did, as the Yanukovych regime was clearly in full control of every arm of the government. The failures of the Opposition leaders to respond effectively to the legislation meant that their coalition was functionally useless and meaningless to protesters. This generated even more instability in political alignments and encouraged the consolidation of previously disparate umbrella groups, such as Right Sector. Finally, this type of repression was different than the direct violence that was used before the laws were passed. It was an attempt to end the protests through threat of repression, rather than active repression itself. Perhaps this is because Yanukovych was concerned, given protesters' previous re-action to the use of force, that he would lose too much credibility if he mobilized troops to raze the square. Perhaps he felt that this legislation would appear to be a more legitimate way to end the protests.

The response to these laws, however, presumably was not what Ya-nukovych and his allies had expected. Instead of instilling fear into the protesters that they would all be thrown in jail – which was a legitimate possibility – it galvanized them. For many leftist activists, the passage of the laws was the proof that they needed that to be on Maidan was to be on the "right" side. Specifically concerning the left, the legisla-tion was unifying in a way that no previous mass protest on Maidan had been. It changed the aims of leftist protesters from simply want-ing to present their own ideas to other protesters to having a strong motivation to influence the direction of the protests, particularly into a massive, nationwide strike. Here, leftists began to see Maidan as a space of possibility, which characterized stage three. But the response of non-leftist protesters to the laws was confirmation that violence was a legitimate response against an arm of government – the police – that the legislation especially protected. The use of violence, more than the laws themselves, was the focus of conversations following the passage of the Dictatorship Laws.

"All the lines have already been crossed"

In the afternoon of 19 January, protesters on Maidan decided to march to the Rada in order to protest directly against the members who had voted for the Dictatorship Laws. Before them stood a massive column of Berkut across Hrushevs'koho Street leading up the hill to the Rada. Although the protests had been largely peaceful until then, some peo-ple on Hrushevs'koho decided they had had enough and attacked the Berkut blocking their way. What followed was a standoff that included throwing Molotov cocktails and cobblestones at the Berkut; tear gas, rubber bullets, a water cannon, and finally live ammunition directed at protesters; and the construction of massive barricades backed by tire fires used to protect protesters. In the end, two protesters, Serhii

Nihoyan and Mykhailo Zhizdnevs'kyi,[7] were shot and killed. On 21 January, two protesters, Igor Lutsenko and Yuri Verbits'kyi, were kidnapped from a hospital and tortured; Verbits'kyi's body was found in the woods near Kyiv a few days later (Kotaleichuk 2014). On 22 January, Roman Senyk died from gunshot wounds suffered on Hrushevs'koho (*Ukrains'ka Pravda* 2014).

Because of Opposition leaders' perceived weakness in challenging Yanukovych's laws or in protecting the protesters in any capacity, protesters' use of violence was somewhat unexpectedly supported by a large majority of Maidan participants (Kulyk 2014; Onuch 2014b; Shevchenko 2014). Over the course of the winter, the Opposition leaders, including the leader of the right-wing Svoboda Party, Oleh Tyahnybok, had lost credibility for the majority of protesters. Where Opposition leaders attempted to compromise with Yanukovych, protesters preferred radical responses. Right Sector and its leader Dmytro Yarosh responded with strong rhetoric and self-organized military-style battalions, ready to fight against the Berkut. The group claimed "headquarters" on Hrushevs'koho, its members appearing exclusively in black masks and military fatigues. Yarosh and Right Sector clearly supported the use of force against the Berkut, and protesters looked towards the organization as a strong leader for others aiming to create self-defence groups in a similar manner.

I photographed a small poster near European Square just over a week after the attack on protesters (figure 4.5). It featured the faces of the killed Verbits'kyi, Nihoyan, and Zhizdnevs'kyi, underscored with the fully capitalized phrase proclaiming *Vsi mezhi vzhe pereideno* (All the lines have already been crossed). It symbolized the disbelief that people who had been spending every day on Maidan felt – while many had suspected the police would use violence against them, the graphic manner in which each of these men had been killed was beyond what anyone had imagined. The sentiment of the poster showed what had galvanized those who otherwise might have been critical of protesters responding with violence to refuse to accept the disparity of force between the Berkut and the protesters.

This image marks the beginning of the third stage of Maidan, which I have referred to as a "space of possibility." In this space, the protesters faced a constantly shifting political atmosphere, which created possibilities that might have been unimaginable under a stricter political regime able to enact control and repression. To some extent, it led to the consolidation of protesters against the government, including leftists who previously had been unwilling to commit to the pro-Maidan camp. At the same time, it placed violence at the forefront of the protests, because

Figure 4.5. "All the lines have already been crossed"
Source: Author's photograph.

protesters could no longer see any way to avoid using violence as the government became more repressive.[8]

"Put your mask on": Proof and Displays of Violence

Throughout the month of January, violence became the focus of most conversations around Maidan. Because of the major crackdowns on media services and freedom of the press following the passage of the 16 January laws, it was extremely difficult to access accurate information, or the accuracy of the information available was always in question. One way Maidan became violence-focused after 19 January was through the collection of materials and weapons used against protesters, a practice that continued on an even greater scale through February. Many people displayed photos of tear gas canisters and rubber and live ammunition casings they had found, and one man living in a tent on the square collected a large amount of these materials to display for passersby. The man painstakingly displayed what had been collected with descriptions, and he was always available outside the tent to answer questions (figure 4.6).

A second way Maidan became more focused on violence was through participants' own displays of their ability to become violent. There was a growing number of people wearing military fatigues and black masks or balaclavas, and people began carrying weapons as well. The weapons ranged from home-made clubs to shields made from wood or road signs (figure 4.7); several times, I saw people openly carrying guns. Molotov cocktails were another weapon of choice, and empty bottles filled the streets around the tents for the later manufacture of cocktails – a task often completed by women otherwise not invited to the front lines. Violence became a central factor in the protests, and the dominant opinion was that the violence used against protesters justified a violent response. Behaviours indicating that violence was possible, such as carrying weapons and dressing as if in a military brigade, was evidence that many protesters now sanctioned violence.

The organizations that were central to these discursive shifts – including Right Sector and the Svoboda Party – took care to represent their violence as the logical next step in the protests, because the government and its representatives had crossed a line. Right Sector's media liaison – the same Artem Skoropadskyi who started the violence at the *Ukrainian Trotsky* event I described in chapter 3 – publicized the group's wide access to weapons and declared the government responsible for *any* violence on Maidan, including protesters' violent responses to government repression. An interview with a Svoboda Party

Figure 4.6. Police and protestors' weapons on Maidan
Source: Author's photograph.

representative at the occupied Ukrainian House also reflected new attitudes towards violence.[9] These attitudes were an attempt to normalize
violence through organizational practices that would appear justified
to observers – namely, by creating hierarchized, militaristic structures
that appeared responsible for and protective of protesters, in contrast
with *provokatory*, who would appear irresponsible and reactionary. In
this way, these groups were able to justify their actions, including radical tactics of occupation and occasional violence.

The Svoboda representative, wearing camouflage pants and a bulletproof vest, first spoke against the police who had previously occupied the Ukrainian House in order to stage attacks against protesters
on Hrushevs'koho Street. According to him, the police had broken into
the archives on the fourth and fifth floors, damaging the building in
the process. When Maidan protesters occupied the space, in contrast,
one of their first steps was to place security at those archives so no
one could damage them. This, he said, showed that Maidan protesters were different from the police – while the police were supposed
to protect Ukraine and its citizens, instead they showed disrespect to
its spaces and history. His description also distinguished Maidan protesters – average, respectable Ukrainians – from the image of the paid

Figure 4.7. Protesters turn transportation signs into shields
Source: Author's photography.

protester who might be drunk, unemployed, or a criminal (see Carroll 2019 for more on the exclusion of these and other groups from the protest space).

He described the makeup of the occupants: middle class, with higher education, and no one was paying them. "We ask people to help," he said, "and they gladly help." His concern with bettering Ukraine's future also allowed him to justify the violence being used by everyday people: "There are always people who are more or less radical, but a lot of these people are teachers, lawyers, doctors, and will take a Molotov cocktail to fight the police if they have to make a better future for their children. The police are criminals and are just there to protect Yanukovych and his family." By creating a stark contrast between the protesters as ordinary people and the police and paid protesters as criminals, the Svoboda representative justified violence in order to protect Ukraine. At the same time, the space of the Ukrainian House – sparkling clean thanks to the use of cleaning machines found in the basement – was organized in a way that reflected the hierarchical organizations in control of it (figure 4.8). These Maidan activists were very aware that media representations of them and their actions were central in gaining sympathy for the protesters, despite their use of violence and radical, illegal tactics.

But other buildings, including the city hall and private businesses that were taken over to house food and medical supplies, or Right Sector headquarters – which I stumbled upon near Hrushevs'koho, identifiable only by the threatening armed man standing outside and the sign reading "Put your mask on" – still showed signs of vandalism and chaos that did not appear at the Ukrainian House. A layer of ice remained outside the occupied Agricultural Ministry, as police attempting to vacate the building had sprayed the sidewalk with a water cannon despite the freezing cold, a tactic that backfired and simply prevented the police from entering the building. By this time, the Opposition leaders were still negotiating with President Yanukovych, who had extended an Amnesty Law through which the regime would not prosecute those guilty of breaking the 16 January laws if they vacated the government-owned buildings they occupied around Maidan. (In theory, the Ukrainian House did not count under the Amnesty Laws because it was not a government building.) But protesters refused the terms of these laws, and by this time they had more clout than the Opposition leaders.

The political shifts during phase two of Maidan led to the discrediting of Opposition leaders and the rise of groups such as Right Sector, whose members legitimized the use of force by presenting themselves

Figure 4.8. Protesters in the occupied Ukrainian House clean the entrance
Source: Author's photograph.

as non-aligned and uncorrupted by the current state of Ukrainian politics – key elements that reflect self-organization. The legislation passed on 16 January only threatened mass repression, but it generated an unprecedented response among protesters, including among leftist activists. Ultimately, it meant the end of stage two, marked by a clash between the police and protesters that led to the deaths of one hundred people at the end of February.

Leftist Responses to the Use of Force

At least one self-identified anarchist, Serhii Kems'kyi, was killed in February 2014 during the violence against protesters. Kems'kyi had participated in some leftist-organized protests through the mobilizations but was not an active member of any of the leftist groups in Kyiv; he published a manifesto in the news outlet *Ukrains'ka Pravda* in December 2013, calling for self-organization and a system of direct representation (Kems'kyi 2013). In the first two stages of Maidan, leftists had focused on peaceful protest, highlighting their stance against violence, and for peaceful organizing on their protest signs as well as in the literature they distributed about self-organization. This was related to their oppositional relationship with members of radical right-wing groups, who regularly used violence against leftists. Leftists largely presented their position as against violence – which they even confirmed during their *krav maga* training (discussed in chapter 2) – whether by the state or by members of radical groups. But the third stage of Maidan prompted leftists to renegotiate their relationship with violence.

The Rada's passage of the anti-protest laws on 16 January, followed by the deaths of several protesters on 19 January, began the third stage of Maidan – what I refer to as a "space of possibility." As many activists recounted, the Dictatorship Laws had solidified the need to participate on Maidan for any leftist who had yet to decide. In an interview (in English) in March, Anton described the impact of the laws on leftist activists: "Each group started actively participating on Maidan after these Dictatorship Laws because everyone understood [what] that [meant]. There were still a lot of far right and that shit, and it's dangerous for the left, but if Yanukovych will stay, there would be no place for far right, left wing. Each one, because we would all be foreign agents, extremists. We would have no chance at all."

To some extent, the obvious effectiveness of a violent response to police force in bringing protesters together against the regime and its representatives made some leftists reconsider their attitudes towards violence. Several active leftists posted on Facebook after 19 January, considering how to move forward now. Maria, a leftist and feminist, wrote that, personally, she was against violence, but that, "since it was already used, it must be seen through to the end – after today, tomorrow will be worse." But she also recognized the confusion wrought by violence, creating a situation in which "young and very young people don't know what to do." Referencing the physical standoff on Hrushevs'koho Street, she described that everyone was grappling for control but neither side could move more than a few metres in either direction. While Maria did not participate directly in the violent standoff, she observed gas and stun grenades used against protesters and heard many people mention the water cannon that was being used to disperse the crowds (figure 4.9).

Another leftist activist, Vitalyk, was even more provocative: "Let's be honest," he wrote. "It makes your head spin. The success of the militarized protesters, especially the ultra-right, makes us think, and even envy. Political life will now be even more connected with violence." Vitalyk's assessment was that groups like Right Sector had gained some validity with their presence during the violent clashes because they were understood to have moved the stagnating protests forward in an effective way. Because of the failures of the political Opposition's

Figure 4.9. Protesters on Hrushevs'koho Street
Source: Author's photograph.

leaders, it seemed likely that Right Sector and other self-organized groups would take part in representative politics, as well as during street demonstrations. For Vitalyk, this logic suggested that leftists would also have to participate in similar forms of political organization – and would have to accept the use of violence as part of the validation of those forms – in order to continue to be part of that "political life." But, in his view, "many leftists today are not ready for such a responsibility and cannot effectively do it," despite their training in self-defence practices. This was both because Vitalyk did not see leftists as willing to use violence against others in an offensive way, and because he felt that such use of violence went against leftist philosophies and self-images: "Bravado with helmets and batons – it is childish. A stick must be used to beat someone, not just held in one's hands. In general, we understand that agitating for the left using the example of military units is not possible. People reaching only for power – it's not us. But it's power we need to show and prove." Vitalyk suggested organizing more small groups for various kinds of training, including in self-defence, but without necessarily adhering to the right's established mechanisms of effectiveness – that is, as military brigades. These concerns also resonated with discussions among feminists about the women's self-defence brigades created in January and February that also mirrored right-wing and militarized organizations and that met with extensive criticism from some feminist groups (see Channell-Justice 2017 and chapter 6 of this volume).

Vibrant Re-creations: The Hospital Guard

Amid their criticism of the use of violence and its embrace among protesters, leftist activists' responses to the violence of Maidan followed Carolyn Nordstrom's observation that, "in the midst of a violent breakdown of order … *most* people [do] *not* respond with disorder and discord, but with vibrant ways of re-creation" (Nordstrom 1997, 213). As she concludes, the statement people are making when they choose re-creations over violence is that "they did not need political institutions to forge community structure and keep social order" (220). Instead, they self-organize in order to create communities to sustain life – precisely what leftist activists promoted.

Vitalyk's message about violence reflected both the desire to participate in the continuing protests, particularly now that they were so clearly against the oppressive governing regime, but also the conundrum that the protests had become violent and to support the protests meant to support the use of force. Vitalyk's idea of small groups that could be organized and trained around particular issues or with particular goals became a prominent way leftists engaged with the protests in order to support them. Many leftists began to participate in an initiative called *Varto u Likarni*, or the Hospital Guard,[10] following the violence against protesters on Hrushevs'koho. One leftist activist described it this way:

> When it began, there was no one who did [this kind of] thing. The problem was that people were hurt on Hrushevs'koho and the ambulance took them, and after the ambulance got to the hospital, the police and Berkut waited for them. They were unconscious, many of them couldn't respond or say their names, so [the police] just took them and they could do anything, make them sign anything. They arrested them at first, I guess there were even people who were kidnapped. They were kidnapping them and they hit them hard [beat them up] … on the first day, when *Varto* was only starting, some people were really hurt. So we had to know where the ambulance is going, which hospital, do these people need to stay at the hospital? Or can they just go? The point is they couldn't [leave the hospital] so easily. But after it became clear that police and Berkut can just kidnap a person, there were many activists, and not even left activists, many people came there.

On 22 January, a leftist activist sent the following message to the leftist Maidan-based email list:

> Comrades, you all know that victims are now being surrendered for trial *en masse* from hospitals. At the strike meetings there was an idea that it's necessary to mobilize in order to get [one of the] hospitals among those in the Centre [of Kyiv] under control. Now, volunteers went to explore several options. But to begin to put the plan into place, we need a normal mobilization. So we request for everyone to try to come themselves and agitate others. We will gather in approximately two hours. It's also important, if someone has contacts, to draw other protest communities into this issue now or later. And also contacts with heads of hospitals for potential support of our actions in their hospitals.

The coordination of the initiative was extensive and meticulous; most of my interlocutors participated in some aspect of *Varto* at least once. From following ambulances and protecting people when they entered and left hospitals, to recording their hospital stays on camera, to bringing food and medicine to victims, the volunteers for *Varto* made sure there was a protective presence in hospitals at all times.

A volunteer for *Varto* was featured in a book of stories of people on Maidan by journalist Kristina Berdyns'kykh,[11] who called the initiative "an important and very necessary service." Berdyns'kykh wrote that the volunteers would record the names of the injured, as well as any other identifying information, so they could pass the information on to families and to aid groups such as Euromaidan SOS. She observed that the volunteers provided a holistic service: "Volunteers also ask the injured if they need legal aid. Then they find out which medications are needed for treatment and in all kinds of everyday moments, even if they need toothpaste and a toothbrush … Volunteers supervise the injured. For example, there is no problem with food in general: people bring homemade dishes to the hospital. A man came to me and said that his wife made lunch for five to seven people, and only later asked for her pot back" (Berdyns'kykh 2014, 108). This idea of *Varto* – which one leftist organizer later referred to as a "humanitarian project with a leftist view" – proved resonant with leftist activists for a number of reasons. First, it allowed them to fight against violence *and* against the police without engaging in violence themselves. Second, it enabled them to use their leftist networks and small-group strategies to do very effective activism. Finally, as their ensuing conversations show, it was an initiative that leftists used to draw in other activists and would-be Maidan participants who were uneasy about the idea of engaging in violent actions against the police.

Much of the early discussion about *Varto* focused on which hospitals would be most effective to take control over. Vitalyk suggested Oleksandrivs'ka Hospital in the centre of Kyiv (commonly known as "October Hospital" after its Soviet name, October Revolution Hospital), while another activist suggested the emergency hospital across the river, because it appeared that more police were attempting to take victims from that location. Initially, one group of leftists went to October Hospital while another went to the emergency hospital. But eventually, the group decided to concentrate on October Hospital, since many Maidan victims were being taken there and it was close to the action on the square. But throughout the next few weeks, leftists travelled to various hospitals around the city, checking to see if people needed help that the initiative could provide. One activist even used his laptop to live stream the protests so that hospital patients could watch what was happening around Maidan while they could not participate.

Most of the coordination for "duty" or "rotations" (*cherhuvannia*) was done via Facebook or by calling a central number to see where help was needed. When activists described the work they were doing to me, I felt that it sounded extremely dangerous because of the proximity to clearly ruthless police. However, they did not perceive it as such, partly because, to them, it was safer than being on or around Maidan – as one male activist put it, "It's less dangerous than Hrushevs'koho!" – and partly because so many other leftists were participating. The initiative's intent was to re-establish hospitals as safe spaces for protesters and victims, for those of both right and left views. Indeed, I never heard any leftist participant in *Varto* use any judgmental words about the people they volunteered to protect. Leftists further used the initiative to encourage others, including non-leftists, to participate in a "safer" way. Vitalyk mentioned a classmate who had wanted to go to Maidan, but, with two small children, was convinced that it was too unsafe. Vitalyk felt that working with *Varto* was a better option for this classmate, as it was perceived in a very positive way as a necessary citizen-driven initiative on Maidan.

Varto was also a crucial way for women to engage in the protests on equal footing with men. The space of Maidan became defined by military masculinity. Women were excluded from militarized roles and limited to behind-the-scenes work in kitchens, on cleaning crews, or as medical care workers. *Varto u likarni* was an initiative that allowed men and women to participate together in a non-hierarchical way. Several of the main coordinators were women, but equally as many women participated in the initiatives by going to hospitals. I knew women who volunteered to escort ambulances and women who worked until two o'clock in the morning on hotlines helping people find hospitalized family members or connect with legal aid organizations. In this way, *Varto* was an effective reflection of leftist principles of gender equality, even if creating an opportunity for men and women to participate equally in Maidan was not an overt part of the initiative's ideology.

In an interview much later, Maria mentioned to me that everything that was successful on Maidan was done without the help of the state. In the context of having completely lost faith and trust in the state and its representatives, from the president to his cabinet to the police, she could have gone so far as to say that many of these initiatives were citizens' ways to challenge the state, which, instead of taking care of its citizens, was actively *endangering* them. From the beginning of the protests, leftists were focused on "self-organizing" outside of *any* political party, but initiatives like *Varto* were their most successful examples of self-organization, which other participants on Maidan recognized as making a positive, and even necessary, contribution to the protests. That *Varto* did not overtly promote leftist ideas did not seem to detract from leftists' willingness to participate, nor did it prevent them from mentioning it to me when I asked them about the most successful events or actions during the protests. This is a distinct aspect of the shifts described earlier in this chapter, when the 16 January laws and the ensuing violence convinced leftists to take a more unified stand in support of the protests. *Varto* was one of the best ways of doing this without committing to the tactics or ideologies of the majority of protesters. Initiatives like *Varto* showed that leftists were not anti-Maidan, as radical right-wing Maidan activists often accused them of being. More than anything, leftists were against state violence, and their motivation and ability to organize outside party frameworks allowed them to create one of the most successful initiatives during the violence on Maidan. People continued to volunteer with *Varto* through the February violence, by which time the coordination was much easier because the initial networks and infrastructures already existed.

The presence of the use of force on Maidan created a conundrum for leftists. Some, including anarchists of the Black Sotnia and members of other leftist groups, did support and participate in the standoff against police forces and snipers in February. Others condemned the violence but wanted to work against the police and the state, and formed extremely useful and successful initiatives such as *Varto u likarni* and the crucial Student Assembly (discussed in the next chapter). Most significantly, neither of these forms of participation on Maidan focused on promoting a leftist platform, as activists had attempted to do in the first weeks of Maidan. Instead, leftists discovered how to support the protests on their own terms. This led to some additional fragmentation on the left, because many did not agree with those who were present on Maidan in late February during the major violence.

18–20 February 2014

The narrative that follows describes the events of 18–20 February. It is reconstructed from live updates by various news sources, as well as from my observations of internet live streams. It is not based on ethnographic evidence because I did not enter Maidan during these days; it is also not based on interview data, because the actions that took place during those days were illegal and violent in nature. I did not ask any interviewee to describe what they did on Maidan during these days because I did not want to implicate them in these actions, nor did I want to collect such information. This was in part because, when I was completing interviews, it remained unclear who would gain power in Ukraine and whether people would be prosecuted for their actions or if this information would be dangerous to have. Furthermore, the experience of these three days was extremely traumatic, for me as an observer and more so for my friends and colleagues who were present on Maidan. I felt that questions about their experience during these days would be invasive and would contribute to the trauma they were certainly already feeling. For this reason, this section is written in a more detached manner than the rest of the ethnography, but the information is central to understanding the context of the discussion.

Early in the morning of 18 February, gunfire erupted on Maidan between protesters and police. Fighting continued throughout the day, and at 4 p.m., the head of the SBU (*Sluzhba bezpeky Ukraïny*, Security Services of Ukraine) and the Interior Ministry issued a warning for people to clear the streets of Maidan within two hours. By 4:30 p.m., the metro was closed and much other public transportation shut down. Roads leading to the centre were blocked by the police, and the only exit from Maidan was up the hill to Mykhailivs'ka Square and Cathedral, where there was a field hospital as well as food and other supplies.

Police forces surrounded the entire Lypky district around Maidan in the afternoon, gaining higher ground above Maidan itself from Hrushevs'koho and Instituts'ka Streets and beating protesters as they claimed territory. The police also evacuated the occupied Ukrainian House and took it over for their own purposes. In Marins'kyi Park, next to Hrushevs'koho Street, government-hired thugs known as *titushky* beat and captured protesters, whom they turned over to the police in the area. The police continued to advance on protesters in Independence Square, using live ammunition, water cannons, and an armoured personnel carrier (a small tank) against the protesters.

In response, protesters set massive fires with tires they had collected around Maidan, creating a giant smoke screen to protect protesters from the police and their weapons. Protesters continued to use Molotov cocktails and fireworks against the police, and they began to tear up the cobblestones around the square and into Hrushevs'koho and Instituts'ka Streets to lob at police. Protesters remained on Maidan through the night, with the *Kyiv Post* counting 20,000 people on the square at 11:30 p.m. on 18 February, including many women, who remained on the square despite specific requests that they leave and allow men to fight. The Trade Unions building on the square had been evacuated, but it remained under protesters' control.

At the end of the day, twenty-five people were reported dead, including both civilians and police officers, and doctors guessed that thousands were injured. In the following two days, police began to install snipers in the tall buildings around Maidan, who shot and killed protesters. In the early hours of 19 February, the Trade Unions building was set on fire by police who had retaken the building – this according to Euromaidan PR, whose office had been in the building. Even though the building supposedly had been evacuated, people were still trapped inside, and police blockages of the streets delayed and prevented rescue crews from getting to them. *Titushky* continued to attack people around the square, even shooting and killing a journalist.

Opposition leaders continued to meet with Yanukovych and Rada members throughout these days. The Opposition leaders attempted to balance support for protesters with brokering a ceasefire, which failed. The leaders spoke out about their frustrations with the president, who viewed the problem as one-sided and continued to try to force protesters to give up their arms and stop fighting. But protesters continued to reinforce their barricades, stoke their tire fires, and make Molotov cocktails. More protesters were attempting to join those in Kyiv, but many cities were blocked and buses of protesters prevented from coming to the capital.

On 19 February at nearly 5 p.m., the SBU confirmed that an "Anti-Terrorist Operation," or ATO, had begun. According to the *Kyiv Post* (2014), this meant that the SBU could "search, seize property, detain protesters at will, without a court order or other legal safeguards. They can detain and interrogate anyone who they suspect of being a terrorist. They can kidnap you from the street and keep you in jail without notifying families for up to 72 hours. Moreover, the SBU can force mobile phone and internet service providers to cease operations." Kyiv's metro remained closed, along with schools and other service centres. (I lived in an apartment in walking distance from where the protest camps began, and all the businesses in that area were closed for several days. This was partly because there were no customers, as there was no transportation, but also because no workers could have reached these places either). Police used the ATO status to search vehicles trying to enter the city through blocked roads, looking for weapons, tires, or other supplies (including food and medical supplies).

At 11 p.m., Yanukovych and opposition leaders declared a truce. But by 8:30 the next morning, 20 February, explosions began again on Maidan, as police and protesters exchanged fire with Molotov cocktails. A *Kyiv Post* writer found the absurd humour in the "shortest truce in history," writing, "It appears the politicians forgot to tell the police and front-line fighters there was a truce, or the protesters and police simply are following different orders." Sniper fire continued from Shovkovychna Street above Maidan, but protesters began a new offensive up Instituts'ka Street, occupying buildings and capturing police officers as they went. From all sides of Maidan, protesters reinforced barricades and created new field hospitals in the Hotel Ukraina and in the city hall.

By 11 a.m., *Kyiv Post* journalists counted thirty-five bodies around the square.[12] They found that most victims had been shot by police, sometimes with armour-piercing ammunition, against which protesters' shields and bulletproof vests were no protection. As the body count grew, members of Yanukovych's Party of Regions began to show a change in allegiance, declaring their support for "the people of Ukraine" and asking the police to stop their attacks. But the violence continued through the day, with the eventual toll over the three days of seventy-seven people killed.[13]

On 21 February, President Yanukovych offered a truce in exchange for early presidential elections and a coalition government. At around 2:30 p.m., *Kyiv Post* journalists reported that police had begun to pull back from their own barricades in several places around Maidan. According to the journalists, many protesters were suspicious that this meant a deal had been reached. While Opposition leaders supported the deal, protesters and protest leaders, such as Dmytro Yarosh of Right Sector, made it clear that they did not, and, importantly, that they would not support Opposition leaders' efforts to make a deal. Amid this disagreement between protesters and Opposition figures, lawmakers and members of parliament from the Party of Regions continued to defect from the party.

The next day, Yanukovych and most of the remaining Party of Regions ministers had disappeared. The Rada had convened in order to vote to impeach the president; instead, members voted for an interim government. Rumours floated that Yanukovych had fled Ukraine entirely or was in the eastern city of Kharkiv, but his estate, Mezhyhiria, was abandoned, with obvious efforts to destroy documents left behind there. The remaining members of the Party of Regions continued to defect or flee, while journalists flocked to Mezhyhiria to salvage what was left and explore the greatest evidence of Yanukovych's appropriation of government funds for his own projects.

Ultimately, Oleksandr Turchynov was elected interim speaker and acting prime minister by the Rada convened by Opposition parties and recently defected Party of Regions members. That Rada also immediately voted to release Yulia Tymoshenko from prison in Kharkiv. The discussion of impeachment of the disappeared president continued, as rumours circulated that he had resigned before he fled, and later that he had planned to resign but changed his mind. Eventually, around 5 p.m., the new government voted 328–8 to impeach Yanukovych and set an election date for 25 May. In the following days, the Mezhyhiria estate remained open for journalists and visitors, and eventually the masses of art and other collections from the estate were exhibited in a fantastically curated exhibit at the National Art Museum of Ukraine. Eventually Yanukovych reappeared in Russia, claiming he still saw himself as the president of Ukraine and intended to return to reverse the illegal seizure of power by the Opposition.

Many have discussed whether the Opposition's seizure of power was, in fact, legal. During his tenure, President Yanukovych had reverted Ukraine to its 1996 constitution, which gave the president significantly more power than the Rada. Although the 22 February government, as one of its first moves, voted to restore the 2004 constitution, which gave the Rada the power to impeach the president, the vote technically was not sanctioned by the existing 1996 constitution. Thus, in legal terms, there are grounds to refer to the 22 February vote as a *coup d'état* or otherwise illegal seizure of power, based on existing laws. This argument was mobilized, however, only by those attempting to discredit the interim government; most others, including Maidan protesters, saw the new leadership as legitimate (figure 4.10).

"It's better to forget humanism": Maidan's Influence on the Left

Maidan remained a tent camp for several months following the end of the violence, in part because people largely saw it as an ongoing memorial site for those who had given their lives for Ukraine. Through the month of March – the two hundredth birthday of national poet Taras Shevchenko – poetry readings continued on the main stage and the flowers and other commemorations remained (figure 4.11). By this time, the general

Figure 4.10. Protesters celebrate the departure of the Yanukovych regime,
22 February 2014
Source: Author's photograph.

consensus seemed that Instituts'ka Street, where most of the protesters
had been killed, would be renamed Heaven's Hundred Street (*vulytsia
Nebesnoï sotni*) – the "Heaven's Hundred" referring to all those killed on
Maidan. Maidan continued to represent a victory for many protesters,
and those who remained on the square now began to discuss mobilizing against Russian encroachments in Crimea and the eastern regions, as
well as implementing lustration against Yanukovych and those Party of
Regions members who had stayed by his side through the protests.

Among leftists, however, there was no consensus about whether
or not they could consider their experience and efforts on Maidan as
a success. Leftists even organized an extensive conference, "Left and
Maidan," about the subject and published a special edition of their
Spil'ne journal with a similar name. Some simply said that no, Maidan
was not a leftist space and was not successful for leftists, but others
considered that whether or not Maidan was "left" did not matter as
much as the real changes in society that had appeared directly because
of Maidan. Some felt that, although Maidan had an overall impact on
changing Ukrainian politics, leftists were limited by the small scale of
the initiatives they had created and the stronger public sympathy for

Figure 4.11. Memorials to the fallen protesters around Maidan
Source: Author's photograph.

right-wing organizations. Danylo reflected on this problem in an interview in the spring of 2014.

> There are cool initiatives, but in comparison with these common ideas
> [achieved by], for example, Right Sector, right? That they in some sense
> had a kind of hegemony, even, on Maidan. It started everything. They
> just put up some tents and gathered these activists from the right circle,
> ultra-right circle, and in the left there wasn't anything like this. Well, there
> were some tents, there were anarchists who didn't especially push them-
> selves forward. Ultimately, social rhetoric from the left movement didn't
> succeed. Other than some things, like the open accounting of the Ministry
> of Education, it's cool, it's good.[14] But in comparison with the scale of this
> protest, which affected all of Ukraine, the president, at this scale, we can
> say it's almost nothing. That's why I can say that on Maidan, the left didn't
> conduct itself like it needed to. It's important that more about these ideas
> would be heard and taken to people. I have the impression that only now
> do they start to bring this consciousness to the majority of activists. They
> must also be able to defend their own views, including physically, right?
> In other words, be able to give opposition, defend their views in the street,
> against whatever encroachment of nationalists, Nazis, and others.

Danylo did not necessarily think the left had failed, but their presence was not as strong as that of the radical right, who were able to take advantage of the situation and promote their political ideology. He saw the positive effects of initiatives such as *Varto u likarni* in bringing something positive to Maidan, but he did not see the left's social platform as successfully disseminated among the larger protest body.

Alternatively, Havryil, my friend with whom I visited Maidan on its first day, told me, in a second interview near the end of my fieldwork after he had had significant time to reflect, that he had really "awesome" impressions from Maidan, and he felt that "we [leftists] won some stuff" and had done more than he had thought possible, given their lack of resources. He specifically mentioned *Varto u likarni* and the Student Assembly as examples of "winning" for leftists, initiatives that arguably were some of the most successful in recent leftist history in Ukraine. At the same time, Havryil recognized that there was a long way to go and that another "revolution" was necessary: "The revolution is time for intensive change. We can do more than we can do in normal life. We have resources to manipulate. We did more during Euromaidan than we did in the last five years. And Euromaidan wasn't even such a fucking awesome revolution. We will get new wind and people can do a lot, but now they are tired from the winter. So they didn't get all the way to the last step. I was really sick after being in the ministry, physically exhausted … And these are people who will give their last breath for fighting." He contrasted beautiful, tranquil moments standing on the roof of the occupied Ministry of Education, describing his nice impressions from watching the streets, with eight-year-old boys making Molotov cocktails and old women bringing militants bricks to throw at the police on Maidan. He captured the contrast poetically: "It was terrifying while you are in the violence but it is also emancipatory, the spirit of violence. You have to be the first one to kick, be more aggressive. You can be dead in one moment so it's better to forget humanism."

Havryil might have presented one of the more radical perspectives, but many other leftists assessed Maidan as having been a positive experience. These assessments were built around the notion that people learned that they had the ability to make change happen based on their own skills and commitment – precisely the way leftists framed "self-organization." In other words, leftists felt that self-organization became a common organizing point for all people on Maidan, even if it was used for diverse goals.

It is important that so many leftists said that their experience of Maidan was positive. Each of these people was a target of violence, first at the hands of the radical right, and later at the hands of the state. Yet they felt pleased with how they had continued to participate despite these setbacks. They assessed the centrality of self-organization and state criticism as discourses provided by the left. They recognized the importance of Maidan for Ukraine and knew that it was necessary to participate in some capacity.

But whether the impact of Maidan on the left can be assessed in such a positive way remains to be seen. Certainly, leftists were not satisfied with the lack of change in social programs during the Poroshenko presidency, and the continued presence of right-wing groups at leftist events – and their continued violence against leftists – suggests that not much has changed for leftist activists in Ukraine, despite their successes and positive experiences during Maidan. Although leftists felt it necessary to participate on Maidan and, in their Kyiv-based participation, were able to assess the mobilizations as a positive experience, they were also critical of its impact on the left and on protest action in general.

Chapter Five

"For free education": Education Activism and Maidan

In the early days of Maidan, participants in the mobilizations associated their protests with the European Union, although protesters' conceptualizations of "Europe" were diverse. Leftist activists focused on EU member states' social policies that they felt would be beneficial in a European Ukraine. On the first day of mass marches around the Kyiv city centre, Sunday, 24 November 2013, I met with a cohort of almost twenty leftist activists to march to Maidan. One of their large signs told fellow participants that they were "For free education" ("free" here in the monetary sense; *za bezkoshtovnu osvitu*), "like in Germany, France, and the Czech Republic." A sign used the following day among a much smaller audience linked Europe not only with better support for education but with better education overall: "Europe: Quality education" read the sign (*Yevropa: Yakisna osvita*). Education was tied fundamentally to leftists' conceptions of social justice, in which they linked their own demands for free health care and transportation with a redistribution of oligarchic wealth to these social needs.

Activism focusing on higher education presents a lens through which to think critically about practices of self-organization. First, leftist students had been organizing around education since Ukraine's independence, and most noticeably since 2009, in response to a series of legislative attempts to force students to pay for university services such as libraries and laboratories. Activists always intentionally organized these campaigns outside the confines of political parties in order to gain the most interest from the broad student body of universities across Ukraine, as I show below. Second, campaigns around education required students to negotiate with a state apparatus and its representatives – the Ministry of Education and Sciences (*Ministerstvo osvity i nauky*, often known as MON), as well as university rectors. While their campaigns were based on principles of self-organization, because they were organized for and by independent student groups rather than political parties, student activists often had to make their demands to specific government entities. Thus, self-organized higher education activism showed a willingness to compromise with state bodies in order to achieve activists' demands. Self-organization allowed activists to access the government more effectively when needed because student groups were not affiliated with one or another political party.

Leftist activists have seen success around issues of higher education much more frequently than around issues perceived as more explicitly leftist or more politically radical. I suggest that this is because the educational system in Ukraine – including curricula, standards and evaluations, and instruction – is controlled by state bodies and therefore subject to political shifts in government representatives like Dmytro Tabachnyk, Yanukovych's widely hated minister of education. Centralized in the Ukrainian Ministry of Education and Sciences, the government controls not only primary and secondary education but also most universities and other institutions of higher education across the country.[1] In focusing on issues of higher education, leftists have criticized state policies that were already widely unpopular in Ukraine. Their criticism is grounded in leftist critiques of neoliberal capitalism, but the protests they have organized in response to policies on higher education did not necessarily use leftist language. Thus, leftist-organized activism around higher education has not been as alienating as other, more explicitly leftist actions, such as their pro-feminist protests or their criticisms of the European Union.

An additional factor helping leftist-organized protests around higher education become more popular among non-leftist students is that students can often see how higher education policies will affect them individually. Because of this, leftist student groups have more easily gained the support of non-leftist and non-activist students. Leftists have also been more willing to compromise with broader (non-leftist) student bodies on education issues than in other realms of their activism. As we will see at the end of the chapter, however, these compromises often have shown how leftists' ideas of Europeanization – oriented towards social welfare programs and equality legislation – are at odds with those of the people who gained power after Maidan. In the sphere of higher education, legislation bringing Ukraine's educational system closer to Europe's has been more focused on competition and profit, aspects of the marketization of education that leftists had worked against in the years leading up to the mass protests. Thus, while leftists were more willing to frame their demands around policy when it came to education activism, post-Maidan policies created new challenges for leftist student activists.

Higher Education Activism as a Critique of Neoliberalism

Leftist activism around higher education presents an enlightening lens through which to explore critiques of neoliberalizing processes at work around the Euromaidan protests. Education itself has long been analysed as an important component of socialization that reinforces social and political hierarchies (Althusser 2001). Schools are presented as neutral sites, free from ideology, in which knowledge – a necessity in capitalist societies – is imparted equally to the population. Pierre Bourdieu (1967; Bourdieu and Passeron 1990) expands the conceptualization of the *goals* for education: educational systems do not simply reproduce a labour force to exploit, they also reproduce sets of values – "cultural capital" – which some students can obtain, while others, based on their background and existing status in society, cannot. In other words, schools establish "cultural fields" in which "certain themes" are "brought to the fore while others are set to one side without being completely eliminated, so that continuity of communication between intellectual generations remains possible" (Bourdieu 1967, 342). Only educated people – not just those who have gone to school but those who are able to gain, through their own work or by inheritance, a generation's established cultural capital – can engage with these themes that have been secured as representative of a person's level of education and valued knowledge.

Increasingly, ethnographers use studies of schools as sites of resistance to show that educational policies and systems are not simply mechanisms of social control, despite their strong influence on social stratification. Many scholars further explore the role of schooling in nation building and citizen creation – stratified and stratifying processes in themselves. Catherine Wanner noted that, in Ukraine, educational reform in the 1990s was a task of national-democrats, including then-president Leonid Kravchuk (Wanner 1998, 80). Schools were the best site for naturalizing a new (non-Soviet) Ukrainian identity among the first post-Soviet generation. Wanner pointed out, however, that schools had a similar function during the Soviet period, essential in the creation of ideal Soviet citizens (81). Anna Fournier's later study of Ukrainian schools shows that young people also learned of themselves as citizens and "rights-bearers," not only through their formal education but also in the streets, where they engaged with the unpredictabilities of socialization by the "bandit-state," the "perceived entanglement between government and violent entrepreneurs" (Fournier 2012, 14) that played out starkly during the Orange Revolution.

Wanner noted a decrease in the attraction of higher education because it could not guarantee prestigious jobs at the time of her writing in the mid-1990s. But promises of Europeanization reinvigorated higher education in the 2000s. The European Higher Education Area (EHEA) was implemented in Ukraine in 2005. Established as a result of the Bologna Process in 1999, it helped create a compatible European educational system in which credits earned in a higher education institution in one signatory country would be of equal value in another.[2] The enactment of the EHEA system in Ukraine made degrees that would be recognized in the European Union and the possible promise of European jobs of particular interest, in addition to the possibility of Ukraine's becoming a desirable destination for European and other international students looking to complete higher education abroad. But, as Elena Aydarova writes, the introduction of European standards and other Western models "infuse[s] educational systems and institutions with neoliberal ideology, manifested in prioritizing choice, competition, individual responsibility, and market values" (Aydarova 2015, 147; see also Rizvi and Lingard 2010; Shear, Hyatt, and Wright 2015; Stein and de Oliveira Andreotti 2017).

Activists in Ukraine have pointed precisely to these processes as central to their critiques of neoliberalism's influence on higher education. When I began fieldwork with Ukrainian leftists in 2012, they were concerned about what they called the "marketization" of higher education (Gebel and Baranowska-Rataj 2012). In addition to the problems of right-wing attacks on student activists and the infiltration of religion into secular higher education institutions, students were particularly concerned with the ways universities were becoming sites to generate profit and competition, rather than institutions that made education accessible for all Ukrainians. As political parties appeared sympathetic to these neoliberalizing demands on higher education – especially inasmuch as these changes were perceived as bringing Ukraine closer to Europe – student activists self-organized, working intentionally outside representative politics in order to access political change.

I begin this chapter with a brief discussion of a student activist campaign that took place in the years before Maidan; nearly all the student activists I interviewed pointed to this campaign as a foundation for the effective organizing they did on Maidan. From here, I show how students were essential participants on Maidan from the earliest days of the protests, and I explore how leftist student activists constantly shifted their goals as they navigated student-run spaces on Maidan. I conclude by addressing one of the many post-Maidan challenges in the sphere of higher education activism, pointing to the ways neoliberal processes have infiltrated Ukrainian universities, just as activists feared.

National-level Success: The Campaign against Paid Services

My research with student activists focused on the independent student union, Priama Diia (PD, or Direct Action). With active branches on university campuses around Ukraine, PD has been a self-organized initiative since its earliest iterations. Political parties have never made the kinds of changes PD activists demand, because students are not generally seen as an important voting bloc. Further, broadly defined leftist activists typically are critical of *all* political parties because of their reliance on neoliberal structures and institutions in order to gain and hold onto power. PD activists have seen that street activism and university-level campaigning have been more successful in making students aware of how neoliberal processes have affected higher education in Ukraine.

Significant changes to national policies began soon after the founding of the most recent iteration of Priama Diia, in 2008. At this time, Yulia Tymoshenko was prime minister, and Ivan Vakarchuk was minister of education. The first change was an effort to introduce new student fees for publicly funded universities. These fees included requiring students to pay to work in laboratories, for using libraries and sports centres, and for internet access. Nearly all the student activists with whom I discussed PD's activism before Maidan mentioned the campaign against this policy as the group's most successful one.[3] The issue of paid services overlapped with the government's attempts to introduce new higher education legislation, which would govern the requirements of students and professors at higher educational institutions and the functioning of those institutions. These concurrent issues mobilized thousands of students around Ukraine, and showed that PD's self-organization could be successful in making demands on the governing regime.

Most activists described the second part of the campaign against paid services, in 2009, in which record numbers of students gathered around the country to protest the fees. But protests had started a year earlier, in 2008, when Vakarchuk first introduced the resolution. In an interview, one long-term PD member, Petro, made sure to point out the origins of the entire anti–paid services campaign: "That campaign included a smaller mobilization, but it had a very quick result … We learned late about, well … The government's statement that it was going to introduce a concrete resolution, it came late and unexpectedly, before the summer vacation. And so it was necessary to react effectively, do everything immediately before vacation, but it was practically impossible to gather students." To Petro, the timing was an important part of their mobilization: "It was the end of the academic year, already June, there were exams. So we organized several meetings around universities: Shevchenko, KMA, KPI.[4] Priama Diia was just born, this was its first big campaign." After meeting to inform students about the campaign, PD was able to mobilize 100–150 students to protest in front of the cabinet of ministers. As Petro put it, "It was a single action, but we were ready for it to be a week-long campaign, maybe to continue to autumn, after vacation. But literally on that same day we got the reaction from the side of the government, and the Minister of Education announced, about the resolution for paid services, that it will not be introduced. The government stepped back, they even rejected what they planned to do. It was almost an instantaneous victory."

This quick resolution surprised the organizers from PD, a new organization without widespread support. For a disparate group of leftist activists with no party affiliation but significant experience in street politics, getting the government to renege on its resolution on paid services was an unprecedented success. It gave PD and its ally, the Foundation for Regional Initiatives (FRI, a liberal youth organization focused on legislative changes), important momentum. As another activist described, the alliance between PD and FRI was beneficial, as FRI representatives negotiated with ministers and administrators while PD members were "in the street." The groups worked together on a campaign based on principles of self-organization, avoiding political parties and each contributing based on its skillsets and on its access to important figures within the education administration.

Government ministers knew the possible impact of mass street protests, but such actions were not especially common at that time, particularly among young people and particularly about education issues. Thus, an organization of young people that was able to gather people to the streets – people who were willing to remain in the streets for as long as it took to get the government's attention – was clearly a threat to that government. Perhaps this was why the government backtracked so quickly to a demonstration of only a hundred people. As one activist noted, PD was the first group "whose main aim was to become a mass movement." Perhaps the Tymoshenko/Vakarchuk ministry was attempting to stall the success of PD; perhaps the government was simply trying to regain something of its plummeting popularity. Activists saw themselves as working against the neoliberalization of education, a process that, in their eyes, was not limited to a certain kind of regime. Activists did not spend time reflecting on exactly why this particular government backtracked on its policy because PD assumed that most governments would pursue a similar policy change.

Indeed, the next year, a new government was in place. In 2010, Viktor Yanukovych was elected president. He named Mykola Azarov as prime minister and Dmytro Tabachnyk – already known as a notorious Russophile who had made claims against the legitimacy of the Ukrainian language and in favour of aligning the Ukrainian higher education system with that of Russia instead of Europe (Lozowy 2011; Sindelar 2014) – as minister of education. Proving PD activists' point that any governing regime would support neoliberalizing policies, that same year, Tabachnyk's ministry attempted to introduce a list of university fees nearly identical to those the Vakarchuk ministry had rejected a year earlier. Again, PD banded together with FRI to campaign against the fees, and this time thousands of students came to the streets.

Significantly, this campaign was a broad-based, national one. While Kyiv was the centre of PD's work and of the campaign, students mobilized in various cities across the country. Anton, a PD founder and organizer of the anti–paid services campaign, claimed that a thousand people came to the protests in Kyiv: "At that time," he said, "everything was very passive and a thousand people was a very big demonstration." Anton claimed seven thousand students came to protest in L'viv, in western Ukraine, and another activist said ten thousand students had mobilized across the country. Again, the government responded quickly to the student mobilization and the resolution for paid services was not adopted. As the only organization committed to street protest to shut down unpopular government policies, PD became a widely known group following the successful second part of the anti–paid services campaign, recognized for being able to bring thousands of students into the streets for extremely visible, well-informed protests.

Following the anti–paid services campaign, other organizations attempted to reproduce PD's successful widespread mobilizing, including far right groups and right-leaning liberal groups. The latter included Vidsich, an independent (non-university, non-partisan) organization similar in structure to that of PD but that diverged in ideological affiliation, leaning towards nationalist sympathies. Despite their differences, PD began to work with Vidsich on large-scale campaigns, including the anti–paid services mobilizations and a following campaign against the new higher education legislation. Although Vidsich was based on self-organization and not affiliated with any party, other, more right-wing groups began to become more present in universities than before. This included the youth wing of the Svoboda (Freedom) party, a right-wing group whose leaders saw that students could be more mobilized around particular issues. As PD activist Anton described it, "It became popular [to organize street protests] and it became harder for us. They did the same, a lot of far-right student unions after this. It became harder to work because far right ideas are more or less popular in our society and left ideas are not. They did a lot of stupid things but they had much more resources, especially the Svoboda Party [which supported a youth-oriented wing].[5] So it became harder for us to function." At the same time, Nadia, a leftist and feminist activist, saw that the right-wing unions were not really "student unions" because "they didn't engage in student issues, student problems." Rather, they "had a cultural agenda," which they promoted by organizing poetry and literary readings, for example. And, Nadia said, "people are more receptive to them" because they were removed from political action. This type of activity began to blur the lines of self-organization for student activists, most of whom felt it necessary to work with groups like Vidsich in order to gain ground against the education administration, especially concerning the campaign against the 2010 higher education legislation, in which both Vidsich and FRI participated alongside PD.

For many activists, the campaign against the adoption of the higher education legislation was a key part of becoming an activist. PD was continually successful not only in getting students to mobilize, but also in securing the government's retraction of the law. The legislation was brought to the Rada three different times, and each time PD was essential in ensuring that the law was not adopted. Activists had different ideas why PD was so successful. One Kyiv Polytechnic Institute graduate suggested that the variation in tactics was key: "Sometimes they were mass actions, sometimes they were some kind of informational picket, sometimes a theatrical performance. They couldn't adopt [the law] because we protested it." Another activist, Natalia, saw the campaign's symbolism as the reason for its success, because symbols unified students where political ideologies could not: "I remember that the primary symbol of the campaign became a pencil. Not a portrait or some symbol. In other words, it was clearly a student protest, not from some political organization, just students who weren't passive about their lives. And the law was never adopted. They attacked painful points for students. This mobilized students because they straightforwardly didn't want it." But Heorhiy, a student activist who began actively participating in PD in 2013, felt that exactly this point – that students mobilized because the legislation was painful for them – was a problem for future student organizing. People mobilized because it was in their "private interests," as he put it. For example, the proposed legislation would have changed the status of Kyiv-Mohyla Academy from a national university to a less prestigious type of institution. Because students were so concerned about the status of KMA, they were willing to mobilize. And only in these types of cases can a "mass of students who are not connected to an organization" be mobilized. Nadia saw a similar conflict in the affiliation between PD and Vidsich, because "PD wanted to put the emphasis on structural issues and Vidsich, they were focusing on persons."

This individualizing effect is a component of neoliberalizing processes (see also Fimyar 2008; Goodman 2018). Students are not independently concerned about the state of higher education in Ukraine but pay considerably more attention when faced with problems that directly affect them. Certainly, the notion that "the personal is political" has successfully mobilized otherwise disinterested people around all sorts of issues. But, returning to the foundational principles of PD, the group was attempting to create a self-organized political movement that could attract a mass of students from universities across the country who were motivated to support structural changes in Ukraine's educational system. This meant not simply responding negatively to legislation that would obviously hurt students, but also creating what PD activists called a "positive program" (*pozytyvna prohrama*). Many activists noted that PD was not very successful in "promoting something," only in rapid response protests, even if those were creative and often achieved organizers' goals. As Natalia noted, it is only when you press people that they begin to react; only a response to negative issues allowed PD to mobilize students. "Unfortunately, that's how it is," said Natalia.

This general passivity was a commonly mentioned problem facing PD when I began interviewing members in 2013. As Natalia described, students were passive, even in the face of issues including common practices of bribery and gift giving to secure grades and university places. "Students aren't doing anything about it. They aren't even thinking about it. So if you say to them they have to pay for student cards, they'll say okay, that's fine. But it's not fine, they don't have to. [But] it's easier to pay and that's it. Students think that the education process is a repressive, authoritarian one." Other activists recognized that general passivity in society contributed to students' views that their efforts wouldn't change anything: "Very few people believe that collective action can change something," said another PD member – before the mass mobilizations on Maidan began in late 2013.

PD and other non-leftist student activist groups united in their criticism of state practices around education for several years before the mobilizations began. Because they saw all governing regimes as having the same neoliberalizing goals – making education competitive and profitable rather than a right for all Ukrainians – PD activists were able to mobilize students continually, even when a new regime took power. Because they worked outside political parties, they used self-organization to make education-based protest relevant to students regardless of their political ideology. This unifying factor was encompassed most clearly in the pencil that symbolized the campaign. These campaigns also set up various student activist groups to be able to mobilize in an effective coalition, even on Maidan, where stark differences in political ideologies became apparent.

"Bring umbrellas, tea, coffee, and friends": Students Turn to Maidan

On 21 November 2013, students gathered around Independence Square at least in part in response to a widely shared tweet by journalist Mustafa Nayem:

> [Retweet]!! Meet at 10:30 p.m. at the independence monument [on Independence Square]. Dress warmly, bring umbrellas, tea, coffee, and friends.[6]

The quick spread of the tweet and the subsequent mobilization of bodies led many to perceive the protests as youth driven – not necessarily incorrect in those first weeks.[7] It was immediately evident that students would play a large role on Maidan and, in retrospect, many credited Nayem for mobilizing students with this tweet.[8]

Katia, a student activist, was hesitant to give Nayem's tweet too much credit. "But he didn't believe the students would come," she told me, because "he wasn't involved in any of the student organizing." In other words, while Nayem expected virtual social networks to allow him to reach many young people, he did not anticipate the massive role students could play and the possible effectiveness of student organizing. Katia suggested that students had more at stake when President Yanukovych refused to sign the Association Agreement – she believed more university-age students had been to Europe than any other contingent of Ukrainians, and they therefore "know what is the difference with the EU." This included knowledge of the better quality and less expensive educational opportunities available in the European Higher Education Area, which many students were anxious to access.

The students who participated most actively on Maidan are part of the first generation in Ukraine to be educated under a fully Ukrainian system, reformed in 1992 following Ukraine's independence. Student-specific actions began on Maidan in the first weeks of the protest, when students organized city-wide strikes across Kyiv in November and December 2013. Violent police crackdowns on student protesters led university administrations to support protesters while concurrently undermining university-based strikes. In January 2014, students gained access to the occupied Ukrainian House, where they set up the Student

Assembly, a consensus-based body that used small working groups to achieve goals ranging from providing arrested students with legal counsel and creating media liaisons to organizing workshops, lectures, and film screenings for the occupants of the Ukrainian House. In response to violence that led to the deaths of a hundred people at the end of February, students successfully and non-violently occupied the Ministry of Education in Kyiv for one week, after which a new minister of education was selected, new legislation for higher education was drafted, and a system of open accounting was adopted in the ministry.

Leftists played a central role in organizing and promoting student strikes as well as the occupation of the ministry, an idea which had been circulating among leftists since the first week of December. Leftists realized that bringing education into the broader picture of Maidan was a way to make student activism more effective in the long term, and they also knew that education was one way to engage with the nationalist groups that had begun to dominate the protests, because, as citizens, the nationalists were also concerned about education. They saw a focus on improved higher education – reforms that would be supported by most other protesters – as a way to participate in the central threads of Maidan, rather than on the margins.

Student activists on Maidan had three interrelated goals: (1) to mobilize student bodies by making something that was personal to them (their education) into a political issue; (2) to bring together various political ideologies into an effective coalition that shifted higher education policies after the new government was installed; and (3) to continue critiques of *both* the state and the EU, critiques that could be made only because students had been criticizing policies of *all* governments since the late 2000s. Importantly, this history also confirmed that students were a self-organized group and not reliant on a party to mobilize.

The Emergence of Police Violence

Students were the first victims of police violence on Maidan. During the night of 30 November, students who were sleeping on the square were beaten and arrested by the Berkut, the government's militarized riot police. That day, riot police and contracted security workers in long, black coats and rounded helmets stood behind metal barriers protecting the small wooden houses that would make up the market as well as the metal structure of the giant New Year's Tree, or *yalynka*. For hours, protesters came to Maidan to berate the police protecting the promised festivities for supporting the Yanukovych government and for beating the students. The metal barriers had been plastered with pro-Europe signs, such as "Students for the EU"; other signs claimed that a variety of Ukrainian towns were "Europe," – for example, "Rivne is Europe!" Protesters had inserted carnations into the barriers, just below eye level of the helmeted officers behind the metal wall. From this day on, these Berkut officers became the symbol of the Yanukovych regime on the ground on Maidan, and they were vilified by protesters throughout the winter.

The atmosphere on Maidan on 30 November was tense. For the first time, protesters realized that the Yanukovych regime – previously largely the target of mockery rather than perceived as intensely threatening – would not hesitate to use force against its own citizens. Not only that, but these citizens were students, a privileged group of young people doing what many, especially in Kyiv, saw as the *right* thing in standing up against Yanukovych's refusal to sign the EU Association Agreement. The presence of protesters on Maidan that day suggested that most participants found it outrageous that students – educated, political citizens who, to reiterate Katia's description, were likely actually to have experienced Europe and knew what was lost in Yanukovych's refusal – had been the targets of this attack. One protest sign, hung on the skeleton of the promised New Year's Tree, referenced the students' sacrifice clearly (figure 5.1).

Students on Maidan were playing a positive role as active, political citizens by protesting against the government, as they had done before in the Orange Revolution (Fournier 2012). Katia described to me that, before 30 November, most students on Maidan were unorganized groups of individuals. Even leftist activists said in later discussions that they did not form an organized group with a recognized opinion or statement about Maidan before that date, which ended the first stage of Maidan; indeed, many claimed that the left remained a disparate group of participants until the 16 January laws were passed, when the second stage of Maidan ended. Students had attempted to organize a general strike on 27 November, marching from their various universities to Maidan, but too many students were sceptical about the effectiveness of such an action, and concerned about potential ramifications of participation, to give the strike much momentum. The Berkut attack on students, however, provided a catalyst for leftists to begin talking about police violence and anti-state activism. These ideas were adopted throughout the protests, including among student activists.

After 30 November, leftists and some other student activists began to focus their energies on more radical tactics, particularly in targeting the Ministry of Education and universities in Kyiv to criticize their complicity with the regime. Inspired by the widespread support on Maidan for the occupation of various government buildings around the city, leftist

Figure 5.1. "Students do not forgive": Sign hanging on the New Year's Tree on Maidan
Source: Author's photograph.

students decided that an occupation (*okupatsiia* or *zakhoplennia*; activists I knew used both words) of a university building was the essential next step to show that students were serious about holding the government accountable for problems in higher education. The organization of several unsuccessful occupations highlights the problems leftist activists faced when attempting to work with other student organizations. Important to note is that the most active organizers considered themselves members of Priama Diia but had recently graduated and were no longer technically students in Ukrainian universities. A few others were master's-level students, and a few were about to finish their bachelor's degrees. Furthermore, because PD had not taken a unified stance on Maidan from the beginning, it was unclear to participants whether student activists were working as PD or as independently interested parties. Maidan caused (or at least confirmed) several significant splits among leftist and radical groups, as questions about fascism, unionizing, and Europe versus Russia forced many to show their true colours. PD members wanted to be cautious about how their organization represented itself, if at all, on Maidan, particularly while trying to draw in student support and protect activists from attacks.

"Everyone on strike!": Early Student Responses to Repression

On the first of December, leftist activists joined a massive demonstration in response to the Berkut's clearing sleeping students off Maidan. I noted that the demonstration seemed more upbeat, though I didn't know for sure if this was because people knew that they had been right about Yanukovych all along, and they were just trying to figure out what to do next. I went to meet the leftist group at Shevchenko Park, but I was late and there were so many people that the cell lines were jammed and it was impossible to find out where anyone was. I ran into a woman from self-defence, and we found some other activists; once the cell lines cleared, we heard that other leftists were already much farther down Khreshchatyk than we could hope to get, so I marched with a small group of eight activists to the square. After a few hours, I went with some of them to a café to warm up; from there, we heard updates about violence that had broken out in front of the presidential administration building on Bankova Street, where several leftists from our network were beaten and injured. When we heard that Havryil was on Mykhailivs'ka Ploshcha, we went back into the freezing cold to hear his ideas for what to do next. Havryil was proposing a general student meeting and peaceful protest, and other leftists agreed that, in general, they should support students' efforts to organize a general strike by all the universities in Kyiv.

At this point, an activist mentioned that there would be a meeting the next day at Taras Shevchenko National University's Red Building, as the university's administration would be deciding what to do about students who were going on strike. While the university administrations would not necessarily speak out in favour of the Berkut's actions, they were also not especially supportive of students who were spearheading protest action on Maidan. Students reported administrators making lists of students who were absent from classes and even from their dormitories, and threats that administrators would turn these lists over to security services, jeopardizing student stipends and possibly resulting in expulsion. Here, students broadly – leftist and otherwise – understood the stakes and felt that encouraging students to take action in response to these threats was a necessary step.

On 2 December, I went to the Red Building at 10 a.m. to join around a hundred other students to protest the potential repression of student action (figure 5.2). Encouraging more students to join, I heard slogans advocating for "student solidarity" and trying to get more students to go on strike: "No one in class, everyone on strike!" (*Zhodni na pari, vsi na straik!*). One leftist activist, Vika, who had recently moved to Kyiv

Figure 5.2. Student protest in front of the Red Building, Taras Shevchenko
National University
Source: Author's photograph.

to continue her studies, said that day's action was the first time she
felt compelled to do something related to the Maidan protests. She told
me that, in her dormitory, someone from the administration came not
only to see which students were in their rooms, but also to ask them
if students were missing and had gone into the streets to protest. On
principle, she refused to talk to the administration, but the threats of
repression became real after this experience, and she joined the student
protest movement the very next day.

After a few more rounds of slogans in front of the park's statue of Taras
Shevchenko, representatives of the university administration came to
tell us that they would indeed be supporting student protesters – as long
as no one was a *provokator*, trying to instigate violence. Students from
Shevchenko University went around to other campuses in the area to try
to gather more students and together we walked to Maidan. The leftist
organizers of the earlier part of the protest by then had fallen back, and
now other student leaders came to organize the student column. These
students seemed overly cautious, making sure everyone in the group
was aware of the threat of violence and suggesting that women stay
in the centre of the column so men could surround and protect us. "If

something happens," one of the leaders said, "we run straight home." Despite his fear, the student march did not face violence, and I saw no police of any kind on Khreshchatyk as we marched down the street.

Although students had been supportive of the protests' original pro-European aspect, the protests began to diverge from those original goals. One student at the 2 December demonstration said outright, "Now it isn't very important whether or not Ukraine becomes part of the European Union," as the stakes had changed dramatically with police violence against protesters. As I argued earlier in the chapter, students were inclined to respond to threats to their universities and to their student status, and the events of the night of 30 November and administrators' response to student protests showed that both were in jeopardy. Because university administrators split from the official government position on the protests in order to support students, the student protests began to focus explicitly on the Ministry of Education itself and the potential of a general student strike.

"Tomorrow, stand down": The Challenges of Planning an Occupation

Student protests on Maidan reflected the typography I laid out in the previous chapter. The night of 30 November ended the first stage of Maidan, a "reactionary space," and moved to stage two, the "space of uncertainty." A student protest on 4 December at the Ministry of Education and Sciences (MON) is one of the events that reflects that uncertainty most clearly (figure 5.3). The protest was organized by students – not necessarily leftists – and was supposed to be *bezpartiina*, or non-party affiliated; as soon as I arrived at the ministry with a few other leftist activists, we could see that party representatives were hoping to co-opt the protest. Representatives from the Udar ("blow," in reference to party leader Vitaly Klitschko's boxer past) party were already there before noon when we arrived; later, members of the Svoboda Party's youth wing brought their party's representatives with microphones to take over the protests. Not long after we arrived, a massive column of Berkut officers dressed in pale blue camouflage broke through the student column in front of the MON to run into the building – one activist joked that it was just to save Minister Tabachnyk; they didn't care about the building itself or anyone else.

At first, the protest was more celebratory, with students advocating non-violence, speakers talking about improving schools, and a drumming group encouraging everyone present. Before long, however, one young man tried to break down the gates in front of the ministry. One

Figure 5.3. Student protest at the Ministry of Education
Credit: Photograph courtesy of the author.

activist, Nastia, told me that there were rumours that he was planning to blow up the ministry – they turned out to be untrue, but it put everyone on their guard. Then, Svoboda Party members took the microphone, completely against the will of the protest body at large. For the first time in my life, I joined the protesters in shouting "*Han'ba!*" – "Shame!" at the non-student speakers, who were intentionally, as someone put it later, occupying the student protest. Together with the other leftist activists, I continued shouting and making noise to get the Svoboda representatives to give the microphone back to the students, but then some unknown men came over and began to harass our group. This, combined with the sight of Berkut officers and rumours of violence led our group of leftists to jump on the next bus that passed so that we would not become the targets of that potential violence. Here, the student protest reflected precisely the uncertainty of the second stage: could violence happen? We had seen it before. Could a student have a bomb? We couldn't rule it out. Could neo-Nazis infiltrate a student protest and call us *provokatory* in order to justify attacking our leftist group? We felt nearly sure that this last possibility would come to fruition. None of these things had to do with the original pro-Europe protests; anything had become possible.

But this space of uncertainty also meant that leftists were inclined to pursue what had previously seemed impossible. After the protest at the ministry, leftists decided to discuss occupying the main building at Shevchenko University. This was the first instance of a serious discussion of occupation among leftists: the Kyiv city hall and the Trade Unions building had already been occupied by other Maidan protesters. The first planning meeting with leftists did not begin until 10:30 p.m. and continued until nearly midnight. Everyone was exhausted, but they continued to discuss even the tiniest detail. As I wrote in my notes,

> They didn't wany any symbols, any flags, no representation from any kind of party. But how could they enforce this so it didn't become like the march on the Ministry of Education? Maria and Yuri were especially grilling Andriy on how the action was going to be presented. Should they say it was Priama Diia? If there are non-students there, or non-PD students, should they still say it was a PD action? Organized with the support of PD? What if they want to interview Andriy, how would he represent himself? As a PD activist? It was a long discussion with little resolution.

They were trying to make every possible contingency plan, as one participant kept continually asking "what if?" questions. But because of the uncertainty surrounding everything, there was no way they could be sure they had covered all the possibilities. In any case, I planned to attend the occupation the next day. When I got back to my apartment, however, I received a text message at 12:04 a.m. from Vitalyk that said *"na zavtra vidbii"* (Tomorrow, stand down). My field notes end with: "So nothing? After all that?"

The next day, I attended an afternoon action against the financial group owned by oligarch Rinat Akhmetov near Mikhailivs'ka Ploshcha. I ran into a few activists, including Havryil, who was supposed to get other students on board and whom we bombarded with questions about the plan. Havryil explained that the SKR (Students'ka koordinatsiina rada, Student Coordinating Committee), a new group trying to coordinate student action around the city, had decided not to support the occupation because the Minister of Education, Dmytro Tabachnyk, said on television that someone was going to occupy the Red Building (which had indeed been the plan). Havryil also said the SKR did not have enough time to come to a decision about the occupation, not because it did not support the idea of an occupation, but only because it had had such little time to make a decision. Havryil also claimed that he didn't know that we had been at the meeting for so long and planned everything together. In my notes, which I wrote just after this conversation and when I was aggravated about the last-minute cancellation after spending hours listening to activists nail down every detail, I said:

> He didn't know, or he didn't understand something, or someone didn't explain something to him, or he simply didn't know. He didn't realize we were planning on *doing* it, that we were ready, that we had planned the whole thing. He also said that the committee, in general, supported the idea, but they don't know anything about how to do it. So, we have to explain it to them very clearly. For example, the first step, the second step, where the toilets are, how to pack a backpack, etc. These students want us to do the occupation together, but they don't know *how*.

In the end, Havryil felt it was positive that many students from different universities supported one another in the occupation, that we could really do something better and make it more widespread in the city. Like Havryil, I concluded that it would be better to take such action with broader student support. The SKR was very active, but it was poorly coordinated, despite its name – Havryil described it as *"amorf,"* an amorphous group rather than a clear unit.

The next evening, we had another planning meeting regarding the occupation of the Red Building of Shevchenko University – or, more accurately, of one auditorium there. Some activists supported the idea, while others were strongly against it. Still others discussed the possibility of occupying Kyiv-Mohyla Academy, but this idea did not take hold, as the rector, Serhii Kvit, had so far been the most supportive of students among university administrators in Kyiv. In terms of occupying an auditorium in the Red Building, the organizers thought it would take ten to fifteen people to block the auditorium, but others disagreed, suggesting it would be necessary to block the whole floor. Havryil stated that the SKR needed a detailed, rational plan, including questions such as where the toilets were. Petro, however, retorted that we had been discussing this issue for a week and that we were ready to occupy. Havryil countered that it was a complex action, so we couldn't just plan it for tomorrow. There were three elements to the plan: first, how we were going to occupy; second, a list of demands; and third, the plan of the occupation, including the toilets, how to deal with security, and how to bring cookies and tea into the building.

Havryil explained that the SKR had already prepared a list of four demands: the resignation of Yanukovych; freedom for those arrested on Bankova Street on 1 December; legislation about higher education and accessible information; and something about the Berkut (which he could not remember). He argued that the SKR was focused on specific demands and that, after Maidan, activists could return to issues of so-cial change. As he described, most members of the SKR were not as radical as those in PD, even if they were not as welcoming of nation-alist language as were the majority of people on Maidan. They sup-ported solidarity with students from other cities, and they wanted to mobilize their resources and bodies that were prepared to support the occupation.

Havryil later explained to me that he became a central, active mem-ber of the SKR. He felt that he had more power and control over human resources at a basic level, and he felt strongly that he wanted to mobi-lize that power. At the same time, he felt rather unproductive because of a lack of a concrete plan, as was obvious when he tried to represent SKR's interests to PD activists who were ready to make an occupation happen. He described the structure of SKR as something between a parliament and a government, and called it a "revolutionary elective body of students" (*revoliutsiinyi vybornyi orhan studentiv*). But the is-sue of communication was not easily resolved. Havryil would end up caught between his personal politics and the SKR's efforts to influence the future minister of education: despite his central role in organizing students, Havryil ultimately got pushed out of students' representative committees during the occupation of the ministry in February.

The failed attempts to agree on an occupation for students is an ex-ample of how Maidan became a space of uncertainty in December. Students were motivated, and they certainly had the numbers to do massive, radical actions. But only Priama Diia was capable of organiz-ing such events, and because it ultimately insisted on working with the SKR and the university student body at large, it did not pursue an occu-pation unilaterally, even if most of its members wanted to do so. A few days later, at a protest in support of students who had been arrested in the past weeks, Zhenia admitted to me that they had not actually been ready for an occupation. She said it would have been terrible to move forward with the occupation without the support of the SKR, but she was still upset that, after all the hard work to plan the action, it had been cancelled at the last minute.

Student activism was essential during stage two of Maidan, but it truly became integrated into the fabric of the protests during the final stage, what I call the "space of possibility." In the next section, I pick up on students' response to the passage of the Dictatorship Laws on 16 January and discuss their most significant moment, the occupation of the Ministry of Education. Later, I consider how this changed the potential for students to influence policy on higher education following the end of the protests.

"Today you sit in class, tomorrow an innocent sits in jail"

On 16 January 2014, President Yanukovych signed the Dictatorship Laws, adopted by the Rada.[9] For many, including members of Priama Diia, these laws were the last straw. People who had been sceptical of the mobilizations and tent camp participants began to come to demonstrations and protests following the adoption of these laws on "Black Thursday." Students called for another strike in a pamphlet they distributed during a rally at KMA:

> After the adoption of the Dictatorship Laws, it became clear that in these conditions, the university cannot remain a bastion of freedom and free thought. On the 20th of January students of Kyiv-Mohyla Academy were called to strike against the anti-constitutional changes in the state.
>
> In the minds of activists, in the current conditions only a full strike is an effective, nonviolent form of protest action. Further, thanks to the suspension of studies, we will be able to attract students in solidarity from other universities to decisive action. Finally, this is just the first step in preparation for a general Ukrainian strike.[10]

Students circulated the flyer around the campus, a Ukrainian "Strike FAQ" that claimed a strike was necessary because of the "adoption of absolutely illegitimate and anti-constitutional laws which cultivate a police state." These laws also provoked violent clashes between protesters on Hrushevs'koho Street and a line of Berkut protecting the Rada at the top of the hilly street. Snipers shot and killed two protesters, Serhii Nihoyan and Mikhail Zhizdnevs'kyi, on Hrushevs'koho Street, the first two people to die in the protests. The Strike FAQ evoked this, asking students to "look at what happened yesterday and today on Hrushevs'koho. If we don't do anything now, we will be lost to this police regime."

The Strike FAQ distanced the current strike from previous ones, however, referring to the first strike in November as "only an imitation of a strike" because "students did not stop studying and only went to protests and marches after class." Activists had suggested strikes many times on Maidan, with some labour activists also calling for a general strike around the country that did not materialize. Because of these previous missteps, the Strike FAQ was designed to advise students on how to proceed with an effective political action in the form of a strike. According to the FAQ, "a real strike (*spravzhnii straik*) is a full suspension of the educational process. During the strike, all participants should spend all their time on resistance ... Don't be a strike-breaker, set an example."

It referenced past examples of student strikes during the Revolution on Granite of 2000 and the Orange Revolution of 2004 that were successful for the broader movement. To allay students' fears of strikes being illegal, the flyer declared that students had a de facto right to protest, which they used in these historical examples, and, anyway, "Now, any peaceful protest is officially against the law" (according to the 16 January laws).

A further concern had prompted KMA students to call for a strike: as the protest camp on Maidan began to become more entrenched and violence seemed inevitable, self-defence brigades that had formed there expanded to other areas of the city. One of those areas was Podil and the student-heavy Kontraktova Ploshcha, where multiple KMA buildings stand. Also present in the area were *titushky*, or government-hired thugs, who appeared on Maidan as *provokatory* or who came to harass students at Kontraktova Ploshcha. In the morning of 20 January, some unknown men detained seven students from the Karpenko-Kary National University of Theatre, Cinema, and Television around Kontraktova Ploshcha. Students noticed unfamiliar cars and jeeps that carried police or other militarized persons. The strike call warned students to be careful in the area, but also called them to action, asking them to come to the main police station to support the students.

For strike organizers, all of a sudden, it appeared that being a student was a crime, because the students from Karpenko-Kary University were assumed to have been on Maidan. According to the authorities, "an examination showed that there were traces of substances for Molotov cocktails on their bodies," which, under the 16 January laws, made them subject to arrest. The seven students were taken to a jail outside the city centre and threatened with up to fifteen years' imprisonment. According to the Dictatorship Laws, wearing helmets or uniforms while participating in a gathering could result in arrest, as could distributing so-called extremist materials and mass disruption. For months, many students had been doing what could fall under these new laws, and the detention of the Karpenko-Kary students was a terrifying reminder of that reality. The understanding of the implications of this reality encouraged students – even non-activists – to take action against the Yanukovych regime.

"Free thought – it isn't extremism"

I arrived at the main building of Kyiv-Mohyla Academy around ten in the morning on 20 January. About thirty people were amassed in front of the building, which swelled to around fifty before we entered the building. We listened to several speakers discussing through megaphones the importance of the strike in light of the new laws, linking the laws to education and academic freedom in Ukraine. They reiterated the claim that, "in a police state, the university cannot remain a bastion of freedom and free thought," and stated that "in a police state, everything is outside the law. In it, we can't study and work normally!" The goals of the strike were the repeal of the anti-constitutional laws, dismissal of the Berkut, university autonomy, a ban on defence groups from entering university territory, a guarantee that (university) teachers would be paid their wages for all of 2014 (changing the current guarantee for only nine months of wages), a decreased workload for students, and a guarantee of the right of (university) teachers to strike. "Our goal," they said, "is to melt down the dictatorial system and create a new society!" Whether these rallying cries were being heard outside the initial group is questionable. The crowd was noticed by passersby and students attempting to enter the university, but only a few protesters actually used the megaphones, while others stood quietly with signs or stood slightly aside from the main crowd, seeming unsure about whether to join the chants of "Freedom! Equality! Student solidarity!" (*Svoboda! Rivnist'! Students'ka solidarnist'!*)

At this point, students were still coming to classes, although KMA rector Serhii Kvit had suspended studies and imposed a "distance education" program on the university. Striking students were encouraging the last remaining students who were in classes – and their professors, whose interests students were also hoping to represent – to walk out of their classes and support the strike. Strike organizers, many of whom were recent graduates and a few of whom were KMA professors, tried to draw in students, teachers, and workers in a more general strike, which would be more effective and could possibly grow into a general, nationwide strike. Leftist organizers mobilized rhetoric about the police state, linking to its effects on education, to draw people into the strike. By the time I left the main building in the afternoon, over a hundred people – including KMA and other university students, recent graduates, and some professors – had gathered in the "strike hall," a large staircase leading into the building that most students would have to pass or go through in order to attend class.

Many students on the staircase created and hung posters highlighting the harsh language of the Dictatorship Laws, with slogans such as "Free thought – it isn't extremism" (*vil'nodumstvo – tse ne ekstremizm*) and "Today you sit in class, tomorrow an innocent sits in jail" (figure 5.4). At the suggestion of Inna Sovsun, a KMA professor who was one of the main strike supporters and who later became deputy minister of education, many students travelled to different departments in the university in order to spread the word to students and faculty about the strike and its

Figure 5.4. Protest signs in the Strike Hall, Kyiv-Mohyla Academy; at top left, "Free thought: it isn't extremism"
Source: Author's photograph.

goals. A group managed to set up a computer with a live stream of the standoff between protesters and the Berkut on Hrushevs'koho Street, where the first protesters had been killed the day before.

Student organizers, many of whom were also leftist activists and used their experience with PD to connect with non-leftist students, worked hard to link language about police violence and the police state with universities and free thought. Particularly, KMA had been known to stand independently from the Ukrainian government and Ministry of Education, taking a stand against Dmytro Tabachnyk and his attempts to pass laws that would seriously hinder the education system. KMA is often seen as a beacon of free thought within Ukrainian higher education both by its own students, who choose this school because of its reputation, and by the Ukrainian diaspora,[11] so KMA students and professors were already well versed in linking state and education politics, as they understood the effects of government policies on education and students. In so doing, they were attempting to confirm the position of students as a unified political voice against repressive government policies. By showing the ways higher education would be affected by the Dictatorship Laws, students would *have* to stand against the laws and the government, no matter their ideological stance. Although many of the students who participated in the strike did not necessarily agree on tactics, they did find unity in their condemnation of the 16 January laws.

Strike organizers even hoped to get Kvit to support the strike, as suggested in the Strike FAQ: "To strike or not to strike can only be the decision of students … [But] when Serhii Myronovych [Kvit] sees that the strike is a real power, we believe that he will join our call and begin to organize a teachers' strike." This attitude towards the administration was different than during the December mobilizations, when students were cautious because administrations had threatened to punish student protesters. In the context of late January, it was clear that all student protest would be considered illegal. Therefore, having the support of Kvit as well as of professors at KMA would have a massive impact in gaining student support as well as providing new fuel to the protests on Maidan. A group of strikers was organized to speak with the university administration, where they were told that Kvit would not stand in the way of striking students or punish them, but that he would not encourage other students to strike either. By the evening of 22 January, however, Kvit decided to close the university entirely and banned from the campus two important organizers, both recent graduates of the university and leftist activists. The rector claimed this was in response to the current political situation, but the decision was also connected to the effect of the occupation of the main building on the university and Kvit's perceived ability to control the student body.

Several student activists told me that the 16 January laws were the first instance since Maidan began when all leftists could come together and support the protests, because the laws had crossed the line: the laws were a clear effort to make protest illegal and to threaten those who would participate. In theory, the implementation of the laws would solidify the power of state representatives; in reality, the protest body was large and diverse enough to continue despite attempts to enforce the laws. Students were still the targets of repression based on these laws, and they wanted their universities to help preserve their right to protest. Even Kyiv-Mohyla Academy, one of the most independent universities in Ukraine, was beholden to the Ministry of Education, so its rector's response to the student occupation was still inflected by the state. In other words, the university itself became a site of contention between the state and citizens; university administrations – obligated to both – were caught in a challenging decision.

The response to the Dictatorship Laws and the first deaths on Maidan show several significant shifts in student activism. First, the laws brought students of various political ideologies together successfully for the first time; the legislation made it clear that any political participation – by students or otherwise – was a punishable offence. This was a threat to students with any political affiliation, as well as those who were not part of organizations. Second, mirroring the wider protests, the strike organizers adopted the leftist language of a "police regime" that provided non-leftist students a way to criticize the state's practices. Even without marking the strike as a leftist tactic, students were drawn to leftists' experiences and discourses in organizing, reinforcing the students' ability and desire to coalesce into a stronger protest body.

The occupation of KMA ended on 22 January because Kvit insisted on fully closing the university, but the students did not want to lose their momentum. For three days, they worried about where to go, engaging with the uncertainties that had been prevalent throughout the protests. They contacted a supportive publishing house, but they were unable to obtain a permanent space there. One activist wrote to a Maidan coordinator about the problem, who suggested the students contact the leaders of the newly occupied Ukrainian House at the bottom of Hrushevs'koho Street on the aptly named European Square. On 27 January, students moved into their new quarters, and the Student Assembly began.

Student Centre in the Former Lenin Museum

The Student Assembly (*students'ka asambleia*) was one of the most significant self-organized initiatives from Maidan.[12] The Student Assembly was crucial because it was the first Maidan-based initiative to put into practice not only self-organization but also consensus-based methods, inspired, to some extent, by Occupy Wall Street and other similar recent movements.[13] The occupied Ukrainian House, previously the Lenin Museum in Kyiv and more recently a site for exhibitions and some museum archives on the top floors, was a prime opportunity for students to reach out to other Maidan participants about their educational concerns and even about leftist issues (figure 5.5). One of the organizers, Sasha, told me that the Student Centre created in the Ukrainian House was a departure from previous education-based initiatives such as strikes. It was formed around the governing principle of "assembly": organizers held a general assembly each day in which all students had an equal say and no leaders ran the platform. Flyers posted around the Student Assembly area explained terms such as "assembly" and "working group," on which the Student Assembly's organization relied in order to broaden its reach and potential effectiveness.

Figure 5.5. Student info centre in the occupied Ukrainian House
Source: Author's photograph.

I attended one of the first general assemblies at the end of January, which had about fifty students in attendance from KMA, Taras Shevchenko, Kyiv Polytechnic Institute, Drahomanov National Peda-gogical University, and others. At the assembly, Vasyl', another activist, described the non-hierarchical functioning of the Student Assembly, as well as the importance of remaining outside party affiliation, because existing political parties would not represent students' interests. From the assembly, students broke into smaller action groups (*hrupa diï*) of five to fifteen people around issues or interests, which could then meet on their own time and bring their decisions to the general assembly when they were ready. In this way, the general assembly did not get bogged down with ideological arguments or small details, but was able to gather and share all necessary information from each action group, which could then gain more members. Action groups included those working on a boycott initiative, picketing courts and working with lawyers to support students who had been arrested, and working with other civic initiatives such as the Hospital Guard and other medical services. Vasyl' reiterated the importance of always having a physical presence in the student space, asking those assembled to volunteer to spend the night or at least to bring sleeping bags and mats for those who would be doing so.

The Student Assembly was a unique example of student activism on Maidan in that it was perhaps the moment of students' – and leftists' – most thorough integration into the fabric of the mobilizations. Their presence in the occupied Ukrainian House as part of the Student Assembly was an opportunity to reach out to a new, non-student population about the idea of self-organization and their commitment to non-party politics. One leftist activist, Maksym, posted a reflection on Facebook on the possibility of launching a leftist "Trojan horse" via the Student Assembly's film screenings and discussions:

> Today I was witness to a quite atypical situation. In the occupied Ukrainian House (where our comrades have set up the Student Centre) at the film screening about Argentinian workers' occupation of their factory sat (other than students) older guys [diad'ky; uncles] who came from other regions of the country to Maidan ... Perhaps if they heard about the left, it's only in the spirit of "communists" and "hang them" [a reference to the common anti-communist/anti-leftist phrase komuniaky na hilliaku, "Hang the communists"]. But they sit here and stick with this "red" film with interest, some even giving lively commentary ...
>
> All of this is to say that, although it is not our revolution, we can really launch our own Trojan horse of social-critical thought among the masses, who were previously inaccessible to us... Understand that our Maidan friends are unlikely, immediately inspired by the example of Argentinian workers, to start taking enterprises under worker control. However, it provides a first and very important precondition for some further left political development which, until now, has been absolutely deaf in terms of the regions.

Maksym saw the film screening and similar events that the Student Assembly organized as a chance to introduce Maidan activists to self-organization without its necessarily being linked to leftist political ideologies. He felt that the Student Assembly – because it was not explicitly a leftist group or initiative but was instead broadly associated with students – provided an opportunity to speak to sympathetic Maidan participants about problems such as low pay and poor working conditions. He also seemed to indicate that it would be a way to feel greater ownership over the protests, which he referred to as "not our revolution," because of the past rejection of leftists in earlier protests. Here, Maksym continued what I outlined in chapter 4, that leftists still managed to find ways to participate in the protests even when the protests were not inclined to embrace their politics.

These themes were especially linked to self-organization because they were not part of the platforms of any of the Opposition parties. Thus, the

Student Assembly was a chance to give people exposure to non-party political activism that directly addressed their concerns as workers, creating the kind of union between students and workers that many activists desired from the beginning of the mobilizations. Protesters condemned the Opposition leaders because protesters' first priority was the resignation of Yanukovych, while Opposition leaders were still treating the president as a legitimate leader. Protesters began to look for new forms of representation, as they no longer felt that Opposition leaders had their interests in mind. Because the Student Assembly was so staunchly leader- and party-free, and because it functioned so well and provided daily, visible examples of its success, other participants could see that student activists were not relegated to dealing only with education issues.

The simple proposition of self-organization and self-representation in politics, without relying on ineffective Opposition leaders, was a very timely theme for the occupants of the Ukrainian House. In Sasha's later reflections, she described that, before the Student Assembly, "people often didn't believe that they could show initiative, that their ideas are worthy of attention." Because of the way the Student Assembly functioned, it treated everyone's ideas equally, and participants attracted the attention of other Maidan activists with their interesting films and lectures (capitalizing on the fact that living in the occupied Ukrainian House for weeks on end was not particularly stimulating).

The Student Assembly was further distinguished from other Maidan initiatives because of its short lifespan. As Sasha described, it ceased to exist because "it was relevant to those conditions in which it emerged, and it is not relevant today." But many activists mentioned their experience in the Student Assembly as essential to the way Maidan changed their mindsets. According to Sasha, the Student Assembly gave the mass of students on Maidan the skills and confidence they needed to, for instance, occupy a government building and use it to bring about significant, long-term change. The Student Assembly also provided a certain legitimacy to student activists who were able to organize a space of their own in the physical confines of the Ukrainian House and the broader boundaries of Maidan at large.[14]

Another activist, Danylo, in an interview that took place in April 2014, after the mass violence but when protests were still ongoing, described the consensus methods the Student Assembly used as "the most useful thing I learned in the time of Maidan":

> I had heard of consensus decisionmaking, but in practice, in use, I didn't know how to do it. And here, almost every action we prepared ... really every action, we made decisions by consensus. I really liked those different symbols you

can give, hand signs.[15] That means you work faster when you're talking about anything, you can see at once reactions to words, someone supports, doesn't support. It's maybe the most democratic way I know to make a decision. When you vote 51 per cent, the other 49, or less, they can really be against it, but it's a majority. When you do consensus, when you don't have any categoric opposition, those who have something against it can propose an alternative to change something so that the decision is accepted, or they give a proposition themselves. This counts the ideas of every person. And that's very important.

The Student Assembly was an important moment in January 2014, at the peak of the general protests' momentum that led to more radical action in late February. It was effective both in giving people who were not typically activists confidence in their ideas, enhancing their ability to participate, and spreading the concept of self-organization to other, non-leftist protesters. The Student Assembly disappeared as soon as students occupied the Ministry of Education, where they used assemblies, affinity groups, and consensus methods to create and promote new higher education legislation and name a new minister of education. These same tactics and successes encouraged other volunteer initiatives during and after Maidan: in the end, Maksym's "Trojan horse of social-critical thought among the masses" came in the form of self-organized volunteerism.

The Student Assembly was a crucial Maidan-based initiative that promoted self-organization – in both theory and practice – among students, but also among the protest body at large. It helped spread effective non-party organizing throughout Maidan, especially because of the growing lack of credibility among Opposition parties and representatives. Importantly, the Student Assembly ended in February when students occupied the Ministry of Education and focused on influencing the formation of a new government. It ceased to exist when the need for it no longer existed, which is a fundamental component of a self-organized initiative. Self-organized groups respond to people's needs according to their abilities, so when the need arose for such a group, people like Sasha used their experience to help others. When the circumstances of Maidan no longer demanded its presence, the initiative disappeared, although its impact remained.

"We'll just wait for him inside": How Students (Peacefully) Took Over the Ministry

In the days after the violent clashes between protesters and police in late February 2014, I walked up Khreshchatyk from Bessarabs'ky market to observe the memorials that had been set up along the street and on the main part of the square. The atmosphere was concomitantly sober and jubilant, and I took photos of mothers with their children lighting candles in memory of the dead and of fathers hoisting their sons onto tanks to pose with masked soldiers. As I watched them on a cold Sunday, my mobile phone rang. Kolia, a leftist activist and our *krav maga* instructor, was on the other end. "Emily!" he said, enthusiastically. "We occupied the Ministry of Education! Get down here, I think you're going to want to write about this!"

Throughout the winter, building occupation had been one of the main non-violent tactics used widely among Maidan protesters. As I described earlier in the chapter, students planned an occupation of Taras Shevchenko University's Red Building that did not come to fruition, and they had taken advantage of the occupation of the Ukrainian House, where the Student Assembly had operated. But before February, occupying the ministry was never in students' concrete plans. When I interviewed Sasha about student activism on Maidan, she told me, "The occupation was a secret plan from mid-January … but the idea was to occupy a university building, like either the Pedagogical University … or the Red Building … The idea to occupy the ministry was like a dreamy-dream." Heorhiy, another leftist student activist, credited Vasyl', a longtime leftist activist, with the idea of the occupation: "He really wanted to occupy something … and I told him the only building worth occupying is the Ministry of Education. I didn't think it was a good idea, we were not ready for that and we would just be thrown out of that place, but when they did that, it was a time when nobody was guarding anything anymore, so they just walked in and nothing happened to them."

Students took over the ministry building to reclaim it from the state and for the people it was supposed to represent. Although I was not present at the moment of occupation, several participants recounted for me in later interviews the narrative I present here. I visited the occupied ministry several times over the week in which students lived there. I attended several general assemblies in the ministry as well as invited lectures and organizing meetings, and I observed the final day of occupation, during which the ministry was reopened to workers. I also gathered social media posts and messages from various activists about the occupation, some of which I include below.

On 21 February, students mobilized in response to the deaths of protesters on Maidan. They organized an action at the ministry to request a meeting with Minister of Education Dmytro Tabachnyk to demand he condemn the regime's violence. Several leftist activists, including Sasha and Zhenia, called the demand "stupid," because they did not think the minister would meet with students, no matter what, and they were sceptical of its effectiveness, but they came to the action anyway just to see what would happen. Several columns of students came down Prospekt Peremohy (Victory Avenue, a large main street in the northwestern part of the city), from Kyiv Polytechnic University on one side and from Taras Shevchenko National University on the other. The students asked for Tabachnyk or his deputy Yevhen Sulima to come and speak with them, but an administrative staff member came out to tell the students that neither minister nor his deputy was at work, even at two o'clock in the afternoon on a Friday. The students then asked the administrator to call them, but the administrator did not have either man's phone number. The students then informed him that, until a minister could be contacted, "we'll just wait for him inside." The administrator had no choice and, of course, many of Yanukovych's closest cabinet members – including the education minister – as well as the Berkut and other security forces that would have protected government buildings had fled with the president, and neither Tabachnyk nor Sulima ever appeared. From there, students established medical points and gathered food and other supplies in order to remain in the ministry as long as they deemed necessary.

The students who occupied the building treated their task of protecting it seriously (figure 5.6). Students guarded the front gates from *provokatory* or unfriendly armed groups. Mimicking the self-defence groups on Maidan, the student occupiers had organized a self-defence brigade to protect students from outside attacks, either from the fallen government's own forces or from military wings of radical right-wing parties, which threatened the students multiple times. Sasha claimed the brigade had up to forty people at a given time, led by Vasyl'. The group was made up of anarchist football hooligans for Kyiv's Arsenal team, leftist activists, and other students who had come to support the occupation. Each time I entered the ministry, the guards asked for my student card; unlike my attempts to enter other occupied buildings in Kyiv, which were occasionally denied, I was always able to get into the ministry. In one memorable interaction, three young men asked for my student card, and when I showed them my temporary residence permit, they let me in and said, "Welcome to Ukraine!"

Once inside, the students sorted mountains of donated food and set up a makeshift kitchen with electric kettles for boiling water for tea and instant ramen noodles. "Someone called Maidan and said the students occupied the ministry and they are hungry," Zhenia told me, laughing. "If you are a student and you want to eat, just go to the ministry! You

Figure 5.6. Students in the occupied Ministry of Education
Source: Author's photograph.

can eat really well there." Sasha related that the Student Assembly of the preceding weeks had already amassed enough resources – including food and medical supplies, as well as media contacts and support from Maidan groups – that the occupation of the ministry was automatically seen as legitimate in the broader picture of Maidan and the ensuing political turnover.

The students gathered in a large assembly hall for most of their meetings, including small working-group and self-defence organizing meetings as well as the larger general assemblies, held every evening. General assemblies were organized around consensus methods, suggested by leftist activists beginning during the Student Assembly. Many leftists worked as moderators during these assemblies to keep people from talking too long or about irrelevant issues, and once preventing a fight between members of the self-defence brigade. According to Sasha,

This training [from Student Assembly] to make these gatherings short and productive proved to be useful when we moved to the Ministry of Education. There we had to demand something, we couldn't just come and go, we had to form some groups, deal with the security of the building, defence of the building because there were some attacks and we were informed there would be some attacks. So we had different things to do there in the ministry and we already had a couple [of people] who learned how to manage a big assembly and it was very useful.

These general assemblies did not go as swiftly, however, as they had in the Student Assembly once students around Kyiv understood that a new government was in formation and that students might in fact have a say in what happened. Leftists who had successfully organized the non-hierarchical Student Assembly wanted to keep the structure of the occupation the same, but many other students felt having a "representative committee" was necessary to liaise with government officials. Here, Sasha described an ideological divide between leftists and liberals, the latter of whom represented official university student unions (largely at odds with the independent student union Priama Diia) and who were very interested in how the ministry would function after students left. Because these liberal students knew that many of the leftists would be critical of any government, and because of historic antagonism against leftist students, no leftist student was elected to the representative committee. Furthermore, several of the most outspoken leftists, including both Vasyl' and Sasha, identified as anarchists. In so doing, they marginalized themselves even more in the eyes of "liberal" activists who wanted to find a compromise with state representatives, but they also openly presented themselves as critical of any government formation, even one in which students could have a strong influence.

These ideological divisions presented a challenge in terms of building a student coalition, precisely because students of different political affiliations had differing ideas about *how* to criticize the state. Leftists, including anarchists, based their criticisms on an understanding of an entrenched police regime, and they felt that changing to a new minister of education, or even electing a new president, was not going to make an impact on Ukraine's broader problems. Those whom Sasha characterized as "liberals," on the other hand, believed that changing the people who made up the state could make state bodies become more representative. They felt that influencing who became the next minister would help institutionalize student participation in the governance of education. As student-activist Zhenia put it, "The main question wasn't about educational reform but the new candidate for minister. A bad minister [Tabachnyk] became a good minister [of their choosing], and everything will be okay." Students' perception, particularly the liberal, non-anarchist students, was that a new minister was all that was needed to enact change in higher education. But for students like Zhenia, these changes were not enough. While these two camps were not necessarily the only political voices represented at the ministry, their ideas often came to a head, leading leftists to compromise on their anti-government stance in order to ensure the ability of the student coalition to function.

There was excessive speculation during the last week of February about who would make up the provisional government's new cabinet. Although ministers named by interim president Turchynov would not necessarily stay in their posts following the elections promised in May, it seemed quite likely that, if students helped select a suitable candidate, such a person might remain in the position for the long term. Over the course of the week in the ministry, they deliberated over a list of possible candidates and selected three acceptable people: Serhii Kvit, Lilia Hrynevych,[16] and Mykhailo Zgurovs'ky.[17] Leftists preferred Zgurovs'ky, who had proposed a reform law for higher education that was generally supported by student activists. However, Zgurovs'ky decided not to accept the students' nomination for minister, having served in the position before, leaving them to choose between Kvit and Hrynevych.

Students' influence on the next minister was an important step in confirming their role in establishing new higher education policies. Where once the minister of education was a target for criticism because of his failed national policy, now the minister would have to be seen as a representative of students, because the students had chosen the minister themselves, at least in part. Further, university administrations should no longer be seen as extensions of state practices that worked to students' detriment, but as intermediaries equally positioned between the ministry and students. A particular group of student volunteers worked as liaisons between these new candidates and the general assembly at the ministry – part of what Sasha described as the "liberal" camp of students – while leftist students focused on organizational tactics, legislation, and the defence brigade.

Both Kvit and Hrynevych came to meet with students at the ministry, and both were accepted as possible candidates that students could support. By this time, it was clear that Kvit was Turchynov's top choice as well, and the former rector of Kyiv-Mohyla Academy was offered the position. As I have mentioned, leftist activists had been strongly critical of Serhii Kvit, as he worked against them at KMA. Zhenia did not mince words when describing why she did not support Kvit for the job of minister: "Leftist activists just hate Kvit. The leftist activists from KMA know who this guy is, know that the university got worse because he's authoritarian, nationalist. But for the majority of students [at the ministry], Kvit was more than just the accepted candidate, because he's from KMA and he's a national intellectual. [For other students] the fact that he's a nationalist isn't anything against Kvit, it's just a bad thing for the leftists." And indeed, his nomination was greeted enthusiastically by ministry occupants and in the end, leftists did not protest his assuming the position of minister. Kvit came to the ministry on Friday, 28 February, to meet with students after being named minister. According to both Sasha and Zhenia, he made many promises to student occupiers to support their demands for higher education reform.

Kvit presented himself as an antidote to a state that did not represent Ukrainians – a point he had made before in his political stances as rector of KMA. Kvit's support for and participation in Maidan further made him appear as a more authentic candidate, one who would have Ukraine's European interests in mind. Crucially, though, as many activists told me, Kvit would not have the ability to lustrate the entire Ministry of Education – indeed, the majority of people who worked at the ministry under Yanukovych kept their jobs following Kvit's installation. This continuity was part of leftists' general criticism of "liberal" students' focus on government institutions and establishing a representative face for state bodies.

The student occupation of the ministry was short lived: they vacated the building on 1 March, after Kvit was confirmed as acting minister. When they occupied the building, students and workers had taped and sealed every office so that no one could be charged with having broken into any of them to steal or manipulate documents. Having decided to leave, the students spent Friday live streaming the opening of each office in turn as bureaucrats waited outside to inspect their offices for any problems. Volodia, the activist running the live stream, said he was enjoying the spectacle: usually when students came to the ministry to meet with workers and manoeuvre through the bureaucracy, they were the ones told to wait outside; for once, he was on the other end, telling the bureaucrats to wait for students – as he put it with a smile, "the system is flipped!"

As I have argued, the Ukrainian educational system was an acceptable target for protest before and during Maidan because it was perceived as representative of an ineffective and eventually violent state. Leftist activists successfully used this perception to enact campaigns about higher education before Maidan, and they were again successful in this task during Maidan. However, despite the prominent role of leftists and the wide usage of anti-state language among other student protesters, the majority of students did not hold that position once they felt that the head of the ministry would represent them. Although many leftists understood that their marginalization in Ukrainian political society led to their having a limited impact among students, others felt that the occupation could have convinced the study body even more deeply that they could influence the direction of policy change. Following the broader Maidan protest, however, students ended their mass mobilization once a new government formed.

Because of the mass student support for the new minister of education, leftist students found it a challenge to target him and his administration for criticism. In part, this was because he had named Inna Sovsun as his deputy minister – she was an education researcher who had been involved in leftist think tanks advocating for higher education reform and worked at KMA with many Priama Diia activists. But a student I spoke with following the end of the occupation felt that, despite the seeming successes of students at the ministry, the fundamental problems in the government had not changed. Although Sovsun was in a position to change things – "she can really help students and dialogue with them," the student said – he was concerned that any position of power would change her priorities. As he put it, "She is left wing, but still she doesn't change [the fact] that the government is neoliberal." This reflected problems for leftist activism more broadly: even if leftists were active in student protests, most students were not leftists, and the behaviour of most students towards leftists during the occupation showed that their attitudes about the left had not changed.

Following the occupation of the ministry, many leftist students worked hard to ensure that they could leave their mark on higher education reforms, even with Kvit at the helm of the ministry. Despite some successes, however, Zhenia ultimately was correct that changing the minister from a "bad" one to a "good" would not change the trend towards marketization and neoliberalization of education policies. And, importantly, because the Tabachnyk administration had been so closed to students, even the most base-level efforts to accept student demands at the ministry made Kvit look like he would be different. After the protests ended, however, Kvit continued to work towards changing the system of university stipend distribution – only top students would get state stipends and would be allowed to take those stipends to the university of their choosing, rather than each state university having an allotted number of stipends, broadening access to higher education.

"No Stipends? Eat the Ministers!" Post-Maidan Challenges

As these processes unfolded after the end of Maidan, Priama Diia no longer took the form it did when I began research in 2012. This is largely because many student activists who formed that generation of PD graduated from university, but other students whom I spoke to about activism in 2017 expressed concern about people's willingness to participate in activism at all following Maidan. Further, students now have easier access to a European education because of visa liberalization policies, so systemic problems in Ukrainian higher education are difficult to prioritize. Despite this lack of engagement, some students remain critical of the kinds of marketization that have taken place since the end of Maidan.

The issue of stipend redistribution generated momentum for one of the most radical interventions from PD and other student activists. On 30 August 2016, a group of students from leftist organizations attended a meeting in which various government representatives were discussing the possibility of decreasing university student stipends. In response, student activists expressed their disdain in a creative way by throwing an entire cake in the face of the deputy minister of finance, Serhii Marchenko.[18] The students rallied others in the small room to the chant of "No Stipends? Eat the Ministers!" and called the reforms "anti-social" before they were escorted from the meeting.

At the time, students studying at public universities typically received monthly stipends of 825 Ukrainian hryvnia (UAH; about US$30 in January 2017). Marchenko, one of the representatives at the meeting, advocated redistributing student stipends for several reasons. First, he and other supporters argued that this small sum of money was essential for only 25 per cent of students – in other words, most students had many other, more important sources of income, so that taking away 825 UAH per month was not going to prevent them from attending university. Further, like Serhii Kvit, Marchenko and others advocated for providing stipends only to top students. In this framework, only the best students would receive funding and could choose which university to attend. This would replace the current system in which each university has a certain number of state-funded seats; theoretically, if only the best students got funding and took their funding to the highest-ranked universities, the ministry could leave some universities without any state funding at all. Such a policy would result in competition among higher-ranked universities to produce the "best" students – those most competitive in a European market – leaving the humanities, pedagogical universities, and other regional universities underattended and thus underfunded, even likely to close. Thus, with this process, the "Europeanization" of Ukraine's student body would be limited to those with access to major cities and the university places they offer. Europe, in this scenario, would mean an even greater stratification between Ukraine's rich and poor, made possible through reforms in higher education, creating a spatialized expansion of Bourdieu's conclusions about how the cultural capital created in educational institutions results in class inequality.

Critics of this position believe that this cut in stipends was an extension of further systematic cuts in social services that the government had been implementing since the election of Petro Poroshenko in May 2014. Writing for the leftist journal *Commons*, Viktoria Muliavka (2016) suggested that these ministers adhered to the assumption that European – and by extension, non-Soviet – was better for Ukraine, and that the notion that all Ukrainians should have access to higher education was linked to a Soviet-style social welfare system: "An extensive network of universities, a high quantity of funded seats in universities and a universal stipend system can guarantee access to higher education at the level of more economically developed societies." This type of system, however, is seen more often as a "relic" of the Soviet era, and thus blamed for current ills in Ukrainian higher education. Rather, Muliavka stated, the problem was with "the inability of a capitalist system to guarantee a functional alternative to the Soviet educational system in post-socialist societies."

The conflict around stipend redistribution shows how leftists' ideas about Europeanizing the Ukrainian educational system were at odds with what many leaders viewed as necessary reforms to bring Ukraine into Europe. The focus on competition among universities and students graduating with degrees whose value is assessed based on recognition and employability is a shift to prioritizing education for the market, rather than for the development of knowledge at both individual and national levels. In the case of Ukraine, the implementation of such reforms, rather than improving the educational system, may be used as a mechanism of governance if the standards to which universities are held are based on markets, student perception, and university reputations (see Strathern 2000).

Higher education activism and its effectiveness at various levels helped its integration into the fabric of the Maidan protests. The educational system was important during Maidan because it provided an example of the negative ramifications of the current regime, and the promises of better integration into the European Higher Education Area was presented as a clear example of how Europeanization would benefit Ukraine, particularly young Ukrainians. Education-based activism was also effective because students were a large and mobilizable population, particularly after the use of violence and other repressions became the norm.

The sphere of higher education in the post-Maidan provides an example of the varying ideas about Europe that were present on Maidan. Leftists' success in higher education activism came partly because of their ability and willingness to form coalitions with non-leftists, even with those they distinctly disagreed with about the role of government and what it meant to "Europeanize" Ukraine's education system. Despite their willingness to form coalitions, leftist concerns about the marketization of education and the growth of inequality were largely ignored in post-Maidan policies to Europeanize education in Ukraine. But higher education was not the only site where leftists faced conflicting ideas about "European values," as we will see in the next chapter.

Chapter Six

"These aren't your values": Gender and Nation on Maidan

On 24 November 2013, I gathered with a group of fifteen leftist activists at a bookstore north of Khreshchatyk, Kyiv's main street leading to Independence Square. It was the first large-scale march organized by Opposition parties and their leaders. The leftist column, as they called it, had a variety of signs, including banners about free transportation and education, and a large red-and-gold version of the European Union flag. Two young women, one from southeastern Ukraine and one from the western city of L'viv, brought signs proclaiming feminism and gender equality (figure 6.1). One read, "Feminism is a European value," and the other asked, "Do you want to go to [to be part of] Europe? (*Khochesh v Yevropu?*) Say no to sexism and homophobia!" Both signs engaged with the rhetoric of Europe that was apparent in the beginning of the protests: Ukraine was presented as part of Europe and Ukrainians as Europeans who claimed to have "European" values. But the use of "feminism" on one sign, as well as suggesting that viewers contemplate gender- and sexuality-based non-discrimination, was a quite risky step for these two activists to take.

EU-imposed anti-discrimination legislation was already a topic of debate in pre-Maidan Ukraine. Pro-Russian oligarch Viktor Medvedchuk's Ukrainian Choice platform had placed anti–Association Agreement advertisements around Kyiv in fall 2013, including one that read, "The Association Agreement Is Same-Sex Marriage." The statement incorrectly claimed that Ukraine would have to adopt legislation legalizing same-sex marriage as part of the Association Agreement – while Ukraine did have to accept some anti-discrimination clauses as part of the Agreement, same-sex marriage was never proposed as one of them. But the threat to family values was perceived as real by many Ukrainians, contributing to their negative reactions to the feminist signs that connected gender and sexual equality with the EU.

Figure 6.1. Feminist protest signs on Maidan
Source: Author's photograph.

Indeed, even in the relatively celebratory context of the mass march, the woman holding the "Say no to sexism and homophobia!" sign was attacked by a man who tried to hit her over the head with a metal pipe, thankfully only grazing her cheek but damaging her sign in the process. She managed to protect herself from more harm, but without help from others around her except those with the leftist group. After three activists and I got separated from the rest of the group, a woman began yelling at us that sexism wasn't real and it was wrong to bring such rhetoric to the protests, essentially suggesting we were coming to the protests to stir up trouble. We were finally able to reconnect with our column at European Square, where Opposition leaders were rallying the crowd. There, an older man enquired about the "Feminism Is a European Value" sign, and he listened attentively to the women's explanations of gender equality, ultimately taking photos with the women and their signs, smiling broadly. His response, however, was not the most common reaction to the presence of feminists on Maidan.

Over the course of the first week on Maidan, I saw harassment and direct attacks on people with signs referencing feminism three more times, including one evening when extreme-right *provokatory* assaulted feminist protesters with pepper spray. Why were gender-based and feminist themes so inflammatory on Maidan? To understand why protesters responded negatively to feminists, it is important to consider the relationship among feminism, national ideology, and Europeanization. The connection of these particular feminists to leftist activists – also marginalized on Maidan – confirmed what many people already believed about feminism, which is that it is deeply linked to socialism and Soviet communism, as I describe in this chapter. Furthermore, as I have noted, Euromaidan was as much about Europe as it was about negotiating Ukraine's future as a post-communist nation-state within the EU. To a large extent, feminist activism that advocates a better future for women through legislation, such as exists in the EU, is at odds with Ukraine's national ideology, because it might threaten national unity by questioning traditional gender norms and family structures that are fundamental to the national idea. These two trends complicate the problem of how to embody "European values" within Ukraine's traditionalist, anti-feminist national ideology. How has feminism become mutually exclusive with of Ukraine's currently dominant national ideology and, relatedly, what kind of nation do Ukrainian feminists envision?

The Maidan protests were organized predominately around the related themes of anti-communism and Europeanization. While leftists' political positions tended to criticize both anti-communism and Europeanization, feminist activists provide one instance in which a strongly leftist political group took an explicitly pro-Europe position because of its promised benefits for gender equality and LGBTQ+ rights. Over time, however, as it became obvious that these benefits were not part of the vision of Europe that most protesters had, feminists found other ways to integrate into the mobilizations through self-organization. Thus, an exploration of leftist feminism provides an example of the ways Europe is a contested political symbol, not only generally in Ukraine but also among radical political activists.

A discussion of the visions of Europe held by Ukrainian feminists focused heavily on gender equality legislation and anti-discrimination policies. These visions of Europe generated suspicion among other protesters, because they perceived Ukrainian feminists as promoting a Westernized, imported political platform rather than supporting the nation. This suspicion created challenges when feminists tried to "vernacularize" (Merry 2006) or translate their politics for Ukrainian audiences. In this chapter I also discuss how, on Maidan, feminists attempted to create spaces for themselves in the protest, with limited success, but which outsiders promoted through equality discourses. Finally, I consider how women developed their own militarized forms of participation, creating new conversations around feminism that reflect the intersection of self-organization and feminism in Ukraine.

Europe and Gender Equality

The example of gender-based activism can be used to argue that discourses about Europe that gained traction during the Maidan mobilizations were meant to establish a specific vision of Ukraine as not Russian (and therefore not Soviet), rather than an accurate interpretation of European reality. Feminist activists, who engaged in Ukrainian politics throughout the mobilizations, felt they had a more realistic conceptualization of Europe than most protesters, and attempted to intervene in the protests in order to promote it. The majority of protesters, however, quickly shifted its focus away from Europe and onto establishing a Ukrainian nation-state that could represent their demands. This idealized nation-state – based on restrictive gender norms that limited the ways women could participate – was reproduced in the space of the protests through a dominant, militarized masculinity. As critics of these restrictive norms, feminists had to find creative ways to participate in the mobilizations. Feminists adopted language and organization similar to the masculine forms in order to find ways to contribute to the broader protests, shifting their focus away from Europe altogether.

Dominant groups of participants attempted to use the mobilizations to promote specific national narratives about Ukraine. These narratives were deeply engaged with establishing the ways gender roles could and should be enacted by participants and supporters. An examination of the ways gender roles were created and reinforced on Maidan is essential to understanding how these roles influenced the new narratives about Ukraine that appeared during the protests and that became somewhat definitive following their conclusion. Although Ukraine's accession to the EU did not remain protesters' primary concern throughout the protests, contradictory ideas about establishing what Ukraine's European-ness would mean for gender- and sexuality-based equality further informed these national narratives.

Traditional, patriarchal notions of gender roles have become more dominant since Ukraine's independence, supported by attempts to detach Ukraine from its Soviet past and its state-sponsored "gender equality" programs (Bureychak 2012; Riabchuk 2012). This is not unique to Ukraine: Susan Gal and Gail Kligman argue that gender roles, family structures, and state gender and family policies have been contentious across the region since state socialism ended (Gal and Kligman 2000; see also Goven 1993). It is important to note that it is not just men who support these traditional, patriarchal gender roles as anti-Soviet; post-socialist women have also been drawn to the idea of a male breadwinner and a female homemaker/caretaker simply because it was exactly what they had been denied under socialism (see, for example, Drakulić 1993). In many former communist eastern European countries, theoretically, better job opportunities gained by entrance into a free trade area with Europe allow men to sustain their families' livelihoods more easily, thus ensuring women's relegation to the home and male dominance in public society. But in reality, neither men's nor women's roles have followed any predictable development, leaving space for the constant contestation of gender roles and family norms (Mattioli 2020, chap. 5; Utrata 2015).

Although feminist discourses appeared to adhere to anti-communist attitudes because of their support of European accession, their form of anti-communism was not what was promoted in the dominant national ideology on Maidan. An embrace of traditional gender roles was seen as a more effective practice of decommunization because it would further benefit traditional family structures, also understood to have been under attack during the communist era. These feminist interventions allow us to explore not only the dominant national ideology on Maidan but also the way this ideology promoted only certain forms of decommunization and anti-communist attitudes – attitudes that appeared regressive to feminists and leftists alike.

Many feminists perceived Europe as a status for Ukraine that would increase gender parity and protect the rights of LGBTQ+ people. They therefore saw themselves as more representative of Europe than were radical, anti-feminist, anti-gay, right-wing activists because feminists had always supported these ideas. Their first response to their own marginalization on Maidan was one of shock. As Maria, a feminist activist, told me, "It was interesting that these right-wing people, who pursued us because we supported LGBT, because we did some feminist initiatives, they really wanted to get to Europe." She felt that the majority of the protesters did not understand what might be called the *social* values of Europe, in which tolerance of difference is the norm, as is a plurality of political opinions. "What, did you forget?" Maria asked. "These aren't your values. Why are you here? We need to be here, and not you. This was more our theme." She felt that feminist activists better understood what Europe would actually mean for Ukraine as a nation, so their presence was more authentically European than those who were protesting for an economic deal.

Feminist criticisms of the Europe being referenced on Maidan diverged from those of the majority of the Maidan protest body. Here, we can perhaps best see the ways "Europe" was a contested symbol on Maidan (see Verdery 1996, chap. 5). To feminists, the establishment of gender equality legislation and practices would move Ukraine closer to Europe, not only symbolically but also in actuality. The dominant voices on Maidan, however, were focused more on presenting the protests as representative of Ukraine's democratic national voice, which should be included in the definition of "Europe." For most protesters, European "values" meant respect for the sovereignty of the Ukrainian nation, however its citizens defined it. For many Maidan protesters, that nation was based on a certain conceptualization of Ukraine that did not allow space for discussion of gender equality. This resulted in a form of masculinity that dominated the protest space on Maidan and limited women's choices how to participate (Khromeychuk 2018).[1]

Feminist Suspects: "Western" and "European" Narratives

In the years between Ukraine's independence and the Euromaidan protests, feminism was most often met with suspicion. Despite several high-profile historical figures – such as Lesia Ukrainka and Ol'ha Kobylians'ka – who are considered essential to Ukraine's national claims, and the critical role played by women's organizations in nation-based organizing in the nineteenth and twentieth centuries (Bohachevsky-Chomiak 1988), feminism as an ideology or activist movement was most often seen as a threat to nation-building. During the years of the Soviet Union, the Communist Party dominated the narrative about gender-based politics, and gender parity was mobilized as part of the global socialist revolution (Ghodsee 2018; see also Channell-Justice 2020a). After the end of state socialism, international organizations brought feminism and gender-based activism to the region. Because of this connection with funding for women's and civil society NGOs in the post-independence period, feminism was often seen as an elite discourse detached from the local context, a problem North American-based scholars have addressed (Funk and Mueller 1993; Ghodsee 2004; Hemment 2007; Johnson and Robinson 2007; Phillips 2008). In the early 1990s, Nanette Funk documented the problematic hierarchy between "East" and "West" discourses about feminism in which, as she writes, "Western feminist discourse is hegemonic in feminism," and which risked "the suppression and distortion of post-communist women's concerns" (Funk and Mueller 1993, 319). This remains a significant problem for leftist-feminist activists in Ukraine. Many have been educated or have spent extensive time outside Ukraine, in Europe or North America, and have read feminist texts that originate in these places, often in their original languages. With the spread of internet access, more activists spend time finding contemporary feminist materials, from blogs to Facebook groups, available online from sources around the world. At the time of Funk's writing, the author was concerned about the possible collaboration between Eastern and Western women, whose communication seemed to exist on different planes. Now, post-communist feminists face the problem of translating these still-dominant Western models of feminism for a local context.

The family and domestic sphere, considered one of the few sites protected from state intervention during communism, has remained contentious since independence. As such, protection of the traditional family is often mobilized as integral for national development (Gal and Kligman 2000; Guenther 2011). When feminism is understood to be an imported project funded by North American or European donors who do not have the same national priorities as Ukrainians, then feminism becomes a threat to national development. Even women who might reject traditional family roles are often hesitant to embrace the idea of feminism, in part because of the narrow definitions of feminist issues that historically have been provided by what Alex Hrycak (2006) calls "foundation feminism." Further, the word "gender" itself is an adaptation of the English word into the local language (*hender* in Ukrainian),[2] which reinforces its distance from post-socialist women.

Leftist feminists are placed in a dually challenging position: engaged with Western feminist discourses, seen as imports and foreign to Ukrainians, while their ideas are still associated with state socialism because of connections to Soviet-era gender equality policies. These Soviet policies were more often a co-optation of feminist ideas rather than genuine feminist reform (Ashwin 2000; Goven 1993; Verdery 1996, chap. 3), but they now discredited leftists' attempts to promote feminism.

When state socialism ended, new national narratives were prominent counter-histories to Soviet narratives. Many of these narratives returned to a traditionalized view of women, men, and the family in which men were public, cultural actors who built and protected the state for the feminized nation. Where Soviet discourses attempted to erase social differences in gender by pretending women and men were biologically the same, post-Soviet national narratives relied on these "natural" differences between women and men, which are often reinforced in post-socialism to reverse the damage done by Soviet-era positions on gender equality (Goven 1993). Thus, "feminism becomes socialist and can be attacked as antinational" (Verdery 1996, 82), limiting possibilities for both women and men in post-socialist gender behaviours.

This process shows how decommunization is deeply linked to gender norms – in other words, an anti-communist national ideology that relies directly on traditional ideas about gender in order to work.

Because ideas about women's equality are so deeply associated with the communist period, only a reversal of these notions can be truly anti-communist. This further explains post-socialist women's own propensity to consider male breadwinners in a positive light, as it reflects their perception of a successfully decommunized family structure. Such ideas are contrary to pan-European gender equality projects that encourage non-discrimination policies for women as well as equal pay; however, these might also be seen as problematic because of their reliance on major state interventions in order to implement such plans – an apparent reflection of the socialist state.

At its worst, this "restoration of patriarchy" takes the form of "STOP Gender" or "Anti-Gender" campaigns, found across eastern Europe and documented in Poland, Ukraine, and Russia (Johnson 2017). Using the term "genderism" and driven by the Roman Catholic Church in Poland, this right-wing mobilization aimed "to demonize gender as an enemy of the family, to link it with pedophilia and to equate it with moral chaos" (Graff 2014, 432). In Ukraine, the STOP Gender campaign also claims to stand in favour of protecting children and family values, suggesting that gender-based policies are "bound to result in the dictatorship of a pro-homosexual minority over the tradition-oriented majority" (Rubchak 2015, 14). This type of language has remained popular among right-wing groups in Ukraine organizing against LGBTQ+ Pride Parades across Ukraine since 2014. In 2017, Right Sector suggested on Facebook that the parade would destroy the Ukrainian traditional family and cultural heritage, calling it "Ukraino-phobic" and asking for a counterprotest to protect "honour, dignity, and the fatherland (*Bat'kivshchyna*)." Gender-based policies, including non-discrimination legislation protecting women as well as homosexual and transgender people, are presented in these campaigns as unnatural and non-native stances. As these policies are linked with European integration, then, pro-gender or feminist stances become antithetical to a pro-nation and anti-communist position.

Narratives of Ukrainian Women's Activism

In contemporary Ukraine, feminism's divisiveness is often understood in the context of the continuing national project, in which the status of a unified Ukrainian nation remains tenuous at best. Although feminists have been active throughout Ukraine's history (see Bohachevsky-Chomiak 1988; Kebalo 2011), feminist and other gender-based issues have often been seen as secondary to the establishment of a lasting, independent nation-state (Kebalo 2007). Women who choose to focus first on feminist issues – even if they *also* consider themselves Ukrainians and/or nationalists – are often stigmatized because they reject the primacy of the nation, even as they continue to try to reconcile the two ideas (Zhurzhenko 2001).

According to many scholars of women's movements in Ukraine, feminism and nationalism inherently have been linked throughout the existence of women's organizations in Ukraine. Nationalist and nation-building groups from the pre-Soviet period in Ukraine failed to integrate women's liberation into the national struggle, even as women were fighting for both gender equality and national sovereignty (Bohachevsky-Chomiak 1988). Although Sovietizing narratives about women and feminism attempted to detach the historical connections between feminism and nationalism in Ukraine, the problems of balancing these political perspectives have resurfaced since Ukraine's independence in 1991. This is at least in part because of the negative backlash about feminism that has been dominant in Ukraine since the end of state socialism (Channell-Justice 2020a).

In Ukraine, a retraditionalization of gendered national narratives has been aided by long-standing matriarchal myths about Ukraine as a nation. The pagan goddess *Berehynia*, or hearth mother, protects the Ukrainian language and culture (Rubchak 2001; see also Pavlychko 2002) and represents the nation itself. Rubchak has interpreted the *Berehynia* model as a basis for Ukrainian indigenous feminism: she concludes that traditional Ukrainian attitudes about gender are based on equal contributions of men and women, even if those roles are understood as inherently different (the traditional man being a warrior, protecting Ukraine's borders (Rubchak 2001, 153). Alternatively, following Solomea Pavlychko (2002), leftist feminist critic Tamara Zlobina calls this *"Berehynia* model" a "conservative discourse about returning to one's roots, national traditions, spirituality, and morality" (Zlobina 2015, 75) – a model quite explicitly linked to women's roles in reproducing a Ukrainian nation, both biologically and spiritually (see also Verdery 1996, chap. 3; Yuval-Davis 1997). Such female-gendered representations of the nation are common to many national ideologies and should not be understood as a "feminist" achievement, particularly as they tend to create a binary model in which the "state" is seen as masculine and the repository of power.

Leftist feminists such as Zlobina see this interest in women's relationship to the nation and the *"Berehynia* model" as one of two bad options for women in post-socialist Ukraine, the other being what she terms the "Barbie model," which promotes the "commercialization and exploitation of women's bodies" (Zlobina 2015, 75; from Kis 2002, who herself draws from Pavlychko's framing [Bulakh 2015, 208n10]). Both models are so focused on women's relationship to men that they foreclose the possibility of the development of a feminist consciousness. Zlobina's view encourages a consideration of feminism's divisiveness in the context of the continuing national project and as a contributing factor to economic instability. The status of a unified Ukrainian nation has been threatened by recent economic challenges and unpredictability. Feminism, which presents alternatives to women's roles as caretakers, reproducers, and supporters of men, is perceived to contribute to the uncertainty of the nation and its economic productivity. This intertwining of nation and economy helps reinforce women's subordinate roles, because they are expected not only to reproduce the nation, but also *not* to gain economic independence (Kis and Bureychak 2015, 136), as this would threaten the precarious balance in which Ukrainians find themselves.

Pre-Maidan Feminist Efforts

The struggle to reconcile feminism with these perceived threats to Ukrainian national unity has made it difficult for feminists to translate their views for a broader audience. Leftist and radical feminists in contemporary Ukraine represent feminisms that draw from Ukrainian women's history as well as from globalized feminist perspectives, all while attempting to reject exclusionary and essentialist tendencies. These feminists combine theoretical engagement along with thoroughly organized protests, street demonstrations, concerts, educational series, and conferences. But despite general support for feminist groups such as Feminist Offensive (*Feministychna ofenzyva*, FO), leftist women still find it difficult to create safe spaces for themselves in general leftist activism.

FO, linked to leftist groups and founded in 2010, attempted to bring attention to women's issues and gender discrimination during the Yanukovych era. Its most recognized work was its continual protests on 8 March, International Women's Day. Each year, FO held feminist parades and demonstrations, attempting to bring a feminist critique of women's roles to the holiday, which since Soviet times had focused on appreciating women's beauty and contributions to the family, usually by presenting women with flowers, candy, and cards. FO's goal was to make International Women's Day a moment to bring attention to women's struggles around the world, and particularly in Ukraine, a goal that continues today. Although FO officially disbanded in 2013, feminists continued to organize street demonstrations for 8 March, especially in Kyiv, all with large numbers of participants.

FO came up in interviews with many activists as a reference point for how leftists thought about feminism. Most activists – men and women – were conversant in general ideas about gender equality, but

the implementation of parity among genders was often more challenging than people wanted to admit. While many female activists pointed
out inequality and discrimination in leftist groups, male activists regularly diminished or disregarded these claims. Male activists often
felt that, because they were associated with feminists and supported
groups like FO, they did not behave in sexist ways in their own lives.
But discussions with feminist activists in various settings before the
Maidan protests tell a different story.

At the student organizing camp I attended in the summer of 2012, feminists organized a "gender block" discussion session in which women
gathered together to discuss problems they had faced as women. These
issues ranged from discrimination at universities to pressure to look
a certain way to annoyance that they were responsible for most of the
cooking at the camp. One feminist representative of the gender block
brought these issues to the group of activists at the camp, suggesting
that everyone – even those who identified as feminists – think about
how to fix these issues at the local level. Although it was important to
create this space within the camp for women to discuss their issues,
the response to the gender block during a general assessment of the
camp was telling. Many male activists claimed they hadn't seen any
discrimination or inequality; others claimed that any sexism present
at the camp was not done on purpose but rather a result of living in a
sexist world. It was largely women who pushed the men at the camp to
really think about sexism: one activist suggested that the group hold a
workshop at the beginning of future camps to recognize sexist practices
so people could improve their behaviour.

Many activists I interviewed before the protests on Maidan began
admitted that there were ways leftist groups reproduced normative
gender ideas in their relationships, even if they felt that they were more
aware of feminism and even considered themselves to be feminists. I
asked student activists if there was a difference in being a woman or
a man in the student movement. One male activist responded in this
way: "Of course there is, because in society there is a difference, so in
the student movement there is a difference. But for the left, or for the
anarchist movement, this difference means less. I've heard people talk
about Priama Diia [the independent student union], that it's maybe
the most progressive organization in Ukraine." Another male activist,
Petro, was rather thoughtful about how these patriarchal views were
reproduced even among leftist groups:

> There is no fundamental [gender] difference. But there is generally a com-
> mon language that comes out in the activism of people of the male sex.

There has always been an argument from that point of view that women are more passive, less politicized, less thoughtful about social problems. These patriarchal relations are often reproduced even in the organizations that think to oppose them. Priama Diia is a case in which the number of women activists (*aktyvistok*) is comparable to the number of male activists (*aktyvistiv*). But outside of this, in society, there isn't much of this. In groups like Feminist Offensive, with other anarcho-feminists, there's more of an understanding – what is sexism, that it is present very often in language, in our groups, and we have to pay attention to it, we also have to fight it.

Tonya, profiled in chapter 2, spoke explicitly about her experiences with sexism as a student activist, stating that it was up to female activists "not to allow yourself to be humiliated … and to make people pay attention to this, say it's discrimination."

Although many feminists were present on Maidan, and leftist men in general supported women's fight for space on the square, it was not until a return visit to Ukraine in 2016 that I heard female activists say they felt as though there was a real shift among male activists in terms of their understanding discrimination. That summer, many of them had participated in the online flashmob "I am not afraid to say" (*ya ne boiusia skazaty*), in which women spoke out online about their experiences of discrimination, harassment, and violence (Antonova 2017; Aripova and Johnson 2018). One woman told me that the male activists in her circle had understood neither the prevalence of sexual violence nor their own contributions to women's marginalization before the flashmob. But a general fragmentation of leftists after Maidan (discussed in the following chapter and in Channell-Justice 2019c) makes it difficult to assess whether any fundamental shifts have been made among leftist groups to adopt a more effective feminist position.

Leftists were clearly concerned with feminism before the Maidan protests began in 2013. It was apparent from the beginning that leftists would support feminist actions on Maidan and that, for leftists, such a presence would be an important intervention. Leftists and feminists regularly worked together on the square to present feminist ideas, despite the challenges they faced to create space for themselves.

Reinforcing the Nation

Maidan had the potential to be a site for the contestation of gender norms, as women were motivated to participate for a variety of reasons (Nikolayenko and DeCasper 2018). Women participated in various capacities, sometimes blatantly claiming a feminist position to draw attention to gender inequality. Ultimately, however, hypermilitarized masculinity won out over more balanced gender roles, limiting both women and men in their expected contributions to the protests and pushing women even further from the front lines. Even after the end of the protests, women tended to remain in caretaker roles in volunteer organizations. Research on women's volunteer roles in the conflict zones in eastern Ukraine reflects this marginalization in its title, "Invisible Battalion" (Hrytsenko, Kvit, and Martsenyuk 2016).[3]

Scholars have shown the links among gender, nation, and militarization in national ideology (Yuval-Davis 1997), and post-socialist spaces are no exception. In an essay analysing the gendered politics of nationalism and its links with the militarization of masculine identities, Cynthia Enloe uses the example of Serbian militias in the 1990s to explore the process through which men and nationalized or ethnic violence become linked. The militias that men volunteered for, she suggests, were "micro-cultures" (Enloe 2004) in which masculinity, ethnicity, and military participation combined to create a gendered politics of privileging male soldiers and creating women's roles to support this type of masculinity. The creation of *sotnia*, or volunteer defence brigades, on Maidan to protect the nation resonates with these ideas about the relationship between gender and nation. These *sotnia* regularly evoked historical ideals of Ukrainian masculinity, drawing on images of Cossacks of the fifteenth through the eighteenth centuries who fought for freedom from Russian imperialism in proto-state formations organized around a military masculine ideal that actively excluded and denigrated women (Bureychak and Petrenko 2014; see figure 6.2).

Similarly, posters for the general Maidan self-defence organization reproduced images resonant of the Ukrainian Insurgent Army (UPA). Although women were active participants in the UPA (Havryshko 2018; Kis 2012), the image most widespread on Maidan was a masculine one: embodied in the face of Stepan Bandera, leader of one faction of the Organization of Ukrainian Nationalists, the Ukrainian male militant was unafraid and prepared to protect the (feminine) Ukrainian nation. The few images of women as fighters that circulated on Maidan represented an idealized female warrior. The most prominent was that of a female freedom fighter (*Banderivka*), based on an image by Ihor Pereklita from 2007, circulated on Maidan in earnest but analysed by Bureychak and Petrenko (2014) as "anarcho-nationalist sarcasm or irony" (figure 6.3).[4] Outside this and a few other sexualized female fighter images, the only prominent woman featured around Maidan was Yulia Tymoshenko, the imprisoned opposition leader.

The images of women presented on Maidan reflected the limited options for women to participate in the protests. In general, women were

Figure 6.2. Men dressed as Cossacks riding down Khreshchatyk
Source: Author's photograph.

expected to work in kitchens or inside the buildings occupied around the square. The images of female fighters were unrealistic and idealized. At the same time, men were expected to be like the Cossacks or Stepan Bandera, who gave their lives fighting for Ukraine. Men who preferred supportive roles were entering into a feminized realm. Thus, the gender roles produced on Maidan were limiting to both women and men.[5] Leftist participants were critical of these limitations from early on in the protests, as reflected in a major feminist event, Women's Solidarity Night.

Vam treba zhinky! (You need women!)

On 28 November 2013, after a dinner at the Fulbright offices in central Kyiv, I walked to the main square to have a look around. I discovered several activists I knew right in front of the independence monument treating Havryil, who had borne the brunt of a tear gas attack. Having missed the attack itself, I read his thoughts about it on Facebook that evening:

> Today I went to Maidan together with comrades from [Feminist] Offensive. We distributed leaflets, spoke and debated with people. We held some social-critical signs that called for joining Europe in a way that would be

Figure 6.3. Ihor Pereklita's *Banderivka* poster taped on the independence monument
Source: Author's photograph.

reasonable and profitable for everyone, and for women in particular. Subsequently, neo-Nazi *provokatory* attacked us. My eyes were filled with tear gas. People and kind policemen washed my eyes.

Havryil still managed to conclude his post with a positive message, that several students from a Kyiv university had joined their protest and that he'd spoken with them about student issues. But this evening was part of a string of negative responses to feminist protests and signs. The responses had ranged from curiosity and occasional support to a man lecturing our protest group about how men are the head of the family, that feminism encourages the feminization of men, who can't be the heads of families if they are emasculated. But the violence against feminists that week – recall the example of a young woman physically assaulted by a man with a metal pipe because of her feminist sign – led feminists, like leftists, to reassess their presence on the square.

Some women used the open microphones around the square to bring up the subject of violence against women, but these small interventions did not have a wide-ranging effect. Women activists wanted to take an active role in the protests, but they felt that they were being denied that opportunity. Riot police had attempted to storm the occupied square on 11 December, and the calls for people to come to Maidan that circulated on social media specifically asked for women to stay home. In response, feminist activists opted to intervene with a Women's Solidarity Night (*Nich zhinochoï solidarnosti*) on 12 December (figure 6.4). Along with drummers from Rhythms of Resistance (ROR, *Rytmy sprotyvu*), a protest percussion group, a dozen or so leftist activists gathered at 1 a.m. near the Trade Unions building on Maidan. The organizers intended the event to bring attention to the ways women's roles had been limited, especially in their exclusion from defending the protest camp (Khromeychuk 2018). They used slogans such as "Night Maidan, you need women!" (*Nichnyi Maidan, vam treba zhinky!*), suggesting that women should also be helping in the camp overnight, rather than only during the day when the camp was unlikely to face violence. The organizers turned the common Maidan slogan, "Glory to Ukraine, glory to the heroes" (*Slava Ukraïni, heroiam slava*) into a feminist chant: "Glory to the heroines, to the heroines glory!" (*Slava heroïnam, heroïnam slava!*). One organizer also referenced the police attack the night before: "I couldn't be here [because I'm a woman], but it's my country, too," she said.

The group first set up around midnight in front of St Michael's Gate on the side of the protest camp opposite from the independence monument, near a kitchen and clothing distribution station. A barricade made of wooden stakes, plywood boards, and snow had been built to protect the centre of the camp, and bonfires in the area helped fight against the frigid night air. Around ten people led the demonstration with ROR, whose players drummed upbeat rhythms and created a backdrop for feminist slogans. The men at the barricades responded positively to the demonstration, enjoying the drumbeats and encouraging the participants to continue. But as we moved down Khreshchatyk towards the city hall, many other people became annoyed with the noisy demonstration, as it was the middle of the night and people were trying to sleep.

Although the demonstration was largely well received, it was difficult to tell if the men at the barricades were actually listening to the message about needing women at the Night Maidan. I spent the rest of the night there with Natalia, one of the drummers, who wasn't sure if the people who encouraged us understood the basic message of Women's Solidarity Night, especially what we were saying about women's participation. We visited the occupied city hall once the Women's Solidarity Night had dispersed, and we found, as expected, women working in the kitchens while men slept in the main hall. Rather than create a space for gender equality, Maidan reinforced existing gender

Figure 6.4. Women's Solidarity Night
Source: Author's photograph.

roles that placed women in the domestic and private sphere and men on the barricades.[6] Reflective of other instances of the devaluation of women's and feminist activism in relation to the activism and political participation of men (Sperling, Marx Feree, and Risman 2001), feminist criticisms were pushed out of the shared, public space of Maidan and into the semi-public but extremely self-contained world of social networks. Organized around initiatives such as "Half the Maidan" (*Polovyna Maidanu*): Women's Voices of Protest," a Facebook group created to promote feminist activities and women-focused initiatives, the diverse feminist voices that had been present early on Maidan retracted into virtual discussions.[7] In the years since Maidan, online spaces have become essential for activist movements, but at the time the action was taking place on the square, and feminists felt strongly that their physical presence was indispensable.

Thus, as with leftist activists, feminists found creative ways to continue to engage in the public space of the square. While some attempted to integrate themselves in the protests by creating women's self-defence brigades, others focused on women-centred protest events that could not be targeted for their feminist interventions. One example took place on International Women's Day, 8 March 2014. Russian soldiers had invaded the Crimean Peninsula just weeks before, so women in Kyiv held an event to support Crimean women's responses to the invasion. Drummers from ROR were present on the sunny, crisp day, and women from across age groups, faiths, and political backgrounds joined the peaceful event. At a table, participants could send messages of support on postcards or record a video message. I was encouraged to write something "nice" – messages of love, health, happiness – because it was such a difficult time for women in Crimea. Women held signs in Russian, Ukrainian, and Tatar languages with phrases including "East-West together," "We support the women of Crimea," and "We love you." One activist, Hanna, stated, "We are showing solidarity from the women of Maidan to the women in Crimea who are standing against Russian armed aggression" (figure 6.5).

Here, a women's action was detached from feminism, and because the invasion of Crimea was so widely condemned, the gender angle of this demonstration was just another aspect of the peaceful protest. Many feminists were present at the event, but it was not an explicitly feminist gathering. Rather, it was an extension of an anti-Russia, anti-war demonstration around the Crimean invasion, and it was a convenient way to mark what was already a women's holiday. But the event reflected one of leftist feminists' major criticisms of the treatment of women on Maidan: women received extensive recognition for their presence, but their participation was not really decided on their own terms.

"Participation, partnership, and the future": Failures of Equality Discourses

In mid-May, a photo exhibition entitled "Women of Maidan" came to the main square, presented on posters around the independence monument. To open the event, several speakers from international funding institutions, including the head of Fulbright, Marta Kolomayets, came to recognize women's participation and representation on Maidan.[8] The photos focused on women's care work in kitchens, in occupied buildings, and at medical points. One woman, a member of a Ukrainian diaspora organization, specifically touted women's "participation, partnership, and future" (*uchast', partnerstvo, i maibutnie*). On the one hand, this recognition was important, because women were essential participants in the protests and would otherwise have remained in the background, in the private spaces, while the men on the physical square were credited with doing the work of the protests.

On the other hand, it was clear that these speakers did not have any awareness about the claims Ukrainian feminists were making on

Figure 6.5. Women of Maidan to the Women of Crimea, 8 March 2014
Source: Author's photograph.

Maidan. They did not understand that feminists had been criticizing women's lack of control over their participation on Maidan since November. Maria, who earlier described Maidan's European values as "more our theme," also attended the event, and we discussed it later. She told me that the international funding agencies seemed out of touch, not recognizing that Ukraine had its own feminist presence and discussions. She felt that these women, most of whom did not live in Ukraine, were making value judgments about women's participation on Maidan without really understanding what women were contributing to the protests – or what they were criticizing. At the photo exhibition opening, Maria gave her own speech, in which she stated outright that sexism and gender-based discrimination were present on Maidan, and that we should not ignore these because we would rather think that women are equal participants (see Popova 2014). In her speech, Maria stated:

> The experience of Maidan has been really important for making concepts like "self-organization" understood, we know what it entails and we can do it … Not everyone was so happy about everything all the time on Maidan, it wasn't this perfect thing. There were xenophobic slogans, and it was far from wonderful. Many times women's voices didn't have the

chance to be heard. So we created the *Sotnia* to unite women and women's society on Maidan. And in this way we can change the views of people. We're not just sandwiches, we're not just *berehynia* (*my ne til'ky kanapky, my ne til'ky berehyni*). It's just a shame that it happened so late. We have to keep struggling against sexism and discrimination.[9]

Pointing to the women's self-defence brigades that grew out of women's criticisms of gender-role limitations, Maria reflected on how women fought for a place on the square and that gender equality had not been achieved. Indeed, some others present thanked Maria for having the courage to bring up sexism and discrimination, even as the event was meant to praise women.

Maria was taken aback by the way these women, based outside Ukraine but clearly invested in Ukraine's future, could have been so detached from actual feminist discussions in Ukraine. "Mainly," she said, "it's that women that are working on a women's program, in an international funding program, can say something like that. I didn't believe it." She couldn't believe that these women had such a stereotypical attitude towards Ukrainians, that they were simply passive, beautiful, flower-crown-wearing *berehynia* women who should just be content with being visible. Maria had assumed that these Western women would be supportive of women's efforts to carve out diverse spaces for themselves and more engaged with discourses about anti-discrimination and gender equality. After fighting so long for the European values of feminism and equality, and after facing violence on Maidan for her beliefs, Maria was disappointed that people representing the West assumed equality had been achieved.

Maria's surprise came in part from her understanding of what feminism is. Like other feminists, and like young leftists, much activist discourse comes from North American and European sources – for instance, many activists were inspired by Occupy Wall Street, which they followed closely via the internet. Feminists, even those who studied in Ukraine, were not necessarily spending most of their time reading about the historical existence of women's groups in Ukraine. Instead, much of their understanding about feminism came from elsewhere; Maria and others expected women who came to Ukraine from the places that produced contemporary feminism to represent precisely that feminism. When those women did not, Maria began to question whether such symbols as "Europe" and "democracy" actually did reflect a stronger commitment to women's rights, as she and many others had promoted in the early days of Maidan. That these women seemed more inclined to support a national ideology that relied on decommunization through the rejuvenation of traditional gender roles challenged Maria's relationship with feminism as a "European value."

In a context in which ideas of feminism and gender equality in political representation are construed as threats to national stability, discourses praising women for supporting roles, like the ones circulated at this exhibition, support local gender-based inequalities. Thus, feminists like Maria were limited not only by the accepted gender roles produced on Maidan that women had to adopt in order to participate actively in the protests, but also by Western conceptualizations of Ukrainian women that encouraged them to accept these limitations. Such events changed Ukrainian feminists' views that "European values" were, in reality, based on tolerance and equality, as they had claimed earlier on during the protests.

The *Zhinocha Sotnia*: Women on the Front Line

One main initiative through which women carved out active space for themselves on Maidan was also the most controversial among Ukrainian feminists. In response to the presence of men's military groups, women created their own *sotnia* (brigades) that theoretically would be ready to fight on the front lines if needed. At least five Women's Brigades (*Zhinocha Sotnia*) cropped up in the days and weeks following the violence in February 2014 (Onuch and Martsenyuk 2014).[10] One particular brigade, founded by feminist and labour activists, called the Ol'ha Kobylians'ka Brigade (after the late nineteenth-early twentieth-century Ukrainian feminist), was championed by Western observers as a successful feminist project (Phillips 2014; Rubchak 2014); I have discussed the brigade in detail elsewhere (Channell-Justice 2017). Here, I use this example to explore the way Maidan created a vibrant discussion among feminist groups in Ukraine about how best to pursue their goals in a context of war.

From its early stages, the Women's Brigade began as a Facebook group following the violence that broke out in February. According to Valia, one of its founders, the Facebook group was started as a joke – she and a friend were sitting in a Maidan kitchen making sandwiches, and she said, "We need a women's brigade!" That would be the only way for women to get out of the kitchen. They wanted to criticize women's lack of roles on Maidan and the militarized structure of the protests. Soon, people were asking about it as if it was a serious project, and about fifteen to twenty people attended their earliest planning meetings. "For me," she said, "it was really a surprise that so many women felt the need for it … For me it became an indicator that yes, we have to do more. Not academic feminism, or some kind of pop-feminism, like the usual example that every woman considers herself a feminist when she says, 'I don't have to cook you *borshch* every day!'" The group organized lectures, film screenings, and self-defence trainings in occupied buildings around Maidan, allowing like-minded women to make connections with one another and share their experiences of discrimination and sexism.

Yet the Ol'ha Kobylians'ka Women's Brigade provoked serious criticism, most notably from other feminists in Ukraine, including Mariya Mayerchyk, a well-known feminist academic from Kharkiv in eastern Ukraine. Having previously worked with many of its members through the Feminist Offensive, Mayerchyk criticized the Women's Brigade for adopting militarized and right-wing structures and rhetoric:

> Inspired by the ideas of justice and equality, these activists planned to demonstrate that women were of equal importance at the Maidan. Then, according to the rules of the genre, their actions took a turn in the direction of right-wing discursive logic. The Women's Company ... used in its very name the rhetoric of military structures, announced its right to carry out its mission on the barricades, and began teaching self-defence classes ... And even though women activists say they are against violence, this has become ... a confirmation of their second-rate status as *women-wives-mothers-sisters-comrades-peacekeepers-helpers*. Women participating in this initiative weren't able to come up with consistent war criticism, or to denounce the destructive role that military hierarchies play in peaceful resistance. In fact, they did quite the opposite: they attempted to "meet" the male standards – *power and barricades* – and became themselves the mechanisms of reinforcing this androcentrism. (Mayerchyk 2014, emphasis in original)

Mayerchyk criticized precisely the *sotnia*'s efforts to vernacularize or translate feminism into the militarized language of Maidan. She challenged the notion that women should have to behave like men in order to be valued, which, in her view, does not actually challenge male dominance.

Mayerchyk's criticism and the existence of the brigade provoked a lively and generative debate around feminism on Maidan and later. One feminist who lived in L'viv felt that the impression that women should be relegated to the kitchen during a revolution had been challenged by women's participation in the brigade during Maidan, even affecting people "who are very far from feminists." However, the Women's Brigade gave feminists "a very popular image of a strong, eroticized, militarized woman who participated in revolution and it's actually the opposite of what we want," she said (figure 6.6).

Figure 6.6. Image of an eroticized, militarized woman
Source: Author's photograph.

Others, however, shared Mayerchyk's criticism of the Women's Brigade. Ania, a feminist living outside Ukraine who watched the events from a distance, felt that women created the brigade only because of their exclusion: "You are pushed to do something, at least something, to show we are here," she said in an interview (in English).

> A lot of people were so proud, there were numerous reports about [the brigade]. But I see it as going along with the only option which people think is left, which is reproducing the militaristic initiatives. At some point when there was such a big threat of physical violence, I feel completely disarmed, literally and symbolically, because any other possibility of having discussions or any other ways are completely devalued. If you are not a man, if you don't have a gun, if you don't have stuff to protect yourself. This is war, and you cannot do anything unless you are participating.

Ania was correct in suggesting that Maidan devalued non-military, non-violent ways of discussing difference and inequality, as early feminist experiences in the protests showed. Feminists adopted masculine, military rhetoric in order to make women's equality seem less threatening and something that could be integrated naturally into the post-Maidan gender order. As an alternative, other leftist groups preferred to avoid vernacularization by creating what they saw as non-ideological initiatives to help protesters. As I discussed earlier, leftists faced similar conundrums in terms of how to deal with the dominance of violent discourses on Maidan, organizing non-violent, support-oriented initiatives rather than participating directly in violence.

Although some women, including those who were involved in the Ol'ha Kobylians'ka Brigade, have channelled their efforts into brigades participating in the conflict in eastern Ukraine (Khromeychuk 2018), others have focused more on the conversation that the brigade generated among Ukrainian feminists. This is best reflected in a conversation I had with Valia from the brigade in June, when members were visiting eastern Ukraine to speak to other women about Maidan and women's and anti-war activism. She described that the brigade had evolved out of the "practical initiatives" of Feminist Offensive, and they were able to meet with the more "theoretical" part of FO in Kharkiv (including Mariya Mayerchyk). Valia understood that the Kharkiv feminists were responding negatively to the brigade based on press coverage of the group, not on the actual goals of its members, and once they were able to meet and discuss these goals, there was no conflict between the two groups. Valia described the rapidity with which the brigade formed, mentioning that they had no documents; they simply had time to create the group and hold events in its name. "We didn't have the chance to think about what we're doing, reflect on it," she said. "Even when we write [about it], we don't have a unified idea." In other words, the perception that the Women's Brigade had caused some kind of rift among feminists in Ukraine was a misunderstanding; instead, these women had always known that there is not only one Ukrainian feminism. While criticism of women's participation in fighting remains, so does the robust feminism generated on Maidan around the questions of self-organization.

Conclusion: Feminism without the State

At the end of Maidan, feminists in Ukraine were left in a precarious position. There seemed to be perhaps less widespread acceptance among politicians of gender equality and anti-discrimination legislation from the EU Association Agreement (eventually signed in June 2014). Leftist feminists realized that their ideas of "European" and "Western" discourses about equality were not grounded in a radical commitment to real political representation but only in the acts of recognition and praise for being present. Both feminist and leftist activists have been more focused on generating effective local initiatives, which fall outside the realm of the state as well as of European policies, to improve their own lives based on feminist and leftist principles.

The shift to self-organization is an essential part of the Ukrainian state's move from communism to neoliberalism. Under communism, women's and men's roles, and their potential to participate in politics, were defined by the Communist Party. Self-organization was not a realistic option for any kind of political activism, including feminism. Following the collapse of the socialist state, however, political participation and self-organization have come to be seen as effective mechanisms to challenge state policy and practice. At the same time, these projects accept the post-Euromaidan neoliberal state's limitations as fact. By attempting to fill the gaps left by the state, these groups are allowing the state *not* to be accountable for gender equality and promoting non-discrimination, an accountability that is supposed to be part of full European integration. This focus on self-organization shifts the burden off the state and onto ordinary citizens to make changes among themselves that, so far, have no promise of being implemented at a higher level.

Although discourses about women and gender have been present throughout Ukraine's history, feminists remain marginalized in the political sphere. This is in part because the issues they present challenge traditional gender norms in which men hold positions of political and economic power and women reproduce and protect the Ukrainian nation. The feminists featured in this chapter are also associated with leftist activists, which further marginalizes their political position because it encourages a view that they support socialist-era notions of gender equality through state policy. In many ways, they do adhere to such notions; in their view, however, this conceptualization of how to enact better gender policies is linked to a progressive Europe rather than a regression to state socialism.

Although the Maidan mobilizations became, over time, a space for leftist activists to find new ways to reformulate their ideology in order to participate in the protests, feminists were less successful. Even when women defined their own ways to participate, such as in the form of a Women's Brigade, they were limited by already-existing discourses about national ideology and political participation, as defined by men. Only when feminist activists adapted to the protests in the same way as leftists – that is, through a focus on self-organization – did they finally vernacularize their positions as feminists who also support Ukraine.

Such a trend has become extremely prominent in Ukraine since the end of Maidan and the beginning of the conflict in the eastern regions. While self-organization began with leftist and feminist initiatives, it has become inextricably linked with processes of decommunization. Because self-organization was not an obvious option under the communist regime, it has now become part of the arsenal of political tactics that proves Ukraine's position as democratic and European. This is not necessarily a great leap away from feminists' original conceptualizations of Europe that were so at odds with those of the majority of protesters. But this linking of self-organization and decommunization has contributed to the further neoliberalization of the post-Maidan Ukrainian state, leaving feminists to continue to fight for gender equality without the help of the state.

Volunteerism after Maidan

In 2020, I had a long conversation with Andriy, one of the leftists profiled in chapter 2, about what had happened in the years since Maidan ended. In 2013 and 2014, Andriy felt it was important to participate in the protests, even if he wasn't sure what would come of it in the end. With a few years' distance, however, we could reflect on what had happened. In his view, the left became even weaker as a political force, and the powers of the state – and the sense of the state's obligation to its citizens – continued to shrink. When I asked why he thought leftist politics had not gained any momentum, even though people were still being disappointed by state actors, he responded,

> It's a combination of the fact that, for some people who tend to be more politically mobilized, everything left wing is associated with the Soviet Union, as it has always been, it never really went away. If anything, Maidan just generated a wave of anti-communism. And … just the fact that Ukraine is a society where people don't trust other people, you don't trust government, you don't trust political organizations, you don't trust them to represent you, that's why hardly any movement has any popular support because people don't do that stuff. They're not members of anything, you trust your narrow circle of friends and family, and … I think it's hard for any movement, it's not just the left that doesn't have any sort of popular base, broad support. I mean, all the NGOs in Ukraine rely on grant funding, and if you take that away, there's going to be nothing left.

Andriy's perception was that the momentum generated by the left during Maidan, as well as other unified political movements, had largely fizzled out since the protests ended. In part, this was because the post-Maidan Ukrainian state became more neoliberal and less reliable, leading people to turn towards narrow, trustworthy circles to self-organize to meet their needs. While the expansion of self-organization is directly related to leftist participation on Maidan, self-organization has also become depoliticized as it becomes more distant from its leftist roots.

How has the post-Maidan period solidified the processes outlined in the introduction and illustrated throughout this book? As neoliberal developments have ensured the shrinking of state bodies – and concomitantly, an inability to rely on state institutions to meet people's needs – other people and groups have taken on those obligations. I argue that, in Ukraine, the proliferation of the idea of self-organization transformed so drastically through the period of the Maidan protests that, by their end, the notion that ordinary people could better serve their own and others' interests than the state derailed any true engagement with state and institutional reform. Instead, volunteer organizations and activist groups came to help where state bodies could not, creating a significant paradigm shift about whom to trust in Ukraine.

As I argued earlier in this book, the notion of self-organization, originally based in leftist ideology, has become linked, if not synonymous with, the notion of civil society during and following Maidan. This discursive shift has enabled an offloading of state responsibility onto citizens – as was proven to be possible and successful during Maidan – with the added legitimating notion that civil society is itself an extension of the values and goals of Maidan (see Shukan 2016b). This shift has two related results: first, bodies and institutions making up the state do not suffer from a lack of trust in these areas because they have removed responsibility for certain needs onto groups that are now perceived as trustworthy. Second, the notion of "civil society" has itself become blurred – now, many groups claiming Maidan origins act in the name of the "people" but would certainly not fall into the category of an NGO or other legitimate institution.

This shift can be traced through the movement of the concept of self-organization following the end of Maidan. Leftists themselves regularly reflected on the possible impact of the spread of principles of self-organization – most fundamentally, this meant the valuing of people's ideas and trust in their ability to accomplish their goals. I suggest that this spread of self-organization began in localized forms on Maidan, but, once the protests were understood as successful and effective, self-organization expanded even further, first overlapping and then overtaking the realm of state practice and policies. Among leftists, this led to a complete re-envisioning of possibilities for leftist forms of governance and for leftist forms of activism. At the same time, it also resulted in a broader societal re-envisioning of the Ukrainian state.

Crucially, the war in eastern Ukraine that began just months after the Euromaidan protests ended has opened the space for the development of new forms of self-organization and the integration of new kinds of volunteerism into the post-Maidan state form.

In this conclusion, I discuss the effects of the illegal annexation of Crimea and the war in eastern Ukraine on political activism following Maidan in relation to the rapid expansion of the volunteer sector. The war has had a powerful impact on the radical left, causing major schisms around the issue of volunteer-based support and the possibility of a unified leftist anti-war position. I argue, however, that the leftist notion of self-organization, promoting non-party political mobilization, underlies these post-Maidan political shifts in crucial ways. I explore three main paths of expansion for self-organization since the mass mobilizations ended: first, various civic initiatives that began during Maidan to respond to the state's limitations; second, leftist efforts to create a party-like structure that would act through direct (internet-based) voting and the varied responses among leftists to this initiative; and third, the conflict in eastern Ukraine, which is supported by myriad self-organized military initiatives as an extension of the principles of Maidan and as a possible criticism of the limitations of the state, even as they fight for Ukraine.

The End of Maidan and the Beginning of the War

The protest camp on Maidan was cleared voluntarily at the beginning of July 2014. Cars again began to use Khreshchatyk, Kyiv's main street, and the occupied buildings were returned to the city. In May 2014, presidential elections were held, and Petro Poroshenko won the majority in the first round of voting. Two months earlier, in March, Russian president Vladimir Putin claimed that the residents of the Autonomous Republic of Crimea, part of Ukraine since 1954, would rather be part of Russia, and offered them a referendum. This was part of Putin's broader strategy to incite instability and thus gain greater control in the region; as Dunn and Bobick have demonstrated, this was one of several "interventions on behalf of 'compatriots,' *sootechestvenniki* – individuals who often are Russian citizens, speak Russian, and consider themselves to be culturally Russian yet who live within the boundaries of other states" (Dunn and Bobick 2014, 407).

Putin's strategy to re-integrate Crimea through a referendum has been widely accepted among scholars and policymakers alike as illegitimate (Dunn and Bobick 2014; Yurchak 2014). The status of the territory was decided based on a referendum of people living in Crimea. Following the Ukrainian constitution and international law, any changes to the territory of Ukraine must be voted on in a national referendum, not just in the territory to which the referendum applies (Bellinger 2014). The wording of the document itself asked voters to choose between two options: support for the reunification of Crimea with the Russian Federation, or support for restoring Crimea's 1992 constitution and its position as part of Ukraine (*BBC News* 2014). A large number of the territory's Crimean Tatar population refused to participate in the referendum because of its perceived illegality (Herszenhorn 2014); following the annexation, the Tatar governing body (Mejlis) ceased functioning within the peninsula (Aydin and Sahin 2019; for more on the Crimean Tatars' struggles, see Charron 2016, 2020; Uehling 2004, 2017).

In the same months, two Ukrainian oblasts, Luhans'k and Donets'k, saw demonstrations in favour of having a similar referendum, led by groups eventually called "separatists" or "rebels." Many people in those regions felt that Russia would provide more economic stability than could the centralized Ukrainian government, and, thanks to Russian news media, many of them also believed that Maidan had been led by the radical right and that Poroshenko's takeover was nothing more than a fascist junta (Humenyuk 2020 also discusses this phenomenon in Crimea). These separatist groups gained major power in certain areas of these two regions, which together make up the Donets'k Basin (Donbas), historically Soviet Ukraine's most industrialized region but one of the hardest hit following the economic downturn Ukraine experienced after independence. Separatists from these regions created the so-called Luhans'k People's Republic (Luhans'ka narodna Respublika, LNR) and the Donets'k People's Republic (Donets'ka narodna Respublika, DNR), neither of which was recognized by Poroshenko's government after his election in 2014.

In this environment, Poroshenko declared an anti-terrorist operation to root out the separatists and reclaim the Donbas for Ukraine. President Putin spent the first year of the conflict claiming that there were no Russian troops in Ukraine, but he admitted that they were there in December 2015. Scholars continue to debate the appropriate terminology to describe the conflict. While some advocate that calling it a civil war will help find an internationally mediated diplomatic solution (Driscoll 2019), I prefer to highlight the international element of the conflict, drawing on Tilly and Tarrow's "internationalized internal" description, in which conflict takes place "between the government of a state and internal opposition groups, with military intervention from other states" (Tilly and Tarrow 2007, 152). This allows us to see the participation of various groups, including volunteer brigades from Russia and Ukraine, which relates to the main subject of this chapter. Since the conflict began in the summer of 2014, there have been several broken ceasefires leading up to the Minsk Agreement of February 2015, which was renewed in 2017.

The self-organized forms featured in this conclusion are part of the continuing rupture between "citizen" and "state" that began before the Maidan mobilizations and that continued after the election of Petro Poroshenko as president in May 2014. Self-organization among leftists was also motivated by the idea that they could create better political structures more representative of Ukrainians than recent administrations had been able to do. After the protests ended, many leftists said they felt that the most important impact of Maidan was that people had experienced *real* self-organization, knew what it entailed, and knew that they could do it. Some activists felt that the impact of self-organization on Maidan was to change protesters' views of the government itself. As one activist put it, "People [are] left in a situation where they have no one to take responsibility for them, [and] they are forced to self-organize. People don't see the government as something sacred."

On Maidan, self-organization took various forms that expanded from leftist-inspired political ideologies. The long-term occupation of the main square, Maidan Nezalezhnosti, as well as of many of the surrounding buildings, was only the most visible. The constant presence of volunteers in kitchens and hospitals and those working as cleaning crews ensured that self-organization was the motor of Maidan. After Maidan ended, many activists told me about other examples of self-organization, such as local efforts to clean up specific districts of the city or even one apartment block. Others were targeted at the municipal level, including the Assembly for Social Revolution, the leftist party-like structure that vied for city council seats in the spring of 2014 (it was not successful). Initiatives supporting the Ukrainian military and volunteer brigades in eastern Ukraine show that discourses of self-organization have spread nationally, in part thanks to the extremely varied forms self-organization can take.

Each of these examples of self-organization (local, municipal, and national) provides important views on the effects of Maidan on the new left in Ukraine. Each initiative is an object of contention, even at the most localized level, because there has been no consensus on the role of the Ukrainian left in the post-Maidan period. Should leftists focus on mobilizing people's newfound ability to self-organize to reclaim city spaces for themselves? Should leftists attempt to reframe the government by infiltrating it? Should leftists aid the resolution of the conflict in the east in order to encourage stability before focusing on social policies? Although most leftists assessed the effects of Maidan positively at the time in terms of its impact on the average Ukrainian, it appears that Maidan had distinctly divisive effects on the left itself. As one activist articulated to me in early 2021, the new dividing lines for the left are attitudes towards (and criticism of) Maidan and the war.

Civil Society and/as Self-Organization

A significant development from this shifting role of the state has been the growth and legitimacy of both the concept and reality of "civil society." Since the 1980s, NGOs, such as churches and development organizations, have taken on tasks that were part of the expectations of the state (West 2010); this was true in the Soviet Union thanks to the timing of *glasnost* and *perestroika*. Following independence, civil society became a measure of democracy across eastern Europe, or a "key symbolic operator" that helped Western observers better understand the progress of post-socialism (see Verdery 1996, chap. 5). International agencies' focus on the growth of "civil society" as a reflection of a country's or region's successful democratization led to a rapid influx of funding for such groups, without an evaluation of their relevance or positive effects. Sometimes the presence of NGOs has been used simply to show civil society development without actually implementing changes. Thus, measuring the strength of civil society by assessing the numbers of organizations or participants inevitably contributes to the widespread perception that many post-socialist countries, Ukraine included, have a "weak" civil society (Gatskova and Gatskov 2015). This assessment, however, can be challenged by shifting one's definitions, measures, and interpretations of the role of civil society (Petrova and Tarrow 2007).

Maidan prompted a renegotiation of the relationship between citizen and state, particularly regarding what can and should be expected from actors representing each sphere. Without forgetting the symbolic role of the civil society concept, the changing measures of civil society in post-Maidan Ukraine show that social participation has changed because self-organization was so effective during the mobilizations (Krasynska and Martin 2017; Udovyk 2017; Way 2014). In a 2014 survey in a Ukrainian weekly asking people in whom they place their trust, the "volunteer sector" – which includes volunteers and volunteer military battalions, civil society, and the church – ranked higher than the state (cited in Puglisi 2015b). This shift does not mean that Ukraine's civil society is more robust or that Ukraine is experiencing greater democratization. Rather, I suggest that people's views on civil society as a concept have themselves shifted following Maidan.

Although this documented shift in attitudes merits a new discussion of civil society in the region, it is important to acknowledge that Ukrainian citizens recognize volunteers as more responsible, more effective, and more valuable than the state. This should not suggest that Ukrainians ever had a particular trust in the state; what it does show is that now they believe there are people who are worth trusting, particularly if they are affiliated with a non-state entity or idea. These new kinds of trust can be beneficial to a retracting state: positive assessments of volunteerism and civil society programs mean that governing bodies can relinquish responsibility when NGOs and volunteers can meet people's needs instead. This is a convenient intervention, given that the Ukrainian government was required to reduce its welfare programs as provisions of the Association Agreement with the European Union. Even if volunteer initiatives are composed of people who are critical of the state's limitations, such programs ultimately might serve the state.

This newfound trust in volunteers has not come exclusively as a result of the conflict in eastern Ukraine. The entire period of the Euromaidan mobilizations influenced people's attitudes about what they believed they were capable of – as one activist told me, this experience changed people's "consciousness" (*svidomist'*) about self-organization and volunteerism. Yet self-organization has shifted far away from its roots since Maidan. What people now call "self-organized" groups range from those volunteering to collect basic amenities for soldiers and volunteer combatants to groups of Afghan War veterans who organize prisoner exchanges across the LNR/DNR front lines because their social networks enable them to complete such exchanges more successfully than state representatives (Lebedev 2016). Like "civil society" before it, the term "self-organization" has become a "key symbolic operator," bringing legitimization to initiatives and used strategically by political figures to link themselves and their positions to Maidan. Self-organization was distanced from its leftist political origins and expanded to include any anti-Yanukovych position (Diuk 2014).[1] To explore how these processes have become entrenched in post-Maidan, Ukraine, I now turn to the civic initiatives that are emblematic of these developments.

Euromaidan/Krym SOS

Two significant humanitarian initiatives were developed in response to gaps in the protection of Maidan participants: Euromaidan SOS and Krym SOS (written in English but pronounced as *sos* instead of as separate letters). One leftist activist, Danylo, who participated in Euromaidan SOS described the origins of the project, when volunteers were responding to the first detentions and arrests on Maidan. According to Danylo, Euromaidan SOS was "the first to propose a hotline (*hariacha linia*) and could help from the legal side. And this was on volunteer principles, in other words, free legal aid." Various people – not one organization – volunteered for the hotline. I visited the offices of Euromaidan SOS in January 2014, when some friends who volunteered for the hotline invited me there for a dinner. The book *Ye Liudy*, which collects stories of ordinary people's participation on Maidan, features Alisa, one of the coordinators of the Euromaidan SOS hotline. A professor of political science at Kyiv-Mohyla Academy, she supported students from all the universities in Kyiv who marched on Maidan at the end of November, even if she had not taken an active part in the protests. Similar to many others' experiences, Alisa recounted how that changed for her after 30 November:

> When the students were cruelly beaten, she understood that it was necessary to do something concrete, and not just stand in the street. Her acquaintances initiated "Euromaidan SOS," and Alisa joined them. Now she coordinates the hotline, which helps connect victims with lawyers. The initiative's website informs [readers] about what to do if someone comes to your house with a search warrant. Volunteers also gather all possible information about missing people. "We are not physically looking for them. But we gather their photographs, we call their families, doctors, regional authorities," explains Alisa. Every day in the "Euromaidan SOS" office one to nine volunteers take turns, depending on the situation in the streets. A few more people work remotely, in the virtual space. They gather and publish information on social networks: Facebook, Twitter, VKontakte, and Odnoklassnyki.[2] (Berdyns'kykh 2014, 95–6)

Euromaidan SOS became a primary source of information about missing people, collecting photos and spreading information across social media as well as on the physical space of Maidan (Figure 7.1).

Krym SOS, created in March 2014, became one of the most prominent self-organized initiatives out of Maidan, in part because of the Russian annexation of the territory. Now that Crimea is under the legal jurisdiction of Russia, many organizations, including the UN High Commission on Refugees, have partnered with Krym SOS to expand its reach. In addition to offering legal aid, there are Krym SOS humanitarian aid centres in Kyiv, Kherson (the first city north of the peninsula in Ukraine), and L'viv, where many evacuees came to try to find new work and housing. Other organizations are working to help with the integration of Crimeans and those who have left eastern Ukraine, who

Figure 7.1. Euromaidan SOS missing persons board, Maidan
Source: Author's photograph.

predominately speak Russian, into communities in western Ukraine, where most people speak Ukrainian. Problematic stereotypes arise at both ends: evacuees assume that western Ukrainians are staunch nationalists and Russophobes, while many in those western communities think that evacuees are sympathizers with separatists and the Russian government (see Sereda 2020 for an assessment of how hierarchies of belonging affect displaced populations from Crimea and the Donbas). While these organizations' platforms are not overtly politicized, they have developed because of the gap left by an absence of state bodies willing on take on such tasks. The description of these initiatives as self-organized collapses the term into the same realm as volunteerism and even humanitarianism, making their contributions seem apolitical even as they present a critique of state limitations.

New Party Forms: Assembly for Social Revolution and Liquid Democracy

Although some leftists supported and participated in these apolitical types of initiatives, others insisted on keeping self-organization expressly political, hoping to change the organization of politics in Ukraine following Maidan. They decided to use the widespread acceptability of anti-party self-organization to create a new political platform, a group called the Assembly for Social Revolution (ASR, *Asambleia sotsial'noï revoliutsiï*), which would function as a party but without relying on single or static party representatives. Ideally, the party would get elected to the Kyiv city council, with designated members running as figureheads (referred to as "administrators"). They would then take a seat on the council and vote based on ASR voting decisions collected online via a platform called Liquid Democracy. While not conceived of as an ordinary political party – many new ones appeared in the months following Maidan, including one formed by the militant group Right Sector – it would have to take party form to allow its members to take part in elections.

According to Sasha, a leftist activist who was a prominent participant in student activism on Maidan, this would work because it was an "Assembly" rather than a party, in which "we don't have representatives but the people who just do what the internet community says to do, so the community decides, and not one person." Sasha and others found the need to be registered as an official party for elections limited the creation of alternative political representations. But, as she put it, ASR was different because people did not conceive of their support for it as having the same "ideology" and expectations for representatives to act based on ideologies. Instead, administrators would act based on issues the community had voted for online. "We are focused on particular demands and particular places," as she put it. This new attitude, which privileged issues over ideology, reflects the shifts among leftists during Maidan, when promoting a "leftist ideology" became secondary to ensuring effective participation in the protests.

In theory, ASR-type representation would be better than the current party system, because the community would have control over its representatives and it would change how people made demands on their politicians. With Liquid Democracy, any community member could propose a vote on an issue, which the administrator would then take to the council. Sasha envisioned that, "in the future, we don't need this [city] council, we're just gonna rule the city through Liquid Democracy and the group of organizers." She further saw the possibility for the internet platform to expand throughout government, allowing people to make demands, for instance, about education reform. Activists envisioned the internet as a way to make politics more accessible and to hold representatives accountable, at least at the level of the city.

However, the Assembly for Social Revolution did not win any seats on the Kyiv city council in the spring 2014 election. It became a volatile point for leftists after Maidan; activists, especially those focused on labour organizing, revitalized the group after the failed election bid. In fall 2017, under the moniker Social Movement (*Sotsial'nyi Rukh*), the organizers circulated across Ukraine a petition, requiring 10,000 signatures, to create a new party. In their words, "We believe that by establishing a new party, controlled by workers, we can build a truly democratic structure." According to their Facebook page, which had nearly 2,000 followers at the beginning of 2019, most events the group organized have taken place in Kyiv, but they have supported other events in Kharkiv, Kryvyi Rih, L'viv, and other cities.

Some activists have vehemently denounced leftist efforts to produce a party-like structure. Those who support ASR feel, however, that there was no other option for effective efforts to change the governing structure than to create a party-like structure. One activist, Anton, made a connection with right-wing, grassroots-type groups that turned local power into a political party: "Something [the] Svoboda [Party][3] has done is something that should be done for the left. There would be a party and there would be some kind of organization that could mobilize people from below. The party should be directly linked to the organization. I think that building up political, I don't know if it could be called a party, but a political organization, it could be elected." However, Anton thought that ASR would not be successful, because it was too focused on getting leftists to join. As Anton put it, leftists "have their own beliefs, no matter right or wrong. Why should you persuade the people who already have their ideas?" Instead, he felt that ASR should promote its platform among people who were motivated to participate in politics to a greater degree following Maidan – those whose consciousness had changed – but who had not yet made up their minds about precisely how to participate. Like Sasha, he felt that many leftists were too dogmatic – as he said, "I guess it's a huge problem of the movement that everyone's too embedded in those theoretical traditions rather than trying to analyse what's happening," both in Ukraine in general and with the left itself.

Despite leftists' continued commitment to ASR and its development since its failure to gain a seat on the city council, Anton was correct that the group would not have much success convincing leftists to support the initiative if they did not initially do so. Volodia, a prominent student organizer who identified as an anarchist before Maidan but became even more militant during the mobilizations, did not mince words: "ASR is ridiculous. They are trying to win elections, but it won't work. To change society in a profound way, we need the emancipation of the people. Their method is the wrong method. This is the moment where the roads go apart. The anarchist movement has enough force to make our own politics. I am beginning to stop identifying as a leftist because 'anarchist' is more concrete and makes more sense." Volodia's perspective rejected any structure that resembled existing ones as able to reflect accurately what people on Maidan had fought to establish. To Volodia, ASR did not even work to criticize the state or its main mechanism of support, capitalism. Volodia felt that the only way to encourage people to see real means to change politics was to make them target capitalism itself: "Most people don't realize it, but they feel it. It's anarchism for a new society."

As Anton described, leftists like Volodia became increasingly committed to ideological terms and positions following Maidan, whereas Anton, Sasha, and others felt that a platform that focused on issues, rather than on naming and uniting, would be more representative for leftists. At their cores, both of these ways of thinking reflect leftists' criticisms of current mechanisms of political representation. In practice, however, this divergence in response to ASR has become a divisive problem for leftists.

Some, like Volodia, hoped that Maidan would radicalize people. He concluded that some participants did become more interested in anarchism the more they saw themselves distanced from the state and future state representatives. But Volodia felt that Maidan was the beginning of a worldwide, anti-capitalist revolution. Those who supported ASR realized that, as long as the current governing system (with a president and parliament elected through parties) remained in place, there were only limited ways for social issues to be represented in the government. This was confirmed when President Poroshenko began the Anti-Terrorist Operation (ATO) in eastern Ukraine, devoting a huge amount of Ukraine's budget towards the military and conscription. Resonant of other localized, self-organized initiatives, the Assembly for Social Revolution's focus on particular issues would allow leftist participants to continue activism around those issues, but with the possibility of greater recognition in government.

ASR was an important self-organized initiative because it continued leftist anti-state activism even as it attempted to integrate leftists into the structures supported by the state. Those who supported ASR truly believed that they could promote discourses critical of state practices without necessarily committing to starting another revolution. Activists like Volodia were fixated on the next revolution, hoping that these discourses would appeal to others frustrated by the lack of change in the government after Maidan. However, austerity measures taken early in the Poroshenko period showed that the government itself was not so concerned about these social issues, even if its representatives had promised to support them during Maidan.

In my interview with Andriy in 2020, reflecting back on the effects of Maidan, he mentioned that leftists running for office was one of the more interesting aspects of post-Maidan politics. Social Movement, mentioned earlier, had ties with unions in Kryvyi Rih, an industrial town in east-central Ukraine – and the home of Volodymyr Zelensky – so one activist, Vitalii Dudin, decided to run in the local elections there. Andriy told me Vitalii received around 400 votes, whereas the winning candidate, from Zelensky's Servant of the People party, received around 30,000. As Andriy said, "Obviously nothing happened out of it, but it was an interesting effort." I asked whether or not it was because there wasn't currently any interest in leftist ideas in Ukraine more broadly, and he responded, "There wasn't ever interest, really." Because of this lack of interest, it became significantly more challenging for leftists to find a unified position once the war in Donbas began, the subject of the final section of this chapter.

The Anti-Terrorist Operation and a Leftist Anti-War Movement

The appearance of separatists in the eastern regions prompted lengthy discussion among leftists in April 2014, some of whom initially considered supporting these groups as anti-state organizations. Once it became clear, however, that the separatists in Donets'k and Luhans'k regions based their principles on military masculinity, Orthodox family structures, and pro-Russian sentiments, leftists quickly distanced themselves from separatists' criticisms of the central Ukrainian state.[4] However, partly because of the divisive effects of ASR, leftists have been unable to present a unified anti-war platform; attitudes towards the war have become the key dividing line among leftist activists. This can be explained partly by the widespread volunteer-based support for the war effort, which has presented a challenge for leftists to develop a unified position in their attitude about the conflict.

Vitalii was one of several radical leftist activists who volunteered their services to fight on the side of the Ukrainian army in the conflict with Russian-backed separatist forces. He had volunteered with a special rapid-response emergency medical[5] unit to deploy to the ATO zone in eastern Ukraine. When Vitalii went public about this work in a Facebook post, he wrote that "this is a division of medical volunteers which has been providing emergency medical aid and evacuation of the wounded in the area of the ATO." Trained as a medical equipment engineer and having worked in hospitals in nearly all the regions of

Ukraine, he volunteered for training instructors and soldiers in Tactical Combat Casualty Care (TCCC) in the ATO zone. He specifically wrote that he was *not* serving in the army or working for other state or private security forces. Instead, he said, he was motivated by his previous experiences as an activist and the events of the past two years in Ukraine, referencing the mass mobilizations of 2013–14. He thanked everyone who had supported his decision and asked people to respect his choice: "If you find this totally unacceptable," he wrote, "do the decent thing and remove me from your friends."

Since 2014, the "side of the Ukrainian army" has been made up of state-funded military units, along with extensive support from contracted volunteer military brigades, many of which were formed on Maidan. The Ukrainian security forces were severely affected by both the dissolution of domestic special forces (including the Berkut, the militarized riot police) and the defection of police and other security forces to the side of the separatists in the east (Puglisi 2015a). As of March 2015, Puglisi had counted forty to fifty volunteer battalions of varied sizes supporting the Ukrainian army; in April 2016, Mykhailo Minakov (2016, 4) counted thirty battalions with 13,500 members.[6] Both volunteer and army soldiers are "clothed, equipped and fed thanks to the generosity of friends and family as well as the relentless activism of the wide network of civil society organizations that emerged in the beginning with the hostilities in the Donbas" (Puglisi 2015a, 15). Importantly, while much of the work on the front lines, like Vitalii's tactical combat casualty care, appears to be the purview of men, Natalia Stepaniuk (2018) has documented that post-war care work – including psychological care – falls into women's hands.

All the brigades formed in the winter and spring of 2014 were eventually officially integrated into the Ministry of Defence structure, so their participants became members of the Ukrainian military (Lebedev 2016; Minakov 2016). Two further developments, however, challenged the success of this tactic. First, several battalions were created or became civilian political structures in the form of parties – including, for instance, the Azov battalion, a far-right group whose civilian platform promotes the same ideology as its military corps (see *Spil'ne* 2016, a response to an attack on an anti-fascist demonstration by the Azov "civilian corps"). Second, oligarchic groups had a strong interest in gaining influence over volunteer military brigades, particularly in eastern regions near the front. Minakov (2016, 18) describes how the "organizational flexibility" of these oligarchic groups allowed their leaders to shift positions according to the political climate of the country. During Maidan, major oligarchs such as Ihor Kolomois'kyi came out in support of protesters in order to distance himself and his beneficiaries from the Yanukovych regime; in the years after Maidan, Kolomois'kyi and others continued this claim for legitimacy by fundraising for and otherwise supporting troops (Minakov 2016, 19). Like the self-organized vigilante justice groups, oligarchic groups have claimed their legitimacy by promoting the "values of Maidan" (Shukan 2016b); in so doing, they have gained control or at least influence over volunteer military brigades, even after the latter have been officially integrated into the Ukrainian army.

The reliance on volunteer, non-unified forces to fight the war appears as an attempt by the governing regime to control these units, which began during Maidan as anti-government activist groups. Theoretically, the incorporation of these battalions into a pro-government platform would help consolidate the regime's power while showing more widespread support for its austerity actions. In this case, however, the great influence of oligarchs, particularly in eastern Ukraine where the conflict zone is located, calls into question whether state forces can effectively coordinate with these battalions. These issues complicate the legitimacy of the new post-Maidan Ukrainian state and the functioning of its governing forces.

Although the volunteer battalions have worked mostly in what Puglisi calls "law and order functions," including at checkpoints and in liberated areas, they have gained both notoriety and "popular trust" – they "rank second, after civil society organizations, and before the church and the army, among the institutions the Ukrainians trust the most" (Puglisi 2015a, 13). Puglisi argues that their popularity comes both from their seeming to embody the spirit of Maidan, which includes a commitment to self-organization, and from their promise of a level of transparency that the Ukrainian government, and therefore the military, cannot provide. Further, citizens' contributions to the military have forced it and related institutions – particularly those dealing with procurement of weaponry and supplies for the armed forces – to be more accountable to them (Puglisi 2015b, 14).

There is little record of the quantity – both monetary and in kind – of donations being made on behalf of the military. When the conflict broke out, according to Natalia Stepaniuk in a personal communication, "Often times, a group of volunteers would pick a voluntary battalion or an army unit (because of family or private ties, etc.) and supply whatever is needed (starting from water, socks, food and finishing with military equipment, cars and military uniforms. The range of support is very wide!)." Some groups simply posted online long lists of what was needed and where to bring supplies. The Ukrainian army itself requested donations: "Responding to an appeal of the Armed Forces, already by the end of March 2014, donors deposited around UAH 70 million (about 5.4 million euros at the exchange rate of the time) on a 'Support the Ukrainian Army' bank account" (Puglisi 2015b, 13). As early as June 2014, advertisements in the Kyiv metro showed that companies would make a donation to the armed forces if customers purchased special products; stores continued to collect funds for the troops as the war went on. Outside Ukraine, there have been many examples of American and Canadian people and organizations collecting money, equipment, and medical supplies to send to both the Ukrainian military and volunteer battalions. In one touching story, historian Olesya Khromeychuk profiled the efforts of one volunteer, Maria (Masha) Berlinska, to train Ukrainian soldiers to use drones donated by diaspora organizations all over the world (Khromeychuk 2020). At the same time that Berlinska was advocating for more state protection of women participating in the ATO, she was training military brigades to use drones for scouting work so that they would not have to use soldiers. Khromeychuk wrote: "I admired her determination. But I also realized that the more Masha and people like her did the job of defending the state, something that should have been done by the professional military, the more the state would feel that it needed to do nothing. When I reproached her for enabling the state to take a passive role while the volunteers did the hard work, she asked me how her stopping flying drones or training others would help the people at the front line." Khromeychuk and Berlinska highlight precisely the conundrum of volunteer work in the ATO: if volunteering can help save lives, how can one justify not helping, even if it contributes to a deepening of the systemic retraction of the state?

Despite the regime change following Maidan, it appears that people's attitudes towards the government, including widespread mistrust, have not changed significantly. Self-organization has allowed and encouraged people to demand and create radical changes themselves. This explains leftists' complex relationship with the largely volunteer-based war effort. Leftists have been offering such criticisms of the state and its limitations for many years. Even if they are critical of war and militarism, the conflict has enabled ordinary people to see the effects of their participation in alternative forms of social supports for one another. Thus, many leftists interpret this obvious adoption of self-organization as a success for the left, while others are critical that widespread self-organization has been successful only in terms of aiding the military, which promotes the militarization of society and ultimately helps the state.

It is in this context that Vitalii used his knowledge of tactical medical combat care to volunteer on the front and to help establish an NGO to train others to continue this work. Importantly, Vitalii made it clear that he was volunteering as an individual person, not as part of some political group, so he was not attempting to change the leftists' position on the war. One activist differentiated Vitalii's work from that of anarcho-nationalists fighting at the front: "Vitalii, you know what he is doing, right? As long as he is a doctor, it's okay. But [there are] guys who are fighting, they're trying to have a left position in support of war, because it was going to happen anyway. But they shouldn't try to make other people think the same."[7] According to this activist, other leftists assumed that war with Russia was inevitable, so the inability of leftists as a collective to create a unified anti-war position was a source of major frustration.

Thus, for many leftists, these uses of self-organization are nothing more than politicians within the government recognizing that they can take advantage of citizen initiatives in the name of a unified "state," which enables them to ignore the responsibilities that are actually expected of state forms. These leftists see Vitalii and others who work as volunteers as aiding the government with their presence and practices.[8] I see Vitalii's volunteerism as part of the longer-lasting effects of self-organization resulting from Maidan that so many activists described to me as the most positive impact of the protests. Vitalii volunteered to serve a population that might otherwise be neglected by the state, applying a similar analysis to Maria Berlinska. In this case, the state's inability to protect its citizens could result in their deaths because they could not be evacuated from the combat zone or, once evacuated, did not have access to medical supplies or technology that would have saved their lives. I see an alternative interpretation of Vitalii's volunteerism as a continuation of leftists' critique of the state through the practice of filling the gaps in its undertakings.

Leftist State Criticisms

In her study of Italian volunteerism, Andrea Muehlebach suggests that leftists are particularly active in adapting the framework of volunteer-as-citizen, because they see its basis in morality as a way to reimagine the neoliberal social order: "Their participation in the privatizing service economy thus appears to them not as a radical break with their political past but as a continuation, even recuperation of it. Morality, in short, allows members of the Left to participate in the moral neoliberal [system] in both wholehearted and yet also critical-complicit ways, and to forge out of this historical moment practices that are both oppositional and complicit at the same time" (Muehlebach 2012, 9). I argue that leftists differed from the other protesters on Maidan because they never assumed that a state form would provide promised services for its citizens when the protests ended. Other protesters, in contrast, assumed they could elect a new governing regime whose policies would provide for citizens, thus rejuvenating the citizen-state relationship. To leftists, their assumption about the state was justified by the austerity measures the post-Maidan government took by the second month of Poroshenko's term. One leftist recognized the irony: "We must really be part of Europe now," he said, referencing the original motivation to mobilize on Maidan in November 2013. "We're implementing austerity just like everyone else in Europe!" While Ukrainian leftists originally saw their notion of self-organization as a mechanism through which to challenge past and current forms of neoliberal governance, the path that the self-organization concept has taken, and its conflation with civil society, has led many leftists to question whether they are contributing to a "reimagining" of the social order or simply reinforcing what already exists.

It is no surprise to many leftists – well versed in the ways the neoliberal order has shifted the relationship between governing and governed – that volunteerist efforts are being co-opted by state bodies, presented as examples of good citizenship rather than understood as anti-state activism. Vitalii and some other medical instructors visited his old school to teach students about combat first aid. The school administrators thanked him and his co-instructors for the "time and energy they gave to the education of the young generation of patriots!"[9] The actions of Vitalii's generation, now seen to embody the honoured ideas of volunteerism and civic duty, are being translated into a new patriotism being taught to the younger generation of Ukrainians. Through these types of discourses, this generation will learn *not* to expect the state to provide such services for them. State discourses take the "activism" out of civic initiatives started on Maidan and depoliticize them through state and national expectations of volunteer participation.

Even now, leftist activists are using connections they made during the Maidan mobilizations to create new networks of support for themselves and to help others where the state cannot. Vitalii described meeting several comrades from the occupation of the Ministry of Education in February 2014 while he was deployed in the Anti-Terrorist Operation zone. "I don't believe in fate," he said. "But I understand the importance and the incompleteness of the occupation of the Ministry and the reconquest of the elite political system more than a year ago. I hope that the war will end soon and we will meet again with friends and comrades and see the thing through to the end."

For Vitalii, volunteering in the ATO zone was not about compromising with the state of which he had once been so critical. Instead, this form of activism enabled him to keep connections with others from Maidan and to support the notion that the revolution was not over. While so many developments – most particularly the ongoing war with Russia – have eclipsed the daily tribulations of the protests, Maidan changed the nature of Ukrainians' relationship to politics, to the state, and to one another. Self-organization was an idea that came with a complex history and, because of its fluidity, became the most important framework of political participation. Volunteering in the ATO zone keeps the idea of self-organization alive because it relies on those brief connections with other activists and volunteers to envision a future for the Maidan generation without war and in critical dialogue with state practices.

Afterword

14 April 2022

"Hi. Nice to hear from you. Everything's okay with me. I joined the territorial defence force. Everything is quiet for now."

Having known Vitalii for more than a decade, I wasn't surprised to receive his message in March 2022 confirming what I had already guessed – that he had joined the territorial defence force after Russia's renewed invasion. After offering to send him money for equipment (he said he already had everything he needed), I spent the next few weeks finding the most banal reasons to send him more messages without seeming overbearing. I'm sure he saw through me.

Every day I find a reason to message someone I know in Ukraine. Most of them are people whose words, ideas, and stories make up the perspectives in this book. Some of them are in territorial defence units – I don't hear from them as often. Others are volunteering and delivering humanitarian aid, and still others are raising money from abroad to send to the defence and humanitarian volunteers. Some have moved to western Ukraine, where it's safer, and others have gone abroad.

The lives of the people in this book were upended on 24 February 2022. Everything they had built together – the tangible and the intangible – and everything they were working towards was destroyed, or at least has entered a long-term hiatus. My own emotions vacillate between outrage at how unfair it all is to people who just wanted to live their lives, and feeling heartbroken that the Ukraine I left in September 2021 when I considered this project to be complete will never be the same. Not because it can't be rebuilt or its physical scars can't heal – they can, and they will. But people have been forced to abandon their projects and priorities, and even their careers. And when people do pick up their projects and go back to work, it's in the context of a genocidal war. It's in a context where they know everything could change again in an instant.

I thought I understood uncertainty in 2013, when the Euromaidan protests were gaining momentum. In chapter 4, I quoted a leftist activist, Heorhiy, who stated that he "lost his sense of prediction somewhere in the middle of Maidan." He said he never would have believed that a hundred people would be killed by the end of it. His statement resonated deeply with me at that time. Now, I feel similarly unmoored, but the stakes are unfathomably higher.

Many experts did not believe that Russian forces would actually invade Ukraine on such a scale in February 2022. Based on everything that made sense at the time, it seemed like a stupid shift in Russia's policy, which until then had relied on the war in the Donbas to prevent Ukraine's joining the EU or NATO. Russia continued to be treated as a respectable geopolitical player even as it continued to violate Ukraine's sovereignty (and as it violated Georgia's in 2008). After the invasion, countries around the world placed unprecedented sanctions on Russia. The horrors being uncovered in Ukrainian towns near Kyiv are being called war crimes – US president Joe Biden has even called Russia's war in Ukraine a genocide.

Did Putin also lose his sense of prediction? Did he simply not see any other outcome than success after three days and the installation of a pro-Russian government in Kyiv? His mistaken calculation has put Ukraine at the centre of world interest, not only because of the sheer scale of refugees flocking to other European countries, but also because of the heroism of the Ukrainians, who continue to outperform any previous expectations. As I write this, on 14 April, Ukrainian forces have sunk the Russian Black Sea fleet's flagship missile cruiser *Moskva*, just another absolutely unexpected Ukrainian victory against the supposedly superior Russian forces.

But these successes, however heartening, leave us unable to guess how long this war will continue and what the state of Ukraine – and the world – will be when it all ends. Uncertainty is difficult to live with; it can be disheartening not to know what the next day will bring. My friends in Ukraine tell me they feel helpless, so they spend every waking hour doing something to help. They deliver tactical backpacks filled with medical supplies to the men and women in the territorial defence forces. They get a smile in return, and suddenly they don't feel so helpless, at least for a while. I hear about how my friends who have moved to safety continue to work because they can't sit still. They are part of the volunteer networks that continue to deliver life-saving body armour across the country. They all continue to help, no matter the odds. And on the days that I feel most useless and uncertain, I think of everything my friends are doing, and it reminds me that we must continue to fight however we can. They just want to return home. To Kyiv, or wherever home is. I can't wait until that day comes.

Notes

Preface

1 According to a 2019 report from the Centre for East European and International Studies (ZOiS), the number of people in the occupied Donbas territories who wanted those territories to become part of Russia decreased dramatically from 2016 to 2019, from 5 per cent to 2.3 per cent of the surveyed population (Sasse and Lackner 2019).
2 Only 28.2 per cent of people supported Zelensky's activities in November 2021 (Kyiv International Institute of Sociology 2021).

Introduction: "We provide the content of Maidan!"

1 All names used in the text are pseudonyms unless otherwise noted.
2 Tymoshenko won 80 per cent of the votes in western regions in the 2010 election runoff against Yanukovych (Kudelia 2014, 21).
3 Additionally, I completed interviews with a dozen university students in the regional centre Cherkasy about their city's local Maidan, which was extremely active but also harshly repressed; see Channell-Justice (2019c).

1. Without Any Help from the State: Self-Organization in Ukraine

1 Most leftist activists with whom I worked in Ukraine would not consider the Communist or Socialist Parties as representative of the contemporary left, if they consider these Parties leftist at all. President Poroshenko banned the Communist Party from participating in elections, which Party representatives have challenged in Ukrainian courts.
2 These two organizations were once one united group, the Centre for Society Research, but this group split after Maidan because of ideological differences. I volunteered as an English-language editor for the Centre

for Social and Labour Research, a job I did previously for the Centre for Society Research. I have been associated with some of the researchers at the Centre for Society Research, but many of them have spent the past few years working in policy areas rather than appearing at street demonstrations or organizing camps, where I met most leftists.

3 I most often hear Ukrainians reference the Turkic origins of the word; I thank Mohamad Junaid for pointing out that the word is related to a much larger linguistic geography.

4 This language comes from Marx's 1875 *Critique of the Gotha Programme*, written in response to a draft program of the United Workers' Party of Germany. Friedrich Engels published the text, along with a related letter Marx wrote, in 1891.

5 Youth are also often examined as a central component of nation-building, a subject that falls outside the purview of this research. For the region, see Blum (2007); Fournier (2012); Hemment (2015); Markowitz (2000).

6 I intentionally did not come into direct contact with Right Sector members, so I draw here from the widespread presence of the group on Maidan and one Right Sector newspaper I collected after February 2014. Although some of the essays in the newspaper feature titles such as "Why It Is Important to Listen to the Ideas of Nationalists" and "Nationalism and Right-Wing Political Power," one essay by Dmytro Yarosh, who became arguably the most visible representative of the group, is surprisingly measured, advocating that "Only the Ukrainian national state can guarantee a dignified life for every Ukrainian citizen, regardless of nationality." Although a deep investigation of Right Sector is outside the scope of this research, the organization and the far right in general are likely more multivocal than they seem, just like leftists.

7 In our interview in Ukrainian, Danylo used both feminine and masculine forms of nouns when he spoke as an inclusive gesture. Here, he said, *kozhen hromadianyn, kozhna hromadianka*, in order to say "each citizen."

8 Since my conversation with Sasha, an entirely new police force has been trained for the city of Kyiv. The training was extremely Americanized, and many new recruits are young people. Many have also been documented because of their attractiveness – through the fall of 2015, I saw hundreds of "police selfies" circulating around social media as civilians posed with the new, beautiful, shiny police recruits (who are, importantly, both men and women). See Pehlman (2020) for more on police reforms in post-Maidan Ukraine.

9 Sasha mentioned that the stadium was being rented by a company that "most likely" belonged to the son of former prime minister Mykola Azarov. I did not confirm this or ask how she knew, but there is a widespread assumption that the companies building high rises tend to be owned by already-existing oligarchs and their families.

10 At the time Dunn and Bobick's piece was written, Putin had annexed Crimea via a referendum, and his position and media propaganda showed major support for separatist groups in the Donbas, but Russian troops were not openly in Donets'k and Luhans'k regions.

2. Twenty-First Century Leftists

1 I attended one of these workshops in December 2013, in the town of Hadiach, in the Poltava region of east-central Ukraine. It included students from Hadiach and another group visiting from the southern city of Kherson.

2 These profiles combine interviews with activists in 2013 and 2014, which I shared with the activist in question, and then discussed in 2020 and 2021.

3 My first on-the-record interview with Andriy took place in May 2014, though we met in the fall of 2013. This profile includes quotes from that interview as well as an interview we did online in summer 2020, in which he reviewed the quotes from 2014 and we discussed how his views had shifted. Andriy and I have spoken almost exclusively in English since we met, so both interviews were in English (quotes are lightly edited for clarity). I thank Andriy for putting so much into this project, giving me helpful suggestions along the way. He has agreed to use his real name.

4 See Commons (n.d.).

5 This profile includes quotes from Tonya's original interview in 2013, which Tonya commented on in response to reading the chapter. In January 2021, we discussed some of the parts of the interview that should be included in the profile, as well as certain parts that should be left out. In September 2021, I was able to see Tonya in Ukraine, and we read through this chapter together. Tonya currently prefers to use they/them pronouns but suggested I continue to use she/her pronouns in this profile when discussing our 2013 interview, which are accurate for that time. I thank Tonya for their time in this process and in general for being extremely patient with my errors and misunderstandings in Ukrainian. Some of the points of our conversation in September 2021 were not easy to address, but they helped me put together the final pieces of this book. Tonya has agreed to use their real name.

6 *Mala arkhitekturna forma* (MAF), or temporary kiosks, are erected near metro stations and used long term even though they are meant to be temporary. There is a large number of MAFs near the metro station leading to the campus Ania references.

7 This section is based on notes taken during a presentation on liberation pedagogy by a leftist activist and Free School organizer in Crimea, kindly translated into English for me by another activist.

8 The Centre for Social and Labor Research has completed extensive research documenting increased repressions against various kinds of protests even

following the end of the Maidan mobilizations (in 2014), suggesting that self-defence is increasingly necessary for those, such as leftist groups, who continue to be involved in protest actions. Recent data from the Marker monitoring organization shows that the most likely targets of right-wing violence in Ukraine are political parties and actors, as well as LGBTQ+ and feminist groups (see https://violence-marker.org.ua).

9 In this section, I refer to police officers with male pronouns. At this point, I had never seen a female police officer in Ukraine, and certainly not among the riot police.

10 Men are required to complete twelve months of military service between the ages of eighteen and twenty-five; students are exempt from service, so many people who do not want to complete it stay enrolled in universities until they are twenty-five.

3. Decommunization and National Ideology

1 I reconstruct the events from 8 December 2013 from videos online and news coverage of the event at the time, as well as drawing from Haidai (2018) and Plokhy (2021).

2 In light of this mention of Kuchma and his outsize influence, it is ironic that he served on President Zelensky's Trilateral Contact Group for one year, from July 2019 to July 2020, in aid of the effort to end the war in the Donbas.

3 See Krytyka (n.d.) in English.

4 Roman Cybriwsky (2014) suggests that Yanukovych used fraudulent methods to win the election. Andrew Wilson recounts that his success was due to divisions among opposition candidates such as Tymoshenko and Yushchenko, which created the opportunity for Yanukovych to win outright (Wilson 2014, 49).

5 The presenters were Marko Bojcun, who wrote the introduction to the book; Vasyl' Cherepanyn, at the time a professor at Kyiv-Mohyla Academy and the director of the Visual Cultural Research Centre; and Yuriy Shapoval, a historian from the National Academy of Sciences, also in Kyiv.

6 Trotsky was expelled from the Communist Party in 1927 and exiled in 1929, having already broken with Stalin. His role in planning and implementing the famine was likely quite limited.

7 Because of widespread homophobia in Ukraine, using "homosexual" as a slur in this case is assumed to provoke homophobic sympathy from the audience and to discredit Trotsky.

8 My reconstruction of this anecdote is taken from my own field notes, a reflection written by Bojcun after the presentation (in English), and various posts on Facebook from leftists that I gathered following the presentation (in Ukrainian).

9 The authors of the Facebook posts agree that of the sixty attendees, about half were from far-right groups.

10 One of my companions half-jokingly referred to this as "positive gender discrimination" – the ultra-nationalists were less likely to attack us than the presenters because we were women.

11 As Snyder has written, "We will never know with precision" how many people were killed during the famine of these years because of lack of documentation; however, "it seems reasonable to propose a figure of approximately 3.3 million deaths by starvation and hunger-related disease in Soviet Ukraine in 1932–1933" (Snyder 2010, 53).

12 In Kharkiv, activists (including the author Serhiy Zhadan) replaced a street named after Vladimir Lenin with new nameplates honouring John Lennon (a nod to both the anti-Soviet and pro-Western aspects of the protests, as well as to the significance of the Beatles' music in challenging dominant Soviet norms; see Yurchak 2006).

13 The Ukrainian Research Institute at Harvard University has mapped the trends of the removal of Lenin statues through its MAPA Project. I thank Kostyantyn Bondarenko, Viktoriya Sereda, and Serhii Plokhy for their work in generating this important resource.

14 In 2020, many writers and scholars, myself included, made connections between Leninopad and the decommunization of public space in Ukraine and the removal of Confederate and colonial monuments in the United States and the United Kingdom, brought more clearly into the forefront of media discussions thanks to the Black Lives Matter movement. See Blacker (2020) for one example.

15 Many historians writing about Ukraine are sympathetic to these alliances. They interpret the motives of these groups as being more afraid of the Soviets than of the Germans, thus making strategic and understandable alliances to protect themselves against the Soviets. Risch (2011) and others, however, have documented extensive sympathy for Nazi ideologies, including anti-Semitism, that must be taken into consideration when discussing the actions of these organizations.

16 Right Sector became a political party and stood in elections in 2014. Several scholars have argued that its electoral failure proved that Right Sector's nationalist rhetoric was not representative of Ukrainians at large (Likhachev 2015; Risch 2015; but see also Ishchenko 2016, 2020).

4. #LeftMaidan: Violence, Repression, and Re-creation

1 I make this suggestion because, during the previous evening, a protester asked me and another leftist activist who paid us to stand on Maidan with signs. He was surprised when the activist responded that no one had paid

us; when she asked him if he was being paid, he replied, "Of course!" (*Kaniechna*, in Russian).

2 The slogan "Glory to Reason" was picked up on Maidan and beyond – I saw graffiti with the slogan all across Kyiv until the summer when I left Ukraine.

3 *Derzhava* indicates "state" in the same, broad sense as the English term; words such as *vlada* or *uriad* refer to the government and governing bodies, but they were not used here.

4 Anthropologist Jennifer Carroll also photographed the banner in the city hall, not knowing that it came from leftist activists.

5 Ukrainian legislation (Ukrainian: *zakonoproekt*; from "law," *zakon*) is always similarly titled. These laws, as well as laws discussed in the next chapter, are officially called "Law of Ukraine 'On …'" – for example, "Law of Ukraine 'On Higher Education.'" Legislation also has a designated number; the "Law of Ukraine 'On Higher Education'" is No. 1187–7. However, laws are often known colloquially by those who introduce them. The Higher Education Laws were introduced by former education minister M. Zgurovs'ky, so they are often referred to as "Zgurovs'ky's Laws." The 16 January laws were a large package of twelve laws and resolutions, each with its own designated number and lengthy title (see Verkhovna Rada 2014). The laws were introduced by Party of Regions representatives Vadym Kolesnychenko and Volodymyr Oliynyk, but I rarely heard these names used in the typical colloquial fashion. This is certainly because most people with whom I spoke about the laws preferred the colloquial "Dictatorship Laws" instead (*zakony pro dyktaturu* or *dyktators'ki zakony*).

6 This last segment was targeted at the growing trend of wearing military-style fatigues on Maidan. While many of these men and women might have been wearing official uniforms from their military service, I also saw an increase in the availability of military uniforms and footwear for purchase at at least one second-hand market on the outskirts of Kyiv.

7 Zhizdnevs'kyi was a Belarusian citizen who had participated in the protests since their early days. Nihoyan was from Dnipropetrovs'k (now Dnipro) and was a central organizer since the beginning, as well; Nihoyan was a Ukrainian citizen, but his Armenian background was often commented upon, as was his use of the Ukrainian language, which was somewhat unexpected in light of his Dnipropetrovs'k origins.

8 Some protesters and groups were likely supportive of the use of force even before the 16 January laws. Indeed, throughout the protests, there were stories of *provokatory* who would instigate violence; some of the time, these provocateurs were assumed to have been paid by the Yanukovych camp, but it is equally possible that they were protesters who wished to promote violent responses to police repression. Ivan Katchanovski has written

extensively on the issue, particularly around the violence that took place in late February, suggesting that Maidan protesters shot police officers first, provoking the response that led to a hundred deaths (Katchanovski 2015). Katya Gorchinskaya (2016) describes the experience of interviewing Maidan protester Ivan Bubenchik on Hromadske TV, who openly discusses having shot police officers with the intention of killing them on 20 February 2014. Katchanovski's conclusions have been debated in the scholarly community, but, as Gorchinskaya points out, police officers were being tried for their crimes in February 2014, whereas protesters such as Bubenchik and others who have admitted to shooting police officers were not.

9 These two interviews were completed with news reporters in public places, where I was able to overhear them. As Skoropadskyi had been involved in several actions against leftist events, I would never be able to access him without putting my interlocutors in danger, so I spoke to the reporter who had interviewed him after Skoropadskyi left. The Svoboda Party representative was speaking to a reporter from a Spanish TV station in the Ukrainian House, so I stood in close proximity to hear his assessment. Given that both were acting as public figures, I consider their opinions useful for thinking through the intentional manipulations of the perception of violence at this moment.

10 The phrase *"Varto u likarni"* is a play on words; *varto* means that something is important or worthwhile; *varta* means "guard." I use the English translation "Hospital Guard," based on an early email correspondence referring to it as the *likarniana varta* and because this rendering makes the most sense in English. I thank Volodymyr Dibrova and Roman Senkus for the discussion clarifying this translation.

11 The book is *Ye Liudy* (There are People; Є (*Ye*) in Ukrainian is also the first letter of Euromaidan, so the title of the book also evokes the name of the protest. Berdyns'kykh started these "warm stories from Maidan" as a Facebook page and brought them together as a book showing snapshots of people on the square from December 2013 to April 2014.

12 Various *Kyiv Post* journalists updated these numbers as bodies continued to appear. The newspaper's live updates would collect each journalist's counts and combine them at various intervals. I found this to be the most accurate count to follow, and it (and injury reports) were corroborated by on-site doctors.

13 This number does not count the four protesters killed in January but it does include police officer deaths; ultimately, close to twenty more people died because of wounds sustained on Maidan, bringing the total number of deaths to one hundred.

14 Students occupied the Ministry of Education at the end of February 2014. An economist and leftist activist created an important initiative to

implement open accounting for the ministry. Now, the ministry is required to publish its financial information online (it is published in raw data form, so one must be trained to read this type of information in order to understand and analyse it). Activists hoped to implement this open accounting system in other ministries to encourage transparency throughout the government.

5. "For free education": Education Activism and Maidan

1 Most universities in Ukraine are still publicly funded, but there is a growing number of private universities. The most prominent are Ukrainian Catholic University in L'viv and the Kyiv School of Economics.
2 See EHEA (n.d.).
3 I was not present in Ukraine during this campaign. However, I had read about each wave of protest online, so when I interviewed activists about it in 2013 and 2014, I had a general idea of the issues surrounding the protest and some of the tactics they used in major campaigns. In these interviews, many activists remembered great detail about the protests. Some of these interviews were completed in September and October 2013, before Maidan began, while others took place during or after Maidan, which also influenced activists' assessments of the importance of the campaign against paid services.
4 Kyiv's main universities are often referred to by various nicknames. Here, Petro is referencing the following universities: Taras Shevchenko National University; its main building is a vibrant red columned structure at the centre of the city, across from Taras Shevchenko Park, sometimes referred to in this chapter as "the Red Building" (*chervonyi korpus*, Ukr.). Next, Petro is talking about the National University of Kyiv-Mohyla Academy, sometimes known as Kyiv-Mohyla, Mohyla, or KMA. Finally, KPI is Kyiv Polytechnic Institute, named since 1916 for aviation pioneer Igor Sikorsky. Universities in Ukraine are sometimes organized around certain specialties – for instance, medicine, film, or pedagogy – and are typically named after a leader in the field of focus – for instance, the National Medical University is named for Alexander Bogomolets; the National University for Theatre, Cinema, and Television is named for Ivan Karpenko-Kary; and the National Pedagogical University is named for Mykhailo Drahomanov.
5 A party-sponsored youth wing is reminiscent of both Soviet and post-Soviet political technologies used commonly in Russia; see Hemment (2015) for a deep look into how these technologies are employed.
6 In the original Russian: RT!! Встречаемся в 22:30 под монументом Независимости. Одевайтесь тепло, берите зонтики, чай, кофе, и друзей.

 7 Dickinson (2014), Metzger and Tucker (2017), and Onuch (2014a, 2014b) document how protesters of various age groups used virtual and real-life social networks to circulate information and mobilize bodies.

 8 Nadia Diuk, personal communication.

 9 I use the charged moniker "Dictatorship Laws" here because students referred to them this way, but their official name was the Kolesnychenko-Oliynyk Laws; see chapter 4 and note 5 in particular for more on this legislation.

10 Students, along with other leftist groups, were attempting to call for a nationwide general strike. However, three days after the adoption of the Dictatorship Laws, three people were killed on Maidan and protesters focused their attention on the violence rather than on calls for a strike. Before the violence, it had seemed feasible that a strike might occur, as it was being strongly promoted around Maidan.

11 This assessment is not always accurate. In 2012, the Visual Cultural Research Centre (VCRC), a leftist artistic and research group housed at KMA, curated an exhibit called "Ukrainian Body" (*Ukrains'ke tilo*), which was shut down by Kvit, who called it "shit" and claimed it was pornographic (*Art Leaks* 2012). Following this conflict, Kvit forced the VCRC to move to a different space. Many activists considered the actions to be a form of censorship. See Zychowicz (2020) for more on VCRC in the context of art and activism before the Maidan protests.

12 The information in this section comes from my field notes and photos, several key interviews, and a reflective article from a Ukrainian journal by a participant and one of my interviewees. I chose not to cite this article so as to preserve the anonymity of the interviewee.

13 *Varto u likarni*, the Hospital Guard, was perhaps the earliest effective self-organized initiative. However, it did not function based on consensus, but rather on volunteer initiative to go to a specific hospital.

14 I thank Elana Resnick for clarifying this point.

15 Danylo is referring to consensus hand signals in which people can signify their dissent, approval, or a point of contention with hand signs. These became popular especially during the Occupy Wall Street protests of 2011 and had a direct influence on student activists' usage of them.

16 A member of the Rada, Hrynevych chaired the Parliamentary Committee for Science and Education.

17 Zgurovs'ky was at the time the rector of Kyiv Polytechnic Institute and previously had been minister of education from 1994 to 1999 under President Leonid Kuchma.

18 In 2020, Marchenko became minister of finance under President Volodymyr Zelensky.

6. "These aren't your values": Gender and Nation on Maidan

1 The most visible "feminist" group since Ukraine's independence is Femen, whose activists famously did topless protests for various issues, beginning with sex tourism. Significant research has been undertaken on this group (for instance, see Channell 2014; Zychowicz 2011, 2020; and the films *Ukraine Is Not a Brothel* [Green 2013] and *Je suis Femen* [Margot 2014]), so I do not include a lengthy discussion of their work here. It is sufficient to note that, while many of the group's participants have engaged with feminist scholarship (from both the Western canon and that of Soviet feminism), they have been widely discredited because of revelations about their funding sources from men encouraging them to use toplessness as a tactic. Leading Ukrainian feminist scholar and activist Oksana Kis stated in an interview that "Femen has nothing in common with feminism" (Lazurkevych 2015). Further, Femen members did not appear on Maidan, and I never found any evidence that they had made statements about the protests at all.

2 When I asked interviewees in Ukraine how to talk about gender in Ukrainian, they overwhelmingly used the Ukrainian *hender*, which begins with the Ukrainian letter г; however, diasporic Ukrainian-Americans often say *gender*, beginning with the letter ґ. According to Ukrainian linguist Yuri Shevchuk, the Russification of the Ukrainian language throughout the Soviet period led to a decreased usage of "g" in Ukrainian in favour of "h" (personal communication, this even though "g" is a letter in Russian whereas "h" is not). Young Ukrainians' usage of *hender* rather than *gender* is a reflection of these shifts in the Ukrainian language during socialism, while diasporic Ukrainians preserve a less Sovietized form of the language.

3 This research and advocacy project did result in a change in Ukrainian law allowing women to serve in combat roles in the military, expanding their protections and benefits as veterans. A second report was published in 2019, detailing the experiences of women veterans' return to civilian life (Martsenyuk et al. 2019).

4 I first saw this image in 2012 as a colour poster being sold at a small shop in L'viv, but it was widely circulated as a black-and-white image on Maidan.

5 One exception to this is *Varto u Likarni*, discussed in chapter 4, in which men and women participated on relatively equal footing. There certainly might have been other gender-balanced initiatives that did not come onto my radar during my research.

6 See also Gal and Kligman (2000, especially chap. 3), to problematize further the notions of public and private for women and feminism.

7 Virtual discussions can certainly create important space for feminism, particularly the aforementioned flash mob #янебоюсясказати, "I am not afraid to say it," about sexual harassment and assault (Aripova and Johnson 2018).

8 Kolomayets was known for her support of women's initiatives and women's representation in politics after Ukraine's independence. As a Fulbrighter that year, I did not work with her on this initiative, but she was involved with this project and with generating support for women's brigades.

9 These comments are reproduced from my notes of the event and translated from Ukrainian.

10 Women's brigades have appeared only since March 2014, after the major violence during Maidan; they were not mobilized during the violence between police and protesters in January or February, although some individual women did participate. Some of these brigades have mobilized to the front in eastern Ukraine.

Conclusion: Volunteerism after Maidan

1 This trend is evidenced both in scholarly work about the protests and in the use of the term across media outlets, often alongside terms such as "self-discipline" and "self-help," both of which echo neoliberal mechanisms of individualization rather than a leftist idea of communality.

2 VKontakte and Odnoklassnyki are two Russian social networking sites. They were both commonly used in Ukraine in 2013–14, during Maidan, but in 2017, then-president Poroshenko banned these and other Russian websites in an attempt to fight the spread of Russian propaganda and disinformation.

3 The Svoboda (Freedom) Party is a far-right party that gained power in the Rada in the 2012 elections. Their leader, Oleh Tyahnybok, was a main Opposition figure during Maidan, but other right-wing leaders, groups, and parties gained legitimacy during and after the protests and have given Svoboda competition on the right.

4 This did not prevent right-wing groups from assuming leftists were sympathetic to the separatists. In two separate attacks on leftist activists after Maidan, one of the epithets used against them was that they were separatists as well as communists.

5 In Ukrainian, *okrema medychna bryhada shvydkoho pryznachennia*.

6 The Ukrainian military does not draft men above the age of fifty-five, so conscripts tend to be young men (largely between eighteen and twenty-five years old; the draft does not extend to registered university students). The volunteer brigades, however, do not have such rules, so

many of these participants were in their mid-fifties and sixties, skewing the statistics about the age of fighters.

7 An additional standpoint among leftists is an anarcho-nationalist perspective, including radical leftists who support the war and fight in the ATO as an anti-Russia, anti-imperial, anti-state position. See Wishart (2019) for more on the politics and activism of this group.

8 Because my analysis of Vitalii's volunteerism comes from what he and others posted on Facebook, I do not examine people's negative opinions of his actions. For the most part, people respected Vitalii's wishes and did not publicly berate him for this choice, although they may have done so in a more private space.

9 This quote is translated from a Facebook post about Vitalii's visit.

References

Abrams, Philip. 2006. "Notes on the Difficulty of Studying the State." In *The Anthropology of the State: A Reader*, edited by Aradhana Sharma and Akhil Gupta, 112–27. Malden, MA: Blackwell.

Althusser, Louis. 2001. "Ideology and Ideological State Apparatuses." In *Lenin and Philosophy*, 85–126. New York: Monthly Review Press.

Antonova, Natalia. 2017. "'I'm Not Afraid to Say' that Something's Changing in Ukraine." *Open Democracy*, 23 August. https://www.opendemocracy.net/en/odr/i-m-not-afraid-to-say-something-s-changing-in-ukraine/.

Appel, Hilary. 2005. "Anti-Communist Justice and Founding the Post-Communist Order: Lustration and Restitution in Central Europe." *East European Politics & Societies* 19, no. 3 (Summer): 379–405. https://doi.org/10.1177/0888325405278020.

Appelbaum, Anne. 2017. *Red Famine: Stalin's War on Ukraine*. New York: Doubleday.

Arel, Dominique. 1995. "Ukraine: The Temptation of the Nationalizing State." In *Political Culture and Civil Society in Russia and the New States of Eurasia*, edited by Vladimir Tismaneanu, 157–88. Armonk, NY: M.E. Sharpe.

Aripova, Feruza, and Janet Elise Johnson. 2018. "The Ukrainian-Russian Virtual Flash Mob against Sexual Assault." *Journal of Social Policy Studies* 16 (3): 487–500. https://doi.org/10.17323/727-0634-2018-16-3-487-500.

Art Leaks. 2012. "Statement of the Visual Culture Research Center, National University of Kyiv-Mohyla Academy (Kyiv, Ukraine)." 11 February. https://art-leaks.org/2012/02/11/statement-of-the-visual-culture-research-center-national-university-of-kyiv-mohyla-academy-kyiv-ukraine/.

Asher, Andrew. 2005. "A Paradise on the Oder? Ethnicity, Europeanization, and the EU Referendum in a Polish-German Border City." *City and Society* 17, no. 1 (June): 127–52. https://doi.org/10.1525/city.2005.17.1.127.

Ashwin, Sarah. 2000. *Gender, State and Society in Soviet and Post-Soviet Russia*. New York: Routledge.

Aydarova, Olena. 2015. "Glories of the Soviet Past or Dim Visions of the Future: Russian Teacher Education as the Site of Historical Becoming." *Anthropology & Education Quarterly* 46, no. 2 (June): 147–66. https://doi.org/10.1111/aeq.12096.

Aydin, Filiz T., and Fethi K. Sahin. 2019. "The Politics of Recognition of Crimean Tatar Collective Rights in the Post-Soviet Period: With Special Attention to the Russian Annexation of Crimea." *Communist and Post-Communist Studies* 52, no. 1 (March): 39–50. https://doi.org/10.1016/j.postcomstud.2019.02.003.

Balmforth, Richard, and Pavel Polityuk. 2014. "Ukraine Parliament Pushes through Sweeping Anti-Protest Law." *Reuters*, 16 January. https://www.reuters.com/article/us-ukraine-law-idUSBREA0F1QV20140116.

Ban, Cornel. 2015. "Beyond Anticommunism: The Fragility of Class Analysis in Romania." *East European Politics and Societies and Cultures* 29, no. 3 (August): 640–50. https://doi.org/10.1177/0888325415599197.

Bar-on Cohen, Einat. 2010. "Globalisation of the War on Violence: Israeli Close Combat, *Krav maga*, and Sudden Alterations in Intensity." *Social Anthropology* 18, no. 3 (August): 267–88. https://doi.org/10.1111/j.1469-8676.2010.00111.x.

Barrington, Lowell W., and Erik S. Herron. 2004. "One Ukraine or Many? Regionalism in Ukraine and Its Political Consequences." *Nationalities Papers* 32, no. 1 (March): 53–86. https://doi.org/10.1080/0090599042000186179.

BBC News. 2014. "Crimean Referendum: What Does the Paper Ballot Say?" 10 March. https://www.bbc.com/news/world-europe-26514797.

BBC Ukrainian. 2009. "'Na Lenini lytsia nemaie!' – ukrains'ka presa u seredu" [There is no face on Lenin! – the Ukrainian press on Wednesday]. 1 July. https://www.bbc.com/ukrainian/pressreview/story/2009/07/090701_ua_press_1_06.

Bellinger III, John B. 2014. "Why the Crimean Referendum is Illegitimate." *Council on Foreign Relations*, 16 March. https://www.cfr.org/interview/why-crimean-referendum-illegitimate.

Berdyns'kykh, Kristina. 2014. *Ye Liudy: Tepli Istorii z Maidanu* [There are people: Warm stories from Maidan]. Kyiv: Bright Star Publishing.

Blacker, Uilleam. 2020. "Lenin in Kyiv, Colston in Bristol: What Can the UK Learn from 'Decommunisation' in Ukraine?" *Open Democracy*, 26 June. https://www.opendemocracy.net/en/odr/lenin-kyiv-colston-bristol/.

Blum, Douglas W. 2007. *National Identity and Globalization: Youth, State, and Society in Post-Soviet Eurasia*. New York: Cambridge University Press.

Bobbio, Norberto. 1996. *Left and Right: The Significance of a Political Distinction*. Chicago: University of Chicago Press.

Bockman, Johanna, and Gil Eyal. 2002. "Eastern Europe as a Laboratory for Economic Knowledge: The Transnational Roots of Neoliberalism." *American*

Journal of Sociology 108, no. 2 (September): 310–52. https://doi.org/10.1086/344411.

Bohachevsky-Chomiak, Martha. 1988. *Feminists Despite Themselves: Women in Ukrainian Community Life, 1884–1939*. Edmonton: University of Alberta, Canadian Institute of Ukrainian Studies.

Bourdieu, Pierre. 1967. "Systems of Education and Systems of Thought." *International Social Science Journal* 19 (3): 338–58.

Bourdieu, Pierre, and Jean-Claude Passeron. 1990. *Reproduction in Education, Society and Culture*. Newbury Park, CA: SAGE.

Bova, Russell. 1991. "Worker Activism: The Role of the State." In *Perestroika from Below: Social Movements in the Soviet Union*, edited by Judith B. Sedaitis and Jim Butterfield, 29–41. Boulder, CO: Westview Press.

Brown, Kate. 2004. *A Biography of No Place: From Ethnic Borderland to Soviet Heartland*. Cambridge: Harvard University Press.

Bulakh, Tetiana. 2015. "Ukrainian Glamour as a Consequence of the Soviet Past." In *New Imaginaries: Youthful Reinvention of Ukraine's Cultural Paradigm*, edited by Marian Rubchak, 89–109. New York: Berghahn Books.

Bureychak, Tetyana. 2012. "Masculinity in Soviet and Post-Soviet Ukraine: Models and Their Implications." In *Gender, Politics, and Society in Ukraine*, edited by Olena Hankivsky and Anastasia Salnykova, 325–61. Toronto: University of Toronto Press.

Bureychak, Tetyana, and Petrenko, Olena. 2014. "Kanapky, Sich, ta 'Banderivky'" [Sandwiches, Sich, and 'Banderivky']. *Zakhid*, 8 January. http://zaxid.net/news/showNews.do?kanapki_sich_ta_banderivki&objectId=1300428.

Bustikova, Lenka. 2019. *Extreme Reactions: Radical Right Mobilizations in Eastern Europe*. Cambridge: Cambridge University Press.

Butterfield, Jim, and Judith B. Sedaitis. 1991. "The Emergence of Social Movements in the Soviet Union." In *Perestroika from Below: Social Movements in the Soviet Union*, edited by Judith B. Sedaitis and Jim Butterfield, 1–12. Boulder, CO: Westview Press.

Caldwell, Melissa L. 2004. *Not by Bread Alone: Social Support in the New Russia*. Berkeley: University of California Press.

Calhoun, Noel. 2002. "The Ideological Dilemma of Lustration in Poland." *East European Politics & Societies* 16, no. 2 (Spring): 494–520. https://doi.org/10.1177/088832540201600207.

Carroll, Jennifer J. 2014. "This Is Not about Europe: Reflections on Ukraine's EuroMaidan Revolution." *Perspectives on Europe* 44, no. 1 (Spring): 8–15.

Carroll, Jennifer J. 2019. *Narkomania: Drugs, HIV, and Citizenship in Ukraine*. Ithaca, NY: Cornell University Press.

Casas-Cortés, María Isabel, Michal Osterweil, and Dana E. Powell. 2008. "Blurring Boundaries: Recognizing Knowledge-Practices in the Study of

Social Movements." *Anthropological Quarterly* 81, no. 1 (Winter): 17–58. https://doi.org/10.1353/anq.2008.0006.

Cervinkova, Hana. 2016. "Producing Homogeneity as a Historical Tradition: Neoconservatism, Precarity, and Citizenship Education in Poland." *Journal for Critical Education Policy Studies* 14, no. 3 (December): 43–55. http://www.jceps.com/archives/3200.

Channell, Emily. 2014. "Is Sextremism the New Feminism? Perspectives from Pussy Riot and Femen." *Nationalities Papers* 42, no. 4 (July): 611–14. https://doi.org/10.1080/00905992.2014.917074.

Channell-Justice, Emily. 2015. "Ukraine's Long Road to 'Decommunization.'" *Anthropology News* 56, no. 11–12 (November–December): 5. https://doi.org/10.1111/j.1556-3502.2015.561105_s.x.

Channell-Justice, Emily. 2017. "'We're Not Just Sandwiches': Europe, Nation, and Feminist (Im)Possibilities on Ukraine's Maidan." *Signs: Journal of Women in Culture and Society* 42, no. 3 (Spring): 717–41. https://doi.org/10.1086/689639.

Channell-Justice, Emily. 2019a. "Thinking through Positionality in Post-Socialist Politics: Researching Contemporary Social Movements in Ukraine." *History and Anthropology* 30, no. 1 (January): 47–66. https://doi.org/10.1080/02757206.2018.1532894.

Channell-Justice, Emily. 2019b. "'Time for Intensive Change': Ukrainian Revolutions in Global Context." *Revolutionary Russia* 32 (1): 110–33. https://doi.org/10.1080/09546545.2019.1603382.

Channell-Justice, Emily. 2019c. "'We Made a Contribution to the Revolution': Shifting Scales of Politics and Unity in Ukraine." *City and Society* 31, no. 3 (December): 462–83. https://doi.org/10.1111/ciso.12236.

Channell-Justice, Emily. 2020a. "Gender, Feminism, and Nation: Contributions of the Socialist and Post-Socialist Worlds." *Feminist Anthropology* 1, no. 1 (May): 24–31. https://doi.org/10.1002/fea2.12001.

Channell-Justice, Emily. 2020b. "LGBT+ Rights, European Values, and Radical Critique: Leftist Challenges to LGBT+ Mainstreaming in Ukraine." In *Decolonizing Queer Experience: LGBT+ Narratives from Eastern Europe and Eurasia,* edited by Emily Channell-Justice, 75–94. Lanham, MD: Lexington Books.

Charron, Austin. 2016. "Whose Is Crimea? Contested Sovereignty and Regional Identity." *Region* 5 (2): 225–56. https://doi.org/10.1353/reg.2016.0017.

Charron, Austin. 2020. "Indigeneity, Displacement, and Regional Place Attachment among IDPs from Crimea." *Geographical Review* 112, no. 1 (January): 86–102. https://doi.org/10.1080/00167428.2020.1780128.

Chase, William. 1989. "Voluntarism, Mobilisation, and Coercion: Subbotniki 1919–1921." *Soviet Studies* 41, no. 1 (January): 111–28. https://doi.org/10.1080/09668138908411795.

Chelcea, Liviu, and Oana Druta. 2016. "Zombie Socialism and the Rise of Neoliberalism in Post-Socialist Central and Eastern Europe." *Eurasian*

Geography and Economics 57, nos. 4–5 (September): 521–44. https://doi.org /10.1080/15387216.2016.1266273.

Chushak, Nadiya, 2013. "Yugonostalgic against All Odds: Nostalgia for Socialist Federal Republic of Yugoslavia among Young Leftist Activists in Contemporary Serbia." PhD diss., University of Melbourne.

Clark, Charles E. 2000. *Uprooting Otherness: The Literacy Campaign in NEP-Era Russia.* Selinsgrove, PA: Susquehanna University Press.

Commons. n.d. Accessed 30 June 2022. https://commons.com.ua/uk/.

Cook, Linda J. 2007. *Postcommunist Welfare States: Reform Politics in Russia and Eastern Europe.* Ithaca, NY: Cornell University Press.

Coronil, Fernando. 2011. "The Future in Question: History and Utopia in Latin America (1989–2010). In *Business as Usual: The Roots of the Global Financial Meltdown,* edited by Craig Calhoun and Georgi Derluguian, 231–64. New York: NYU Press.

Cybriwsky, Roman Adrian. 2014. *Kyiv, Ukraine: The City of Domes and Demons from the Collapse of Socialism to the Mass Uprising of 2013–2014.* Amsterdam: Amsterdam University Press.

Dickinson, Jennifer. 2010. "Languages for the Market, the Nation, or the Margins: Overlapping Ideologies of Language and Identity in Zakarpattia." *International Journal of the Sociology of Language* 2010, no. 201 (February): 53–78. https://doi.org/10.1515/ijsl.2010.004.

Dickinson, Jennifer. 2014. "Prosymo Maksymal'nyi Perepost! Tactical and Discursive Uses of Social Media in Ukraine's EuroMaidan." *Ab Imperio,* no. 3, 75–93. https://doi.org/10.1353/imp.2014.0058.

Diuk, Nadia. 2014. "Finding Ukraine." *Journal of Democracy* 25, no. 3 (July): 83–9. https://doi.org/10.1353/jod.2014.0041.

Drakulić, Slavenka. 1993. *How We Survived Communism and Even Laughed.* New York: Harper Perennial.

Driscoll, Jesse. 2019. *Ukraine's Civil War: Would Accepting This Terminology Help Resolve the Conflict?* PONARS Eurasia Policy Memo 572. https://www .ponarseurasia.org/ukraine-s-civil-war-would-accepting-this-terminology -help-resolve-the-conflict/.

Dunn, Elizabeth, and Michael Bobick. 2014. "The Empire Strikes Back: War without War and Occupation without Occupation in the Russian Sphere of Influence." *American Ethnologist* 41, no. 3 (August): 405–13. https://doi.org /10.1111/amet.12086.

Edelman, Marc. 2001. "Social Movements: Changing Paradigms and Forms of Politics." *Annual Review of Anthropology* 30 (October): 285–317. https://doi .org/10.1146/annurev.anthro.30.1.285.

Eliasoph, Nina. 2011. *Making Volunteers: Civic Life After Welfare's End.* Princeton, NJ: Princeton University Press.

Emeran, Christine. 2017. *New Generation Political Activism in Ukraine: 2000– 2014.* New York: Routledge.

Enloe, Cynthia. 2004. "All the Men Are in the Militias, All the Women Are Victims: The Politics of Masculinity and Femininity in Nationalist Wars." In *Curious Feminist: Searching for Women in a New Age of Empire*, 99–118. Berkeley: University of California Press.

European Higher Education Area (EHEA). n.d. Accessed 30 June 2022. http://www.ehea.info/.

Eyal, Gil. 2000. "Anti-Politics and the Spirit of Capitalism: Dissidents, Monetarists, and the Czech Transition to Capitalism." *Theory and Society: Renewal and Critique in Social Theory* 29, no. 1 (February): 49–92. https://doi.org/10.1023/A:1007086330378.

Fimyar, Olena. 2008. "Educational Policy-Making in Post-Communist Ukraine as an Example of Emerging Governmentality: Discourse and Analysis of Curriculum Choice and Assessment Policy Documents (1999–2003)." *Journal of Education Policy* 23, no. 6 (November): 571–94. https://doi.org/10.1080/02680930802382920.

Follis, Karolina S. 2012. *Building Fortress Europe: The Polish-Ukrainian Frontier.* Philadelphia: University of Pennsylvania Press.

Fournier, Anna. 2012. *Forging Rights in a New Democracy: Ukrainian Students between Freedom and Justice.* Philadelphia: University of Pennsylvania Press.

Fournier, Anna. 2018. "From Frozen Conflict to Mobile Boundary: Youth Perception of Territoriality in War-Time Ukraine." *East European Politics and Societies and Cultures* 32, no. 1 (February): 23–55. https://doi.org/10.1177/0888325417740627.

Freilikher, D. Ia. 1968. "Komunistychni subotnyky na zaliznytsiakh Ukraïny pid chas borot'by z Vranhelem" [Communist *subotnyky* on the railways of Ukraine during the struggle with Wrangel]. *Ukrainian Historical Journal* 88 (7): 92–6.

Funk, Nanette, and Magda Mueller. 1993. *Gender Politics and Post-Communism: Reflections from Eastern Europe and the Former Soviet Union.* New York: Routledge.

Fürst, Juliane. 2010. *Stalin's Last Generation: Soviet Post-War Youth and the Emergence of Mature Socialism.* New York: Oxford University Press.

Gal, Susan, and Gail Kligman. 2000. *The Politics of Gender after Socialism.* Princeton, NJ: Princeton University Press.

Ganev, Venelin. 2014. "The Legacies of 1989: Bulgaria's Year of Civic Anger." *Journal of Democracy* 25, no. 1 (January): 33–45. https://doi.org/10.1353/jod.2014.0006.

Gatskova, Kseniia, and Maksim Gatskov. 2016. "Third Sector in Ukraine: Civic Engagement Before and After the 'Euromaidan.'" *Voluntas* 27, no. 2 (April): 673–94. https://doi.org/10.1007/s11266-015-9626-7.

Gebel, Michael, and Anna Baranowska-Rataj. 2012. "New Inequalities through Privatization and Marketization? An Analysis of Labour Market Entry of

Higher Education Graduates in Poland and Ukraine." *European Sociological Review* 28, no. 6 (December): 729–41. https://doi.org/10.1093/esr/jcs012.

Georgescu, Diana. 2015. "'Ceausescu's Children': The Making and Unmaking of Romania's Last Socialist Generation (1965–2010)." PhD diss., University of Illinois–Urbana.

Ghodsee, Kristen. 2004. "Feminism-by-Design: Emerging Capitalisms, Cultural Feminism, and Women's Nongovernmental Organizations in Postsocialist Eastern Europe." *Signs: Journal of Women in Culture and Society* 29, no. 3 (Spring): 727–53. https://doi.org/10.1086/380631.

Ghodsee, Kristen. 2018. *Second World, Second Sex: Socialist Women's Activism and Global Solidarity During the Cold War*. Durham, NC: Duke University Press.

Gökarıksel, Saygun. 2017. "The Ends of Revolution: Capitalist De-Democratization and Nationalist Populism in the East of Europe." *Dialectical Anthropology* 41, no. 3 (September): 207–22. https://doi.org/10.1007/s10624-017-9464-7.

González-Enríquez, Carmen. 2001. "De-Communization and Political Justice in Central and Eastern Europe." In *The Politics of Memory and Democratization*, edited by Alexandra Barahona de Brito, 219–47. Oxford: Oxford University Press.

Goodman, Bridget. 2018. "Acts of Negotiation: Governmentality and Medium of Instruction in an Eastern Ukrainian University." *Anthropology and Education Quarterly* 49, no. 1 (March): 36–52. https://doi.org/10.1111/aeq.12236.

Goodwin, Jeff, James M. Jasper, and Francesca Polletta. 2001. *Passionate Politics: Emotions and Social Movements*. Chicago: University of Chicago Press.

Gorchinskaya, Katya. 2016. "He Killed for the Maidan." *Foreign Policy*, 26 February. https://foreignpolicy.com/2016/02/26/he-killed-for-the-maidan/.

Gorsuch, Anne E. 2000. *Youth in Revolutionary Russia: Enthusiasts, Bohemians, Delinquents*. Bloomington: Indiana University Press.

Goujon, Alexandra. 2016. "Local State Capacities Facing Multiple Actors in the City of Slaviansk." Paper presented at the Association for the Study of Nationalities World Convention, Columbia University, New York, April.

Goven, Joanna. 1993. "Gender Politics in Hungary: Autonomy and Antifeminism." In *Gender Politics and Post-Communism: Reflections from Eastern Europe and the Former Soviet Union*, edited by Nanette Funk and Magda Mueller, 224–40. New York: Routledge.

Graeber, David. 2002. "The New Anarchists." *New Left Review* 13 (January/February). https://newleftreview.org/issues/ii13/articles/david-graeber-the-new-anarchists.

Graeber, David. 2009. *Direct Action: An Ethnography*. Baltimore: AK Press.

Graff, Agnieszka. 2014. "Report from the Gender Trenches: War against 'Genderism' in Poland." *European Journal of Women's Studies* 21, no. 4 (November): 431–5. https://doi.org/10.1177/1350506814546091.

Green, Kitty, dir. 2013. *Ukraine Is Not a Brothel*. Carlton, Australia: Noise and Light. Documentary, 78 min.

Greenberg, Jessica. 2014. *After the Revolution: Youth, Democracy, and the Politics of Disappointment in Serbia*. Palo Alto, CA: Stanford University Press.

Greenhouse, Carol J. 2009. "Introduction." In *Ethnographies of Neoliberalism*, edited by Carol J. Greenhouse, 1–10. Philadelphia: University of Pennsylvania Press.

Guenther, Katja. 2011. "The Possibilities and Pitfalls of NGO Feminism: Insights from Postsocialist Eastern Europe." *Signs: Journal of Women in Culture and Society* 36, no. 4 (Summer): 863–87. https://doi.org/10.1086/658504.

Haidai, Oleksandra. 2018. *Kam'ianyi Hist': Lenin u Tsentral'nii Ukraïni* [Stone guest: Lenin in central Ukraine]. Kyiv: KIS Press.

Halmai, Gábor, and Kim Lane Scheppele. 1997. "Living Well Is the Best Revenge: The Hungarian Approach to Judging the Past." In *Transitional Justice and the Rule of Law in New Democracies*, edited by A. James McAdams, 155–84. Notre Dame, IN: University of Notre Dame Press.

Haney, Lynne A. 2002. *Inventing the Needy: Gender and the Politics of Welfare in Hungary*. Berkeley: University of California Press.

Harvey, David. 2005. *A Brief History of Neoliberalism*. New York: Oxford University Press.

Havryshko, Marta. 2018. "Love and Sex in Wartime: Controlling Women's Sexuality in the Ukrainian Nationalist Underground." *Aspasia* 12, no. 1 (March): 35–67. https://doi.org/10.3167/asp.2018.120103.

Hellbeck, Jochen. 2009. *Revolution on My Mind: Writing a Diary under Stalin*. Cambridge, MA: Harvard University Press.

Hemment, Julie. 2007. *Empowering Women in Russia: Activism, Aid, and NGOs*. Bloomington: Indiana University Press.

Hemment, Julie. 2009. "Soviet-Style Neoliberalism? Nashi, Youth Voluntarism, and the Restructuring of Social Welfare in Russia." *Problems of Post-Communism* 56, no. 6 (November): 36–50. https://doi.org/10.2753/PPC1075-8216560604.

Hemment, Julie. 2012. "Nashi, Youth Voluntarism, and Potemkin NGOs: Making Sense of Civil Society in Post-Soviet Russia." *Slavic Review* 71, no. 2 (Summer): 234–60. https://doi.org/10.5612/slavicreview.71.2.0234.

Hemment, Julie. 2015. *Youth Politics in Putin's Russia: Producing Patriots and Entrepreneurs*. Bloomington: Indiana University Press.

Herszenhorn, David M. 2014. "Crimea Votes to Secede from Ukraine as Russian Troops Keep Watch." *New York Times*, 16 March. https://www

.nytimes.com/2014/03/17/world/europe/crimea-ukraine-secession-vote
-referendum.html.

Hibou, Béatrice. 2004. "From Privatising the Economy to Privatising the State:
An Analysis of the Continual Formation of the State." In *Privatizing the
State*, edited by Béatrice Hibou, 1–47. New York: Columbia University Press.

Hillis, Faith. 2013. *Children of Rus': Right-Bank Ukraine and the Invention of a
Russian Nation*. Ithaca, NY: Cornell University Press.

Hirsch, Francine. 2005. *Empire of Nations: Ethnographic Knowledge and the
Making of the Soviet Union*. Ithaca, NY: Cornell University Press.

Höjdestrand, Tova. 2009. *Needed by Nobody: Homelessness and Humanness in
Post-Socialist Russia*. Ithaca, NY: Cornell University Press.

Horváth, Ágnes, and Árpád Szakolczai. 1992. *The Dissolution of Communist
Power: The Case of Hungary*. New York: Routledge.

Hrycak, Alexandra. 2006. "Foundation Feminism and the Articulation of
Hybrid Feminisms in Post-Socialist Ukraine." *East European Politics and
Societies* 20, no. 1 (February): 69–100. https://doi.org/10.1177
/0888325405284249.

Hrytsak, Yaroslav. 2004. "On Sails and Gales, and Ships Sailing in Various
Directions: Post-Soviet Ukraine. *Ab Imperio*, no. 1, 229–54. https://doi.org
/10.1353/imp.2004.0033.

Hrytsak, Yaroslav. 2015. "Rethinking Ukraine." In *What Does Ukraine Think?*,
edited by Andrew Wilson, 34–44. London: European Council on Foreign
Relations.

Hrytsak, Yaroslav. 2019. "Ukraine in 2013–2014: A New Political Geography."
In *Regionalism without Regions: Reconceptualizing Ukraine's Heterogeneity*,
edited by Ulrich Schmid and Oksana Myshlovska, 367–92. Budapest:
Central European University Press.

Hrytsenko, Anna, Anna Kvit, and Tamara Martsenyuk. 2016. *Invisible Battalion:
Women's Participation in ATO Military Operations in Ukraine*. United Nations
Entity for Gender Equality and the Empowerment of Women (UN Women).
https://eca.unwomen.org/en/digital-library/publications/2016/08
/invisible-battalion-womens-participation-in-ato-military-operations
-in-ukraine.

Humenyuk, Natalia. 2020. *Zahublenyi Ostriv: Knyha Reportazhiv z Okupovanoho
Krymu* [Lost island: A book of reportages from occupied Crimea]. L'viv:
Staryi Lev.

Humphrey, Caroline. 2002. *The Unmaking of Soviet Life: Everyday Economies after
Socialism*. Ithaca, NY: Cornell University Press.

Hyatt, Susan Brin. 2001. "From Citizen to Volunteer: Neoliberal Governance
and the Erasure of Poverty." In *The New Poverty Studies: The Ethnography of
Power, Politics, and Impoverished People in the United States*, edited by Judith
Goode and Jeff Maskovsky, 201–35. New York: New York University Press.

Ishchenko, Volodymyr. 2016. "Far Right Participation in the Ukrainian Maidan Protests: An Attempt of Systematic Estimation." *European Politics and Society* 17, no. 4 (October): 453–72. https://doi.org/10.1080/23745118.2016.1154646.

Ishchenko, Volodymyr. 2020. "Insufficiently Diverse: The Problem of Nonviolent Leverage and Radicalization of Ukraine's Maidan Uprising, 2013–2014." *Journal of Eurasian Studies* 11, no. 2 (July): 201–15. https://doi.org/10.1177/1879366520928363.

Ishchenko, Volodymyr, and Mihai Varga. 2021. "Focusing on Extremism Won't Counter Far-Right Violence." *Open Democracy*, 3 December. https://www.opendemocracy.net/en/north-africa-west-asia/focusing-on-extremism-wont-counter-far-right-violence/.

Istorychna Pravda. 2013. "Istoriia Pam'iatnyka Leninu v Kyievi" [The history of the Lenin monument in Kyiv]. 12 September. https://www.istpravda.com.ua/articles/2013/12/9/140323/.

Jasper, James M. 1998. "The Emotions of Protest: Affective and Reactive Emotions in and around Social Movements." *Sociological Forum* 13, no. 3 (September): 397–424. https://doi.org/10.1023/A:1022175308081.

Johnson, Janet Elise. 2017. "Anti-Genderism vs. Feminism in Russia: Criminalization and Decriminalization of Domestic Violence." Presented at the Association for Slavic, East European, and Eurasian Studies Convention, Chicago, November.

Johnson, Janet Elise, and Jean C. Robinson. 2007. "Living Gender." In *Living Gender after Communism*, edited by Janet Elise Johnson and Jean C. Robinson, 1–24. Bloomington: Indiana University Press.

Johnson, Juliet. 2016. *Priests of Prosperity: How Central Bankers Transformed the Postcommunist World*. Ithaca, NY: Cornell University Press.

Juris, Jeffrey. 2012. "Reflections on #Occupy Everywhere: Social Media, Public Space, and Emerging Logics of Aggregation." *American Ethnologist* 39, no. 2 (May): 259–79. https://doi.org/10.1111/j.1548-1425.2012.01362.x.

Juris, Jeffrey, and Alex Khasnabish. 2013. *Insurgent Encounters: Transnational Activism, Ethnography, and the Political*. Durham, NC: Duke University Press.

Kaplan, Frederick I. 1965. "The Origin and Function of the Subbotniks and Voskreseniks." *Jahrbücher für Geschichte Osteuropas* 13, no. 1 (April): 30–9. https://www.jstor.org/stable/41042470.

Katchanovski, Ivan. 2015. "The 'Snipers' Massacre' on the Maidan in Ukraine." Paper Presented at the American Political Science Association Annual Meeting, San Francisco, September.

Kebalo, Martha Kichorowska. 2007. "Exploring Continuities and Reconciling Ruptures: Nationalism, Feminism, and the Ukrainian Women's Movement." *Aspasia* 1, no. 1 (March): 36–60. https://doi.org/10.3167/asp.2007.010103.

Kebalo, Martha Kichorowska. 2011. "Personal Narratives of Women's Leadership and Community Activism in Cherkasy Oblast." PhD diss., City University of New York.

Kems'kyi, Serhii. 2013. "Chuiesh, Maidane?" [Do you hear, Maidan?] *Ukrains'ka Pravda*, 19 December. https://www.pravda.com.ua/columns /2013/12/19/7007716/.

Khromeychuk, Olesya. 2013. *"Undetermined" Ukrainians: Postwar Narratives of the Waffen SS "Galicia" Division*. Oxford: Peter Lang.

Khromeychuk, Olesya. 2018. "From the Maidan to the Donbas: The Limitations on Choice for Women in Ukraine." In *Gender and Choice after Socialism*, edited by Lynne Attwood, Elisabeth Schimpfössel, and Marina Yusupova, 47–78. Cham, Switzerland: Palgrave Macmillan.

Khromeychuk, Olesya. 2020. "On the Edge of a European War, Who Gets to Defend the State?" *Open Democracy*, 14 October. https://www .opendemocracy.net/en/odr/who-gets-defend-state-ukraine/.

Kis, Oksana. 2002. "Modeli Konstruiuvannia Gendernoï Identychnosty Zhinky v Suchasnii Ukraïni" [Models of women's gender identity construction in contemporary Ukraine]. *Yi*, no. 27, 38–58. http://www.ji .lviv.ua/n27texts/kis.htm.

Kis, Oksana. 2012. "(Re)Constructing Ukrainian Women's History: Actors, Agents, and Narratives." In *Gender, Politics, and Society in Ukraine*, edited by Olena Hankivsky and Anastasia Salnykova, 152–79. Toronto: University of Toronto Press.

Kis, Oksana, and Tetyana Bureychak. 2015. "Gender Dreams or Sexism? Advertising in Post-Soviet Ukraine." In *New Imaginaries: Youthful Reinvention of Ukraine's Cultural Paradigm*, edited by Marian Rubchak, 110–40. New York: Berghahn Books.

Kopeček, Lubomír. 2010. "Dealing with the Communist Past: Its Role in the Disintegration of the Czech Civic Forum and in the Emergence of the Civic Democratic Party." *Communist and Post-Communist Studies* 43, no. 2 (June): 199–208. https://doi.org/10.1016/j.postcomstud.2010.04.002.

Kotaleichuk, Anna. 2014. "This Is Not a Ukrainian Civil War." *New Eastern Europe*, 26 January. https://neweasterneurope.eu/2014/01/26/this-is-not -a-ukrainian-civil-war/.

Kozyrska, Antonina. 2016. "Decommunisation of the Public Space in Post-Euromaidan Ukraine." *Polish Political Science Yearbook* 45 (2016): 130–44. https://doi.org/10.15804/ppsy2016010.

Krasynska, Svitlana, and Eric Martin. 2017. "The Formality of Informal Civil Society: Ukraine's EuroMaidan." *Voluntas* 28, no. 1 (February): 420–49. https://doi.org/10.1007/s11266-016-9819-8.

Krytyka. n.d. Accessed 30 June 2022. https://krytyka.com/en.

Kudelia, Serhiy. 2014. "The House that Yanukovych Built." *Journal of Democracy* 25, no. 3 (July): 19–34. https://doi.org/10.1353/jod.2014.0039.

Kulyk, Volodymyr. 2014. "Ukrainian Nationalism Since the Outbreak of Euromaidan." *Ab Imperio*, no. 3, 94–122. https://doi.org/10.1353/imp .2014.0064.

Kurkov, Andrey. 2014. *Ukraine Diaries*. London: Random House.

Kurtović, Larisa. 2015. "'Who Sows Hunger, Reaps Rage': On Protest, Indignation, and Redistributive Justice in Post-Dayton Bosnia-Herzegovina." *Southeast European and Black Sea Studies* 15, no. 4 (October): 639–59. https://doi.org/10.1080/14683857.2015.1126095.

Kurtović, Larisa, and Azra Hromadžić. 2017. "Cannibal States, Empty Bellies: Protest, History, and Political Imagination in Post-Dayton Bosnia." *Critique of Anthropology* 37, no. 3 (September): 1–35. https://doi.org/10.1177/0308275X17719988.

Kurtović, Larisa, and Nelly Sargsyan. 2019. "After Utopia: Leftist Imaginaries and Activist Politics in the Postsocialist World." *History and Anthropology* 30, no. 1 (January): 1–19. https://doi.org/10.1080/02757206.2018.1530669.

Kuzio, Taras. 2015. "Competing Nationalisms, Euromaidan, and the Russian-Ukrainian Conflict." *Studies in Ethnicity and Nationalism* 15, no. 1 (April): 157–69. https://doi.org/10.1111/sena.12137.

Kyiv International Institute of Sociology. 2021. "Socio-Political Moods of the Population of Ukraine: The Results of a Survey Conducted on October 25–29, 2021 by the Method of Personal ("Face-to-Face") Interviews." https://www.kiis.com.ua/?lang=eng&cat=reports&id=1069&page=1.

Kyiv Post. 2014. "EuroMaidan Rallies in Ukraine (February 19 Live Updates)." 19 February. https://www.kyivpost.com/article/content/ukraine-politics/euromaidan-rallies-in-ukraine-feb-19-live-updates-337098.html.

Lazurkevych, Sofiia. 2015. "'Zhinky Chasto Maiut' Alerhiiu na Feminizm'" ['Women often have an allergy to feminism']. *Zakhid*, 29 October. https://zaxid.net/zhinki_chasto_mayut_alergiyu_na_feminizm_n1370972.

Lebedev, Anna Colin. 2016. "Civilians at War: Afghanistan Veterans in the Armed Conflict in Donbas." Paper Presented at the Association for the Study of Nationalities World Convention, Columbia University, New York, April.

Ledeneva, Alena V. 2006. *How Russia Really Works: The Informal Practices that Shaped Post-Soviet Politics and Business*. Ithaca, NY: Cornell University Press.

Leksikov, Roman. 2020. "Queer People and the Criminal Justice System in Ukraine: Negotiating Relationships, Historical Trauma, and Contemporary Western Discourses." In *Decolonizing Queer Experience: LGBT+ Narratives from Eastern Europe and Eurasia*, edited by Emily Channell-Justice, 115–32. Lanham, MD: Lexington Books.

Liebich, André, Oksana Myshlovska, Viktoriia Sereda, with Oleksandra Gaidai and Iryna Sklokina. 2019. "The Ukrainian Past and Present: Legacies, Memory, and Attitudes." In *Regionalism without Regions: Reconceptualizing Ukraine's Heterogeneity*, edited by Ulrich Schmid and Oksana Myshlovska, 67–134. Budapest: Central European University Press.

Likhachev, Vyacheslav. 2015. "The 'Right Sector' and Others: The Behavior and Role of Radical Nationalists in the Ukrainian Political Crisis of Late

2013–Early 2014." *Communist and Post-Communist Studies* 48, nos. 2–3
(September): 257–71. https://doi.org/10.1016/j.postcomstud.2015.07.003.

Liva Opozytsiia. 2013. *Ukrains'ky Trots'ky* [Ukrainian Trotsky]. Odesa: Liva
Opozytsiia.

Lobanov, Volodymyr. 2002. "Dveri u pid'ïzd – zasib vid apatiï" [Doors to the
courtyard: A cure for apathy]. *Holos Ukrainy*, 5 December. http://www
.golos.com.ua/article/248639.

Lozowy, Ivan. 2011. "Education: The 'Ukrainophobe' in Charge of Educating
His Country's Youth." *Transitions Online*, 7 October. https://www.ceeol.com
/search/article-detail?id=79574.

Magocsi, Paul R. 2002. *The Roots of Ukrainian Nationalism: Galicia as Ukraine's
Piedmont*. Toronto: University of Toronto Press.

Maharawal, Manissa McCleave. 2013. "Fieldnotes on Union Square, Anti-
Oppression, and Occupy." Society for Cultural Anthropology, *Hot Spots*,
14 February. https://culanth.org/fieldsights/fieldnotes-on-union-square
-anti-oppression-and-occupy.

Margot, Alain, dir. 2014. *Je Suis Femen* [I am Femen]. Lausanne, Switzerland:
Caravel Productions. Documentary, 95 min.

Markowitz, Fran. 2000. *Coming of Age in Post-Soviet Russia*. Urbana: University
of Illinois Press.

Martsenyuk, Tamara, and Ganna Grytsenko. 2017. "Women and Military in
Ukraine: Voices of the Invisible Battalion." *Ukraine Analytica* 1 (7): 29–37.
https://ukraine-analytica.org/women-and-military-in-ukraine-voices-of
-the-invisible-battalion/.

Martsenyuk, Tamara, Anna Kvit, Anna Hrystenko, Lesia Vasylenko, and
Maria Zviahintseva. 2019. *Invisible Battalion 2.0: Women Veterans Returning
to Peaceful Life*. United Nations Entity for Gender Equality and the
Empowerment of Women (UN Women). https://eca.unwomen.org/en
/digital-library/publications/2019/11/invisible-battalion.

Mattioli, Fabio. 2020. *Dark Finance: Illiquidity and Authoritarianism at the
Margins of Europe*. Stanford, CA: Stanford University Press.

Mayerchyk, Mariya. 2014. "On the Occasion of March 8th/Recasting of
Meanings." *Krytyka*. http://krytyka.com/ua/community/blogs/do-8
-bereznya-pro-pereplavku-smysliv.

Merry, Sally Engle. 2006. "Transnational Human Rights and Local Activism:
Mapping the Middle." *American Anthropologist* 108, no. 1 (March): 38–51.
https://doi.org/10.1525/aa.2006.108.1.38.

Metzger, Megan MacDuffee, and Joshua A. Tucker. 2017. "Social Media and
EuroMaidan: A Review Essay." *Slavic Review* 76, no. 1 (Spring):169–91.
https://doi.org/10.1017/slr.2017.16.

Minakov, Mykhailo. 2016. "Civil Society and the Misbalance of a Political System
in Post-Maidan Ukraine." Paper Presented at the Association for the Study of
Nationalities World Convention, Columbia University, New York, April.

Minakov, Mykhailo. 2018. "Civil Society and the Power Elites after the Euromaidan in Ukraine: Competition, Cooperation, and Fusion." In *The Nonprofit Sector in Eastern Europe, Russia, and Central Asia: Civil Society Advances and Challenges*, edited by David Horton Smith, Alisa Moldavanova, and Svitlana Krasynska, 174–90. Leiden, Netherlands: Brill.

Muehlebach, Andrea Karin. 2012. *The Moral Neoliberal: Welfare and Citizenship in Italy*. Chicago: University of Chicago Press.

Muliavka, Viktoria. 2016. "Nova osvitnia polityka – vtratyly chy zdobuly" [New education policy: Lost or won]. *Spil'ne*, 30 August. https://commons .com.ua/uk/nova-osvitnya-politika-vtratili-chi-zdobuli/.

Mungiu-Pippidi, Alina. 2006. "Democratization without Decommunization in the Balkans." *Orbis* 50, no. 4 (Autumn): 641–55. https://doi.org/10.1016/j .orbis.2006.07.005.

Myshlovska, Oksana, Ulrich Schmid, and Tatjana Hofmann. 2019. "Introduction." In *Regionalism without Regions: Reconceptualizing Ukraine's Heterogeneity*, edited by Ulrich Schmid and Oksana Myshlovska, 3–23. Budapest: Central European University Press.

Nading, Maryna. 2022. "Solidarity against Fear." *HotSpots*, 28 March. https:// culanth.org/fieldsights/solidarity-against-fear.

Nikolayenko, Olena, and Maria DeCasper. 2018. "Why Women Protest: Insights from Ukraine's Euromaidan." *Slavic Review* 77, no. 3 (Fall): 726–51. https://doi.org/10.1017/slr.2018.207.

Nordstrom, Carolyn. 1997. *A Different Kind of War Story*. Philadelphia: University of Pennsylvania Press.

Ong, Aihwa. 2006. *Neoliberalism as Exception: Mutations in Citizenship and Sovereignty*. Durham, NC: Duke University Press.

Onuch, Olga. 2014a. "Social Networks and Social Media in Ukrainian 'Euromaidan' Protests." *Washington Post*, 2 January. https://www .washingtonpost.com/news/monkey-cage/wp/2014/01/02/social-networks -and-social-media-in-ukrainian-euromaidan-protests-2/.

Onuch, Olga. 2014b. "Who Were the Protesters?" *Journal of Democracy* 25, no. 3 (July): 44–51. https://doi.org/10.1353/jod.2014.0045.

Onuch, Olga, and Tamara Martsenyuk. 2014. "Mothers and Daughters of the Maidan: Gender, Repertoires of Violence, and the Division of Labour in Ukrainian Protests." *Social, Health, and Communication Studies Journal* 1, no. 1 (November): 80–101. https://journals.macewan.ca/shcsjournal/article /view/248.

Ozolina, Liene. 2019. *Politics of Waiting: Workfare, Post-Soviet Austerity, and the Ethics of Freedom*. Manchester: Manchester University Press.

Pasieka, Agnieszka. 2017. "Taking Far Right Claims Seriously and Literally: Anthropology and the Study of Right-Wing Radicalism." *Slavic Review* 76, no. S1 (August): S19–S29. https://doi.org/10.1017/slr.2017.154.

Pavlychko, Solomea. 2002. "Between Feminism and Nationalism: New Women's Groups in the Ukraine." In *Feminizm*, 37–52. Kyiv: Osnovi.

Pehlman, Nicholas. 2020. "Patrimonialism through Reform: Public Participation in Police Reform, Institutional Capture, and Bureaucratic Independence in Ukraine." *Harvard Ukrainian Studies* 37, nos. 3–4 (January): 323–66. https://www.jstor.org/stable/48626498.

Petrova, Tsveta, and Sidney Tarrow. 2007. "Transactional and Participatory Activism in the Emerging European Polity: The Puzzle of East-Central Europe." *Comparative Political Studies* 40, no. 1 (January): 74–94. https://doi.org/10.1177/0010414006291189.

Phillips, Sarah D. 2008. *Women's Social Activism in the New Ukraine: Development and the Politics of Differentiation*. Bloomington: Indiana University Press.

Phillips, Sarah D. 2011. *Disability and Mobile Citizenship in Postsocialist Ukraine*. Bloomington: Indiana University Press.

Phillips, Sarah D. 2014. "The Women's Squad in Ukraine's Protests: Feminism, Nationalism, and Militarism on the Maidan." *American Ethnologist* 41, no. 3 (August): 414–26. https://doi.org/10.1111/amet.12093.

Plokhy, Serhii. 2021. "Goodbye Lenin!" In *The Frontline: Essays on Ukraine's Past and Present*, 257–82. Cambridge, MA: Harvard University Press.

Polletta, Francesca. 2006. *It Was Like a Fever: Storytelling in Protest and Politics*. Chicago: University of Chicago Press.

Popova, Dariia. 2014. "Seksyzm na Maidani" [Sexism on Maidan]. *Spil'ne*, 3 October. https://commons.com.ua/uk/seksizm-na-majdani/.

Price, Charles, Donald Nonini, and Erich Fox Tree. 2008. "Grounded Utopian Movements: Subjects of Neglect." *Anthropological Quarterly* 81, no. 1 (Winter): 127–59. https://doi.org/10.1353/anq.2008.0005.

Puglisi, Rosaria. 2015a. "Heroes or Villains? Volunteer Battalions in Post-Maidan Ukraine." Working paper. Rome: Istituto affari internazionali.

Puglisi, Rosaria. 2015b. "A People's Army: Civil Society as a Security Actor in Post-Maidan Ukraine." Working paper. Rome: Istituto affari internazionali.

Quinn-Judge, Paul, and Yuri Zarakhovich. 2004. "The Orange Revolution." *Time*, 28 November. http://content.time.com/time/magazine/article/0,9171,832225,00.html.

Razsa, Maple. 2015. *Bastards of Utopia: Living Radical Politics after Socialism*. Bloomington: Indiana University Press.

Razsa, Maple, and Andrej Kurnik. 2012. "The Occupy Movement in Žižek's Hometown: Direct Democracy and a Politics of Becoming." *American Ethnologist* 39, no. 2 (May): 238–58. https://doi.org/10.1111/j.1548-1425.2012.01361.x.

Read, Rosie, and Tatjana Thelen. 2007. "Introduction: Social Security and Care after Socialism: Reconfigurations of Public and Private." *Focaal* 2007, no. 50 (December): 3–18. https://doi.org/10.3167/foc.2007.500102.

Riabchuk, Anastasiya. 2012. "Homeless Men and the Crisis of Masculinity in Contemporary Ukraine." In *Gender, Politics, and Society in Ukraine*, edited by Olena Hankivsky and Anastasia Salnykova, 204–24. Toronto: University of Toronto Press.

Riabchuk, Mykola. 2002. "Ukraine: One State, Two Countries?" *Eurozine*, 16 September. https://www.eurozine.com/ukraine-one-state-two-countries/.

Risch, William Jay. 2011. *The Ukrainian West: Culture and the Fate of Empire in Soviet Lviv*. Cambridge, MA: Harvard University Press.

Risch, William Jay. 2015. "What the Far Right Does Not Tell Us about the Maidan." *Kritika: Explorations in Russian and Eurasian History* 16, no. 1 (Winter): 137–44. https://doi.org/10.1353/kri.2015.0011.

Rizvi, Fazal, and Bob Lingard. 2010. *Globalizing Education Policy*. New York: Routledge.

Rubchak, Marian J. 2001. "In Search of a Model: Evolution of a Feminist Consciousness in Ukraine and Russia." *European Journal of Women's Studies* 8, no. 2 (May): 149–60. https://doi.org/10.1177/135050680100800202.

Rubchak, Marian J. 2014. "A Fiery Euromaidan Ignites a Feminist Voice." *Perspectives on Europe* 44, no. 2 (Autumn): 82–7. https://www.researchgate.net/publication/273402822_A_Fiery_Euromaidan_Ignites_a_Feminist_Voice.

Rubchak, Marian J. 2015 "Introduction." In *New Imaginaries: Youthful Reinvention of Ukraine's Cultural Paradigm*, edited by Marian Rubchak, 1–32. New York: Berghahn Books.

Sadurski, Wojciech. 2003. "'Decommunization,' 'Lustration,' and Constitutional Continuity: Dilemmas of Transitional Justice in Central Europe." EUI Working Paper LAW 2003/15. Florence: European University Institute.

Sasse, Gwendolyn, and Alice Lackner. 2019. "Attitudes and Identities across the Donbas Front Line: What Has Changed from 2016 to 2019?" ZOiS Report 3/2019. Berlin: Centre for East European and International Studies (ZOiS). https://www.zois-berlin.de/en/publications/attitudes-and-identities-across-the-donbas-front-line-what-has-changed-from-2016-to-2019.

Schmid, Ulrich, and Oksana Myshlovska, eds. 2019. *Regionalism without Regions: Reconceptualizing Ukraine's Heterogeneity*. Budapest: CEU Press.

Sereda, Viktoriya. 2020. "'Social Distancing' and Hierarchies of Belonging: The Case of Displaced Population from Donbas and Crimea." *Europe-Asia Studies* 72, no. 3 (March): 404–31. https://doi.org/10.1080/09668136.2020.1719043.

Shear, Boone W, Susan Brin Hyatt, and Susan Wright. 2015. *Learning under Neoliberalism: Ethnographies of Governance in Higher Education*. New York: Berghahn Books.

Shekhovtsov, Anton. 2014. "From Electoral Success to Revolutionary Failure: The Ukrainian Svoboda Party." *Eurozine*, 5 March. https://www.eurozine.com/from-electoral-success-to-revolutionary-failure/.

Shevchenko, Daryna. 2014. "Poll Discovers EuroMaidan Evolution from Dreamy to Radical." *Kyiv Post*, 6 February. http://www.kyivpost.com/content/ukraine/poll-discovers-euromaidan-evolution-from-dreamy-to-radical-336389.html.

Shevel, Oxana. 2016. "The Battle for Historical Memory in Postrevolutionary Ukraine." *Current History* 115, no. 783 (October): 258–63. https://doi.org/10.1525/curh.2016.115.783.258.

Shmatko, Ivan. 2022. "'Even if You Need a Mustache of a Unicorn': Informalities and War in Ukraine." *HotSpots*, 28 March. https://culanth.org/fieldsights/even-if-you-need-a-mustache-of-a-unicorn-informalities-and-war-in-ukraine.

Shore, Cris. 2004. "Whither European Citizenship? Eros and Civilization Revisited." *European Journal of Social Theory* 7, no. 1 (February): 27–44. https://doi.org/10.1177/1368431004040018.

Shore, Marci. 2018. *The Ukrainian Night: An Intimate History of Revolution*. New Haven, CT: Yale University Press.

Shukan, Ioulia. 2016a. *Génération Maïdan : Vivre la crise ukrainienne* [Generation Maidan: Living the Ukraine crisis]. Paris: Éditions de l'Aube.

Shukan, Ioulia. 2016b. "Order and Security from Below: Vigilantism in Post-Maidan Ukraine – The Case of Odesa." Paper Presented at the Association for the Study of Nationalities World Convention, Columbia University, New York, April.

Shukan, Ioulia. 2018. "L'Ukraine, entre tensions politiques à Kiev et guerre larvée dans le Donbass" [Ukraine, between political tensions in Kyiv and creeping war in the Donbas]. *Les Études de CERI : Regards sur l'Eurasie*, nos. 235–6 (February): 11–17. https://hal-sciencespo.archives-ouvertes.fr/hal-03440912/document.

Shulman, Stephen. 2002. "Sources of Civic and Ethnic Nationalism in Ukraine." *Journal of Communist Studies and Transition Politics* 18, no. 4 (December): 1–30. https://doi.org/10.1080/714003618.

Shulman, Stephen. 2004. "The Contours of Civic and Ethnic National Identification in Ukraine." *Europe-Asia Studies* 56, no. 1 (January): 35–56. https://doi.org/10.1080/0966813032000161437.

Sindelar, Daisy. 2014. "As Heads Roll in Kyiv, Few Tears Shed for Divisive Education Minister." *Radio Free Europe/Radio Liberty*, 23 February. https://www.rferl.org/a/as-heads-roll-in-kyiv-few-tears-shed-for-divisive-education-minister/25274495.html.

Sinyavsky, Andrei. 1990. "The New Man." In *Soviet Civilization: A Cultural History*, 114–52. New York: Arcade Publishing.

Siry, Leonid. 1978. "A Ukrainian Worker's Appeal." *Ukrainian Review* 27, no. 1 (Spring): 78–80.

Slezkine, Yuri. 1994. "The USSR as a Communal Apartment, or How a Socialist State Promoted Ethnic Particularism." *Slavic Review* 53, no. 2 (Summer): 414–52. https://doi.org/10.2307/2501300.

Snyder, Timothy. 2010. *Bloodlands: Europe Between Hitler and Stalin*. New York: Basic Books.

Song, Jesook. 2009. *South Koreans in the Debt Crisis: The Creation of a Neoliberal Welfare Society*. Durham, NC: Duke University Press.

Sperling, Valerie, Myra Marx Feree, and Barbara Risman. 2001. "Constructing Global Feminism: Transnational Advocacy Networks and Russian Women's Activism." *Signs: Journal of Women in Culture and Society* 26, no. 4 (Summer): 1155–86. https://doi.org/10.1086/495651.

Spil'ne. 2016. "Zaiava vid Redaktsiï 'Spil'noho'" [Statement from the Commons Editors]. 21 January. http://commons.com.ua/zayava-vid-redaktsiyi-spilnogo/.

Stein, Sharon, and Vanessa de Oliveira Andreotti. 2017. "Higher Education and the Modern/Colonial Global Imaginary." *Cultural Studies↔Critical Methodologies* 17, no. 3 (June): 173–81. https://doi.org/10.1177/1532708616672673.

Stepaniuk, Natalia. 2016. "A Gendered Account of War-Driven Voluntary Engagement in Ukraine." Paper Presented at the Association for the Study of Nationalities World Convention, Columbia University, New York, April.

Stepaniuk, Natalia. 2018. "Lives Punctuated by War: Civilian Volunteers and Identity Formation amidst the Donbas War in Ukraine." PhD. diss., University of Ottawa.

Strathern, Marilyn, ed. 2000. *Audit Cultures: Anthropological Studies in Accountability, Ethics, and the Academy*. New York: Routledge.

Subtelny, Orest. 2000. *Ukraine: A History*. Toronto: University of Toronto Press.

Țichindeleanu, Ovidiu. 2010. "Towards a Critical Theory of Postcommunism? Beyond Anticommunism in Romania." *Radical Philosophy* 159 (January–February): 26–32. https://www.radicalphilosophy.com/article/towards-a-critical-theory-of-postcommunism.

Tilly, Charles, and Sidney G. Tarrow. 2007. *Contentious Politics*. Boulder, CO: Paradigm Publishers.

Todorova, Maria. 2005. "The Trap of Backwardness: Modernity, Temporality, and the Study of Eastern European Nationalism." *Slavic Review* 64, no. 1 (Spring): 140–64. https://doi.org/10.2307/3650070.

Udovyk, Oksana. 2017. "Beyond the Conflict and Weak Civil Society; Stories from Ukraine: Cases of Grassroots Initiatives for Sustainable Development." *East/West: Journal of Ukrainian Studies* 4, no. 2 (September): 187–210. https://doi.org/10.21226/T27W6R.

Uehling, Greta. 2004. *Beyond Memory: The Crimean Tatars' Deportation and Return*. New York: Palgrave Macmillan.

Uehling, Greta. 2017. "A Hybrid Deportation: Internally Displaced from Crimea in Ukraine." In *Migration and the Ukraine Crisis: A Two-Country Perspective*, edited by Agnieszka Pikulicka-Wilczewska and Greta Uehling, 62–77. Bristol, UK: E-International Relations Publishing.

Ukrains'ka Pravda. 2014. "Pomer Shche Odyn Aktyvist, Pidstrelenyi na Hrushevs'koho" [Death of one more activist shot on Hrushevs'koho]. 25 January. http://www.pravda.com.ua/news/2014/01/25/7011296/.

UN Women. 2015. "Women in Ukraine's Military Face Barriers and Abuse, Study Says." *UN Women: Europe and Central Asia*, 14 December. https://eca.unwomen.org/en/news/stories/2015/12/ukraine--invisible-batallion.

Utrata, Jennifer. 2015. *Women without Men: Single Mothers and Family Change in the New Russia*. Ithaca, NY: Cornell University Press.

Verdery, Katherine. 1991. *National Ideology under Socialism: Identity and Cultural Politics in Ceauşescu's Romania*. Berkeley: University of California Press.

Verdery, Katherine. 1996. *What Was Socialism, and What Comes Next?* Princeton, NJ: Princeton University Press.

Verdery, Katherine. 1999. *The Political Lives of Dead Bodies: Reburial and Postsocialist Change*. New York: Columbia University Press.

Verkhovna Rada of Ukraine. 2014. "For the Period of January 14–17, the Verkhovna Rada Adopted 11 Laws and 1 Resolution." 16 January. https://www.rada.gov.ua/en/news/News/News/87088.html.

Wanner, Catherine. 1998. *Burden of Dreams: History and Identity in Post-Soviet Ukraine*. University Park: Pennsylvania State University Press.

Wanner, Catherine. 2005. "Money, Morality and New Forms of Exchange in Postsocialist Ukraine." *Ethnos* 70, no. 4 (December): 515–37. https://doi.org/10.1080/00141840500419782.

Way, Lucan. 2014. "Civil Society and Democratization." *Journal of Democracy* 25, no. 3 (July): 35–43. https://doi.org/10.1353/jod.2014.0042.

West, Paige. 2010. "Making the Market: Specialty Coffee, Generational Pitches, and Papua New Guinea." *Antipode* 42, no. 3 (June): 690–718. https://doi.org/10.1111/j.1467-8330.2010.00769.x.

Wilson, Andrew. 1997. *Ukrainian Nationalism in the 1990s: A Minority Faith*. New York: Cambridge University Press.

Wilson, Andrew. 2005. *Ukraine's Orange Revolution*. New Haven, CT: Yale University Press.

Wilson, Andrew. 2014. *Ukraine Crisis: What It Means for the West*. New Haven, CT: Yale University Press.

Wishart, Alexandra. 2019. "The Radical Left in Ukraine since Maidan: The Case of the National Anarchist Movement." Master's thesis, University of Glasgow.

Yekelchyk, Serhy. 2014. *Stalin's Citizens: Everyday Politics in the Wake of Total War*. New York: Oxford University Press.

Yurchak, Alexei. 2002. "Entrepreneurial Governmentality in Postsocialist Russia: A Cultural Investigation of Business Practices." In *The New Entrepreneurs of Europe and Asia*, edited by Victoria E. Bonnell and Thomas B. Gold, 278–324. Armonk, NY: M.E. Sharpe.

Yurchak, Alexei. 2006. *Everything Was Forever, Until It Was No More: The Last Soviet Generation*. Princeton, NJ: Princeton University Press.

Yurchak, Alexei. 2014. "Little Green Men: Russia, Ukraine and Post-Soviet Sovereignty." *Anthropoliteia*, 31 March. https://anthropoliteia.net/2014/03/31/little-green-men-russia-ukraine-and-post-soviet-sovereignty/.

Yuval-Davis, Nira. 1997. *Gender and Nation*. Thousand Oaks, CA: SAGE.

Zhurzhenko, Tatiana. 2001. "Ukrainian Feminism(s): Between Nationalist Myth and Anti-Nationalist Critique." IWM Working Paper 4/2001. Vienna: Institut für die Wissenschaften vom Menschen.

Zlobina, Tamara. 2015. "Theory to Practice: The Personal Becomes Political in the Post-Soviet Space." In *New Imaginaries: Youthful Reinvention of Ukraine's Cultural Paradigm*, edited by Marian Rubchak, 72–88. New York: Berghahn Books.

Zychowicz, Jessica. 2011. "Two Bad Words: FEMEN & Feminism in Independent Ukraine." *Anthropology of East Europe Review* 29, no. 2 (Fall): 215–27. https://scholarworks.iu.edu/journals/index.php/aeer/article/view/1266.

Zychowicz, Jessica. 2020. *Superfluous Women: Art, Feminism, and Revolution in Twenty-First Century Ukraine*. Toronto: University of Toronto Press.

Index

wealth redistribution: activism for, 7, 19, 37–8, 42, 141; Association Agreement, 7, 141; community, 16, 196; privatization versus, 15

welfare state programs, 213; neoliberalism and, 13, 15; provision of, 54–5, 142, 179

western Europe, eastern versus, 11, 86–8

women, 222; assumptions of, 16, 70, 122, 139, 200; care work of (*see* care work); experiences of occupation, 29–30, 195–9; on Maidan, 131–5, 155, 181–6, 193–9, 205–6; in male-dominated activism, 59, 75–6, 186–94, 198–200; popular representations of, 16, 189, 192–5; self-defence training, 72–7, 128–9, 197–200; Soviet discourse on, 38, 184–9, 205–6; violence against, 70, 91, 155, 182, 195; volunteerism of, 15–16, 193. *See also* gender equality; gender roles; sexism

Women's Brigades, 201–6, 239nn8,10

women's organizations: funding for, 186; nationalism and, 186, 189, 193, 199–201

Women's Solidarity Night, 194–7

World Bank, 12, 54

worldbuilding, leftist, 7, 19, 37, 49

Yanukovych, Viktor, 41, 176, 232n4; constitutional changes, 10, 136; Customs Union, Russian, 4, 10, 42, 95; demands for resignation of, 4, 10–11, 36, 46, 135–7, 159; Dictatorship Laws, 106, 117–19, 161–2; election of, 9–10, 34, 38, 60–1, 99, 229n2; fleeing to Russia, 8, 84–5, 135–6, 172; police force use, 14, 44, 113–20, 134–5, 151–4; public perceptions of, 9–10, 79–82, 112–16, 125–7, 220–1; refusal of EU Association Agreement, 4, 8, 27, 42, 104–6, 150–2. *See also* Orange Revolution; Party of Regions

Yarosh, Dmytro, 99, 120, 135, 230n6

Ye Liudy, 214, 235n11

youth organizing: activist work with, 51, 146, 150; entrepreneurship, 39–40; post-Stalinist, 39; pro-Soviet, 13, 236n5; right-wing, 147–8, 156; in Romania, 39; socialist discourses and, 38–9, 60

Yurchak, Alexei, 38–42

Yushchenko, Viktor, 38, 60, 232n4; public perceptions of, 9–10, 34, 61

Zelensky, Volodymyr, 97, 219, 229n2, 232n3; election of, 20, 88, 103

Zgurovs'ky, Mykhailo, 175, 234n5, 237n17

Zhenia (activist), 112–13, 160, 172–7

Zhizdnevs'kyi, Mykhailo, 120, 161, 234n7

Zlobina, Tamara, 189–90

Anthropological Horizons

Editor: Michael Lambek, University of Toronto

Printed and bound by CPI Group (UK) Ltd, Croydon, CR0 4YY

01/09/2025

14727259-0001